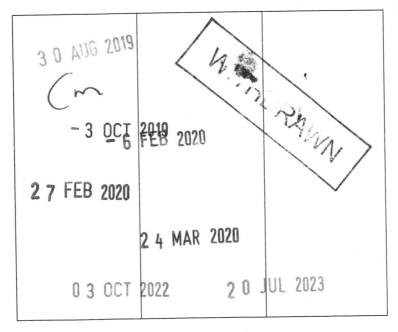

# THE
# BLACK
# WIDOW

# THE
# BLACK
# WIDOW

## LINDA CALVEY

m
B

MIRROR BOOKS

First published by Mirror Books in 2019

Mirror Books is part of Reach plc
10 Lower Thames Street
London EC3R 6EN
England

www.mirrorbooks.co.uk

ISBN 978-1-912624-59-1

Typeset by Danny Lyle
DanJLyle@gmail.com

Printed and bound in Great Britain by
CPI Group (UK) Ltd, Croydon, CR0 4YY

A CIP catalogue record for this book is available from the British Library.

Every effort has been made to fulfil requirements with regard to
reproducing copyright material. The author and publisher will be
glad to rectify any omissions at the earliest opportunity.

1  3  5  7  9  10 8  6  4  2

Cover images: iStockphoto

For Melanie and Neil

# CONTENTS

# PROLOGUE

"Come ON!" I screamed as the men in balaclavas ran towards the van, sawn-off shotguns in their hands. They flung open the doors and threw themselves in just as I slammed my foot down on the accelerator. The tyres squealed. "Get us out of here!" Brian shouted, pulling up his balaclava, a wild look on his face.

"Hold on!" I swung round the corner and screeched down a side passage to the far end, turning into a backstreet residential road, before abruptly drawing to a stop. I glanced in the car mirrors, making sure we weren't being followed by Old Bill.

"All clear," I barked. "Carl. Balaclava in the bag." Carl pulled off his headgear and thrust it at Brian. "Now go!"

Carl jumped out and slammed the door behind him, throwing his gloves back in through the window. We sped away in the van as Carl sauntered off in the other direction towards the bus stop, smoothing down his hair, looking to all intents and purposes like a normal bloke just going about his daily business. Brian packed the shotguns away into the holdall containing the money, and stuffed the balaclavas and Carl's gloves in on top. The sirens squealed in the distance behind us as I rounded the next few corners at full speed, and shuddered to a halt a few streets further along. Every police officer and squad car within a three-mile radius was heading our way.

"It's clear, Brian. Meet you at Harpley Square later." Brian gave me a brisk nod as he leapt out of the van with the holdall, pulling his gloves off and packing them away as he walked towards his own car. He got in and drove off as casually as possible.

My heart was pounding as I tore off once more, alone. Brian had the loot, but the coppers would still be suspicious if they found me in my gloves – I couldn't take those off until I was out of the van, to avoid leaving prints.

I raced round the next few bends, still on full alert, expecting the cops at every turn. I pulled up again 10 metres short of my car, which I had left innocently parked up at the side of the road, took off my red wig and dark glasses, and shoved them into my handbag. Then I jumped out of the stolen van, checking we hadn't left anything in there, pulled off my gloves, walked to the car and set off for home.

As my mind began to clear, I realised that we'd done it. In five frenzied minutes, Brian and Carl had robbed a bank security van in broad daylight on a busy street in London. They'd legged it from the scene, brandishing their shotguns. Weeks of meticulous planning had come off exactly as we wanted. I'd suggested the bank to the boys as a perfect target, and it was me who'd gone to scout the area. We'd discovered the times when the security van pulled up to load up the day's money, and I'd made sure there were three possible exit routes in case of trouble. And I'd stayed cool in the heat of the moment, closing the deal in the getaway vehicle. It was far from over, but I was one of them now. Once Brian had dropped the guns and disguises off at the garage he rented, we'd all be meeting back at my place to share the spoils.

The air was heavy with police sirens as I turned onto the main road, straight out in front of a police car that was hurrying to the scene of the crime. My heart skipped a beat as I glanced in the mirrors, and I drove on at a normal speed with the traffic. But they hadn't paid the slightest attention to me, and the Old Bill soon got fed up of following along behind. I allowed myself a wry smile as the police cars sped past me, sirens blaring, and disappeared up ahead.

*You were born for this, Linda.*

# CHAPTER 1

# EAST END, BORN AND BRED

## 1948-60

I grew up in the East End of London, the home of the underclass, the seething, broiling hunting ground of the city's criminal establishment. My family lived just a stone's throw away from the area ruled by the Kray twins, near the streets that Jack the Ripper once prowled. East London meant gang wars, violence, poverty and brutality. And yet alongside it was a real sense of yearning for a better life: a life where housing wasn't in slum tenements with outdoor shared lavvies, where clothes weren't all bought second- or third-hand at the Mission, where children could play in streets without coming home covered in filthy residue from the nearby dockland industries, where they could breathe in air that wasn't filled with the stench of the tanneries, the boozers and the warehouses. We wanted more than we were born to, and yet we had no way of getting it. Not legally, at least. We survived by ducking and diving, by wheeling and dealing, by looking after our own, under the wing of the women who got us through the post-war deprivations with a grim smile, hot suppers on the table and endless love.

You have to be born within the sound of Bow bells to be a proper Cockney, and I was born in Ilford, so don't quite have that privilege. But nowadays it's a rare honour anyway, as most of the maternity hospitals within earshot have closed down. I was born in 1948, the second of nine children. My mum was the pillar of our family, as most East End mums are. It was only three years after the end of the war, and the country was reeling from the loss of a generation of men.

My father was a soldier, a tall lean man with dark hair and eyes that twinkled with mischief. He'd clapped eyes on Mum back when she was working her coffee stall under the arches at Stepney East Station. The story goes that even when the air raid sirens were wailing across London, Mum resolutely refused to go into a shelter, and carried on serving coffee to those who also didn't care for a night spent breathing in the smells of other people, the unwashed, unshaven masses huddling together on the cold steps or floor of the Underground platform. Mum served steaming hot drinks as the Luftwaffe tipped bombs from the heavens onto our city, as the flames rose and buildings fell to rubble, as the docks ignited and explosions were heard as far away as Bermondsey. She put out incendiary bombs in her spare time. She was an indomitable spirit. She showed how strong the women of East London were back then. She didn't tremble at the sound of the sirens – she just got on with it, like thousands of others. She was fierce when her back was against the wall.

It was there, under the arches, that my dad Charlie found his way to her stall. He was a dapper man, but he didn't wear a trilby or a suit – he went about in braces, a flat cap and a shirt with a grandad collar.

My mum didn't like the look of him at all. He looked like a charmer, a bad boy with far too much confidence about him.

"Can I 'ave a tomato sandwich without the bread, please." Dad looked at her, his head cocked to one side. Mum arched her brow.

"A tomato sandwich without the bread. D'you think I'm daft? What you mean is, you want a tomato?" she replied, caustically.

"Yeah that's what I said, a tomato sandwich without the bread," Dad shot back. My mum always says that at that point, she looked him up and down, and concluded that he was as good-looking as a film star but too tricky for her liking.

"There you go then, a tomato. You enjoy that, won't you," she said, keeping the smile off her face. She wasn't going to give this charmer the satisfaction of seeing he'd tickled her. She knew he was flirting with her. No way was she going to flirt back.

"You got a match?" he drawled, clearly reluctant to move away from the woman he'd taken a fancy to, even though there was a queue forming behind him. Flustered now, Eileen said, "'Ere take this, I've got customers to serve. What would you like, love?" she said as she turned to the person behind him, handing Charlie the silver match case her father had gifted her for her birthday.

Charlie lit his cigarette, a Lucky Strike – which made Mum think he was a real wide boy, as they were hard to get. He casually shook away the flame and flicked the matchstick onto the road.

"You'll get this back when you promise to go out with me," he said, backing away and sauntering off down the street, whistling as he went.

"Of all the cheeky thieving so-and-sos!" Mum huffed. "He's nicked me silver case."

"You 'eard him," grinned the next customer, "if you go out with him you'll get it back… Can't see you've got a choice, darlin'."

With that, the man – who now had his hot coffee – winked at her and walked away, leaving Mum fuming, but also curious about this handsome but tricky bloke. "Well I never!" Mum huffed, her blood boiling as she carried on serving.

Mum wasn't at the stall when Dad returned. Her sister Joyce was manning it for her.

"Tell Eileen I'm going off to the army," Dad said. "Tell her she'll have to write to me, and when I get back she's gotta go out with me."

Dad survived the war, came home, and did exactly as he'd promised. They were wed within weeks of his return, and she got her silver case back.

The docks were the centre of the working men's world. After the war, my dad worked as a blacksmith, making docker's hooks for the longshoremen, the manual labourers who loaded and unloaded the giant ships that brought spices from the East, and grain, tobacco, meat and vegetables from the Americas. The hooks were the stevedores' most important tool and formed the emblem of the dock workers – so Dad managed to forge himself a niche in that uncertain world where men would queue for hours each morning at the gates to be picked for work.

Because of the docks, the East End was a prime target for German bombers during the war, and when I was growing up in the early 50s it was full of demolished buildings. It was heaven for kids. We'd spend hours running over the bombed houses, climbing piles of rubble, rifling through bits of brick and metal and digging out various old household items to take home with us. When we were getting under my mother's feet, her first response was always to tell us to "Go and play on the bomb site."

It seems unimaginable now, but those were some of the happiest days of our lives. We lived in a tight-knit community, and the streets were the perfect playground for us. When our friends came round to knock on the door and ask after us, Mum would chuckle and say, "Oh, they're round the bombed houses."

My brother Terry was three years older, and after me came Tony and Vivienne. Then, when I was five, we all moved from Ilford to Stepney, in the heart of the East End. Dad had been offered a four-bed maisonette by the council in Welton House on Stepney Way, and he'd leapt at the chance. It brought us closer to his work near Limehouse Docks, and Billingsgate and Smithfield markets. The Blind Beggar Pub, where Ronnie Kray later shot George Cornell dead, was a few streets away. So was Vallance Road in Bethnal Green, where the Kray twins had grown up. On the south side of the river were the Richardsons. Even though organised crime and gang warfare was rife by the time I became a young woman, I knew nothing about it.

We thought we'd landed in the lap of luxury in Stepney. The tower blocks were newly built in that familiar boxy shape with flat frontage, arranged in a long straight line opposite a row of bombed houses. Even though it was on a busy main road, dotted with occasional trees and the sound of passing traffic, we loved it.

"We've got stairs!" I shouted at Terry and Tony as we scampered inside. Both my brothers were handsome, both adored by me. Terry was tall and slim with light brown hair, Tony had a stockier build with dark brown hair. The street door to our new home, brand new and painted blue, opened into a passage. The toilet was on the left, the kitchen on the right, and at the end of the corridor was the lounge looking over the small back garden. It felt like paradise. Coming from a poky flat in Ilford, this seemed like a mansion.

"And there's a new bomb site across the road for you boys to run wild in, no doubt," said Mum, peering into her new kitchen, a smile on her lovely face.

I ran up the stairs with glee, Terry and Tony on my heels. We were like puppies let off the leash. It took me hours to arrange my dolls on my little bed inside my room painted pastel blue.

The place had been built to house those whose homes were destroyed in the war. It needed a good scrub, especially the kitchen, which had an oven, a small window looking out to some trees at the back, and cabinets that looked like they hadn't seen a clean in a while. But to us, it was perfect. I shared with my next eldest sister, Vivienne, while the boys slept in the freezing room over the archway. Soon enough, we had more siblings appearing: after Terry, me, Tony and Vivienne came Shelley, Maxine, Hazel, Ricky and Karen. The five of them made do in the third bedroom. Goodness knows how we all squeezed in, but it never felt cramped.

I was sent to the local primary school in Senrab Street with my brothers, and our life as Eastenders began. Both my parents, contrary to first impressions of Dad, were honest, hardworking people who always had enough food on the table to keep us fed, and a new set of clothes every Easter – quite an achievement, with 11 mouths to feed. At the time, it wasn't unusual to see groups of men huddled together, looking for casual work on Commercial Road, the busy thoroughfare close by that linked Whitechapel to Shoreditch. The new road had been built by bulldozing through the stinking slums, the alleys where the Ripper found his victims. It was meant to modernise and "improve" the area.

Gone were the overcrowded Dickensian rookeries inhabited by thieves, prostitutes and the poor, packed together in hastily built housing with no sanitation or clean air, yet the area was still poor. No-one looking at the street market traders gathered around each winter, coats held together with string tied round their waists, burning veg boxes for warmth, would think there was really any real difference. And yet I loved the hustle and bustle of my manor, the boutiques selling mini dresses, the pie and mash shop windows I would squash my nose up against to see through the condensation and breathe in the smell of the meat pies cooking. We didn't have much, but we ate like kings.

Dad would often ask for payment from blacksmith work done at the food markets, in a prime cut of beef instead of cash, or a batch of the freshest scallops. It wasn't unusual to come home from school and be served Dover sole for dinner, or a leg of lamb, when I knew most of my classmates would be greeted by mutton stew or the cheapest cuts of meat with stodgy dumplings.

Looking back, I could laugh at how a family living in a tiny council flat in an estate in London's poverty-stricken East End could be eating as well as our Queen in Buckingham Palace. That was normal life for us. We got by. We lived well compared to many of our peers, and we shared what we had. It was a badge of honour that Mum would never let any visitor leave without a full tummy. She'd take food off our plates if there wasn't enough and create an extra place for whoever was commanded to squeeze round our table. By the time all my siblings were born, we couldn't all fit round it, let alone accommodate guests, but somehow, there was always room. We'd sit on the sofa or stand leaning against the Formica kitchen cabinets to eat. If we were hungry later, she'd make us cheese on toast. We never went to bed without a full tummy. Yet, I always knew I wanted more. My home life was safe, relatively comfortable for the time, and loving, but I wanted excitement like a moth to the flame.

# CHAPTER 2

# LOOKING AT THE STARS

## 1960-68

"Dad, slow down!" I said, as I clung to the cushion propping me up on the seat of Dad's beaten-up old van. I wasn't wearing a seatbelt. Health and Safety hadn't yet been invented in 1960.

"Alright, alright, keep yer hair on…" He laughed as we swayed round a bend, heading along Stepney Way, surrounded on both sides by ugly post-war blocks of flats that had been hurriedly built back in the 50s after the bombings.

It was a Sunday afternoon, and everywhere young couples were out courting, walking together hand-in-hand, or young mums wearing scarves covering their hair, tied under their chins, were pushing prams and gossiping as they walked. Kids weaved in and out of the people, boys with their hair combed to the side, with shorts that looked too large for their spindly legs and woollen tank tops, running in groups, getting the occasional swipe for misdemeanours, while old men sat on benches at the roadside, smoking pipes and passing the time.

We were heading for Mile End, past Stepney Green Park, travelling over to an aunt's house for the afternoon. I was 12 years old, squeezed in the front in-between my parents. We didn't go visiting often, but Mum and Dad were going over for the afternoon and I'd asked specially to come with them. Our world was a small one, encompassing the myriad streets around Stepney and little else, and chances to go further afield were rare. Family was the cornerstone of our lives. It was everything – and it still is.

"Dad, you've done it again," I squealed as the van juddered to a stop at a set of traffic lights, causing the three of us to lurch forwards and laugh at the hilarity of it.

All at once my gaze fell on a large shiny dark red car that had pulled up next to us.

"What's that…?" I gasped, taking in the colour, the expense, the sheer class of the motor purring beside us in stark contrast to the rust bucket we were sitting in.

Dad turned to look, following my line of sight. He snorted. "That, Linda, is a Roller. There ain't no better car on this earth." I couldn't tear my eyes away. I peered over Dad, almost pushing him out of the way so I could see more of this magical sight.

When I finally managed to tear my eyes away from the car itself to look inside, I saw a blonde woman, impossibly alluring, swathed in a fur coat. She was sitting next to a man, who was driving. He stared straight ahead of him, his thick neck set inside a starched white collar and a pinstripe suit. He was puffing on a fat cigar, the car filling with his smoke. I sniffed the air, imagining I could smell the dense, woody scent. Neither of them looked around. I was utterly invisible to them.

Everything I knew about my happy life, my family, school and friends, suddenly seemed drab and small, though I loved them all dearly. It was my first glimpse into another world, into the possibility of a different, bigger, life. I didn't have a clue how to enter their world. I didn't know anyone who drove a car like that or who looked like a Hollywood actress, but I knew that one day, I wanted to be like them, to have a life that reached far out of my tiny experience. It was the first time I realised there really was more to life, and perhaps, I really could look to the stars, as Mum kept telling us we could.

I was spellbound. The lights changed, and we moved on in the wake of that Rolls Royce. I watched it go, a sinking feeling in my tummy, which I didn't understand. I wanted what they had, but how on earth was I going to get it?

Those people, who I was invisible to, were as far from the sights and sounds that surrounded me as it was possible to be. As we carried on driving at a snail's pace, I barely took in the rows of council blocks, the Lyons tea truck, a man selling whelks from his stall, or the children with scuffed shoes playing with pennies in the gutter.

"One day, I'm going to have a red Rolls Royce and a fur coat…" I said, pondering on what I'd seen.

Far from being cross with me for being suddenly ungrateful for the life we had, Mum saw the stunned look on my face and laughed, "I hope you do, darlin'. You can achieve anything you set your mind to. It don't matter where you were born, what matters is your dreams."

I had never really understood that until that moment. Somehow everything I'd ever yearned for, ever felt was missing, ever longed for outside of my small, safe world, was encapsulated in that vehicle in that fateful moment. It wasn't just because it was expensive or shiny, it was more the promise of a bigger world out there, something I couldn't fathom how to find, but something that was real, a glittering example of what might be possible, though surely not for a girl from Stepney?

When we arrived back at the maisonette I had thought was a mansion, I saw it with new eyes. Gone was the vision of loveliness and security I'd cherished. Instead, the road outside looked grimier, the place looked smaller, meaner, with gaudy wallpaper in the lounge which didn't quite meet at the skirting boards. I saw the greying net curtains at Mum's windows, the worn blankets we'd had for as long as I could remember. The air outside smelled of next door's stew, the sounds from the street filtered up with shouts from boys playing football on the road, while a couple were having a row a few doors down. It was as if a harsh spotlight had been put onto my life, and I didn't like what I saw.

"Come on, Linda, help me set the table," Mum said, sensing the change in me.

I smiled over at her, "Course, Mum," and I walked behind her, opening the drawers and laying out the mismatched cutlery, lost in my own confusing thoughts.

That moment had crystallised something inside me. I loved my close-knit family, but over the following years I wanted more and more desperately to be destined for something greater.

After my youngest sibling Karen was born when I was 15, Mum decided to stop being a housewife and set up a stall again, like she used to run in the war. She started selling wigs at Roman Road market, Petticoat Lane and East Street, and as I was the eldest of her girls, I helped her out at the weekends. We'd get there early, around 7am, as the traders arrived, bleary-eyed from the night before, to set up.

"Mum, should I put these out here?" I had a bag filled with blonde wigs – it seemed everyone wanted to look like a Hollywood star.

"Yes, darlin', put those out while I brush out the brunette ones, they got a bit messed up on the way."

I watched as Mum pulled a hairbrush and pair of scissors from her handbag to attend to the wigs. She brushed them out until the fake tresses were shiny in the early morning light, then placed them carefully on the mannequins' heads she had lined up on the rickety wooden-framed stalls which lined the street.

"Here they come, Linda, look sharp," Mum said, "and keep an eye out for the lifters!"

"I will, Mum," I said, steeling myself to stop anyone trying to pull a fast one on us.

"Hello missus, can I help you?" I turned to the first customer of the day, a woman in her mid-forties who was studying the beehive style hairpieces. I almost giggled, wondering what on earth an *old* woman would need one of those for.

"That looks lovely, don't it, Mum," I said, holding the hairpiece underneath a handful of the woman's hair. "Would you pass me the mirror so I can show this lady how nice she could look if she does her hair like this?"

Mum stood holding the mirror as I fussed around the woman.

"Yes, you see that'd look lovely if you backcombed this bit and stuck it in here…" My mother cocked her dark blonde head, giving the impression she was a top professional stylist scrutinising her client, like I'd seen in magazines.

"You're right Linda, and it's your lucky day," she said to the woman, "that one's half price. We're havin' a sale, but just for today, mind. It suits you, darlin', I bet your old man will like you in that, eh?" The woman, who had fair hair pulled back off her lined face, laughed raucously at that.

"I'll take it!" And she handed Mum some coins. The market was filling up. Soon it was almost impossible to pass through the densely packed street. I loved the noise, the hawkers plying their trades, the men standing on boxes with signs saying *The End is Nigh*. I've always loved people. It comes from having a large family where you have to get on with each other, and so the markets were heaven for me.

My family was everything to me. I now had younger sisters Shelley, the clever one, with light brown hair that she wore long, Maxine, who also had long brown hair and a sweet nature, Hazel, the quiet one with a short brown bob, and Karen, the baby of the family with large deep brown eyes and dark hair. Then there was my younger brother Ricky, who had a slim build and mid-brown hair. Somehow, I felt like I was their protector.

I'd left school at 15, when Mum told me it was high time I got a job. My first reaction was one of sadness. I wasn't an A student, but I liked seeing my friends at school, and had been quite happy cruising through life, getting mediocre grades and spending my time gossiping and going to the flicks at the weekend. Suddenly, life became more serious.

"Hello, I'm Linda Welford, do you need anyone in your offices? I'm lookin' for a job?" I said to the receptionist at Smithson's factory in Whitechapel Road. The woman, who can only have been in her thirties, waved me through to the office where I knocked, feeling butterflies in my stomach.

"Hello, I'm lookin' for a job, can you help me?" I said. This time my voice sounded a bit weedy. A young-looking man, with brown hair and a nice suit, looked me up and down. I shifted on the spot. I was wearing one of my favourite Mary Quant dresses, a shade of coral, which was cut almost up to my knicker line.

"Yes, we do need an office girl, actually," he said, winking at me. "Can you type?" I shook my head. "I make a good cup of tea," I blurted out, making him laugh.

"Alright then, you can start next week." He turned away.

"But what will I get paid?" I said, I couldn't go home without telling Mum, she'd skin me alive.

"We'll start you off on £20 a week and see how we go," he smiled.

£20 a week! That seemed like a huge amount of money to me back then. My first week went well. I did what I was told, tidied the office, made the tea and answered the phones.

"Good afternoon, Smithson's Paints, how can I help you?" I perfected my posh secretary voice, and I became part of the team. On Friday afternoon, David, the youth who worked there too, invited me for a drink in the pub across the road, The Blind Beggar. "Go on, Linda, it's where the Krays go, we might get to meet them…" He said, leaning against the doorframe, barring my exit.

"My mum will kill me if I don't bring my wages home," I said, primly. "Thank you, though."

The Swinging Sixties had made London the centre of the universe, and even though I was still considered too young to be out enjoying it, I spent every wage packet making myself look the part: buying mini dresses, kitten heel shoes and the black kohl I still like to wear on my eyes all these years later.

Staring into the mirror in the room Vivienne and I shared, I saw a young woman now, and not a child. I had thick blonde hair, which I wore in the style made fashionable by Dusty Springfield, high on my head and backcombed furiously. My eyes were painted with black kohl, making them stand out. I turned my face from side to side. My skin was pale but clear. I had high cheekbones and a look that seemed to say, "What next?"

I smiled at myself, seeing a familiar twinkle in my eyes as I did so. When I wore the mini dresses I loved, I saw men's gazes follow me as I walked, the wolf whistles accompanied me wherever I went. Something had changed. I had become visible in a way I hadn't been before. I liked it, but didn't really understand it. But I would, in time.

At that moment, Vivienne appeared in the mirror. She was a slim girl with long brown hair, and she looked upset. Immediately, my reverie was over.

"What's wrong?" I said, moving away from the mirror and sitting next to my young sister. A single tear ran down Vivienne's cheek. She sniffed and wiped it away with her sleeve. "Oh, just one of the girls who I used to go to school with…" Her voice was all choked up.

"What do you mean? What's happened to you? What has she done?" I instinctively hugged her, wiping the fresh tears away myself.

"Ivy bullies me… She tells me I'm no good and says nasty things. She's horrible to me…" Vivienne blurted out, then dissolved into sobs. I held her shaking body, my mind whirring. "Where does she live? D'you know where she is?"

Vivienne nodded her head, telling me her name and where her family lived. It wasn't far from us.

"What are you goin' to do, Linda?"

"You don't need to worry about that, I'm goin' to sort it, ok?"

"What d'you mean, sort it?" Vivienne swallowed hard.

"Don't you worry. You just wait here and I'll be back shortly."

I marched across the road, kept walking along Stepney Way until I came to a block of flats, not dissimilar to ours. I knocked on the number Vivienne had given me. It was time to make her pay for what she'd done to my sister.

As luck would have it, Ivy opened the street door herself. She was taller than me, with a stocky build and short dark hair. I didn't care that she was bigger. My outrage at my sister being her victim overruled that.

"That's from Vivienne," I said, punching her squarely in the face. I had no idea that's what I was about to do – my arm seemed to arch over and land the blow before my brain engaged.

We both looked at each other in shock. I stepped backwards, trembling all over. "If you touch my sister again, you'll get another bunch of fives," I snapped menacingly.

"Muuuuuuum!" Ivy burst into tears and slammed the door in my face. I legged it back home, shock and pure adrenalin running through me as I moved.

"It's sorted," I said to Vivienne as I marched into our room. She was still sitting on my bed where I'd left her. Terry poked his head round the door. "What's the wailing?" He snorted when he saw Vivienne's tear-streaked face.

"Never you mind," I retorted stoutly.

I got my fair share of wolf whistles as I walked to and from work, and it wasn't long before boys crossed my radar. I was walking through Victoria Park in Hackney one sunny Saturday afternoon with my friend Pat from the office, who had short, dark hair and a tomboyish look. I nudged her.

"Look over there, he looks nice."

A young man was leaning against his maroon and grey Ford Zephyr, looking every inch the confident, handsome charmer. He had brown hair and wore unusual clothes for the time, reminiscent of Dad's braces and flat cap. I saw him eyeing us up, and blushed. I would never have approached him – only "fast" girls did that – but I did want to play this exciting new game a bit, so I said to Pat, "Let's walk over there, give him a smile and see what happens." We giggled together as we walked over, desperate not to give any indication we were interested in them.

My friend stopped. "I don't know if I like the look of the other one." Another chap had joined the first. He had blond hair and a sneer, and I had to agree with her, but my curiosity was piqued and so I begged, "Oh come on, don't let me down now, I won't leave you with him, I promise." We changed our direction to head towards them, pretending not to look at them as we went, though I caught myself stealing glances to make sure they were aware of our existence. The young men hopped into the car, and within seconds they drew up beside us.

"Goin' anywhere nice, ladies? I'm Frank, pleased to meet ya." The one I liked smiled, leaning with his arm out from the driving seat, looking just like a film star. He had hair styled like Elvis. I thought he looked the bee's knees.

"Hello, I'm Linda, and this is Pat. We're just out for a walk together, aren't we Pat?" I replied, trying to look nonchalant.

"Fancy goin' for a coffee with us?" My friend and I looked at each other. "Alright then," Pat said as casually as she could, and so Frank got out of the car, opened the back door for us to scramble in. Somehow, the decision was made for Pat and "her" chap to go on the back seat and me to sit in the front next to Frank.

"Nice motor, is it yours?" Pat said.

"Thanks, yeah it is, cheeky cow." Frank Chapman replied, winking at me. I blushed again, thinking he was the handsomest boy I'd ever spoken to. We felt very daring, especially as Frank drove for almost an hour.

"Where are you takin' us?" I said, smiling sideways at Frank.

"There's this lovely café we like in Epping. What's it called, mate?" he shouted to the guy in the back. I glanced in the mirror. Pat looked less than thrilled to be cooped up with him when I was in the prime front seat.

I gave her a look of sympathy and she stuck her tongue out at me, making me laugh.

"High Beech Coffee stall," came the answer.

"Sounds lovely, Frank," I said, enjoying the feel of his name in my mouth.

"Four coffees, and four cheese sandwiches – no, make mine spam," Frank said, handing over a one pound note.

I nudged Pat. "He's flash," I whispered. We giggled through that afternoon, the sun shining on our faces, the boys messing about and joking to make us laugh.

"So, what music d'you like?" I asked him.

"'Ave you heard of The Beatles?" he said, leaning intimately across the table towards me.

"Yes, I have," I said, batting my eyelashes at him. I really did fancy him. He had a muscly though wiry build, and his clothes created a striking and unusual effect.

"What d'you do for a livin'? I work in an office, though I can't type yet," I said, which made Pat giggle.

"No, she flippin' well can't!" And we both dissolved into laughter.

"I'm a coalman in winter, and a scrap dealer in summer. I deliver coal then take in their scrap. It's not a bad life…" His brown eyes were boring into mine. I could've melted into them, but my friend nudged me, breaking the spell. I realised she wanted to go home.

"We have to get goin', but it was lovely to meet you both," I said.

Frank replied immediately, "Can I see you again?"

"Oh, alright then," I said, with as much fake languor as I could muster, which wasn't much.

"I'll pick you up on Friday and take you for a drink." Frank winked again. Frank and I chatted all the way back to Stepney, while Pat and his mate sat in awkward silence. I was giddy, thinking Frank Chapman was the height of attractiveness in a man.

When Friday came, I made sure I bought a new dress down Brick Lane market. It was very short, with a design of pretty flowers in reds and pinks. I loved wandering up and down the stalls fit to bursting with fruit and veg, clothing stalls, bric-a-brac and lingerie. Blokes would stand outside The Hospital Tavern nursing their pints, eyeing up the girls and whistling as they passed. It was a thrilling mix of sights and sounds, the smell of spices and unwashed traders, geese cackling from cages, women arguing over prices. I was 16 years old, and about to fall in love for the first time.

On Friday, Frank picked me up from outside work in his car. I felt like a film star stepping into his motor. He'd never take me out in Stepney or any of the nearby boroughs, always preferring to drive me up to Epping or Chigwell. At the time, I didn't mind, thinking he wanted to impress me with the drive. Again, how wrong I was.

A year after we'd started dating, I was sitting in a pub in Epping sipping a port and lemon, when it occurred to me to ask Frank why we couldn't stay a bit closer to home.

"You've promised that I could come for tea, meet your mother, but when will it happen, Frank?" I asked one Friday night. I was beginning to get fed up of the drive.

"It's not a good time, Linda, don't keep askin' me," Frank replied sharply.

"But why not? Why won't you let me come home? You ashamed of me?"

"Mum's sick. I told ya, now leave it," Frank snapped.

I sighed. "Since I met you, your mum's been sick, your sister's been away, your dad's had mates around. What's really goin' on?" I wasn't intimidated by him – perhaps I should've been.

"You say another word and I'll give you a slap. Now, drink up, I'm takin' you home."

Frank got up and marched out, where I found him a few seconds later sitting in his car, looking stony-faced and staring straight ahead. We didn't say a word on the way back.

"I've defended you to my sisters and my friends," I said. "They all said you was a pikey, a gypsy, and you were no good, but I said you was straight up. I'm beginnin' to think my friends were right about you, Frank Chapman. I don't want to see you again."

"Fine by me, now shut yer face, will ya."

A week later, Frank appeared at work, his cap in his hand: "I'm sorry, Linda, darlin', I love ya, will you forgive me?"

Somehow, I couldn't resist him. Soon enough, Frank and I had broken up for a second time, but we kept getting back together again, even though all we ever seemed to do was quarrel.

We were out one night, in a horrible old man's pub in Romford, and he'd had one too many to drink.

"You bitch, you was lookin' at him, I swear it." Frank snarled in my face.

I was sick of our fights, but I couldn't seem to let go of him, though he treated me badly.

"Don't say that, Frank, of course I wasn't lookin' at another man."

Whatever I said seemed to make little difference to him. He was eaten up with jealousy, and it came out in these unfounded outbursts.

"You're a slag. I know you go with other fellas behind my back..." Frank was slurring. I hoped he'd be alright to drive us home.

"I haven't Frank, come on, let's make a move, I don't want you drinkin' any more or you'll be too legless to drive us home."

Frank perked up at that. He got us home, but I was becoming weary of his moods, his possessiveness.

As well as my secretary work and helping Mum with her stall, I went round to babysit a couple of times for my cousin Pat and her husband George. I admired Pat – she was always dressed very elegantly. George was a tall man with a kind face, and I knew he worked as a cat burglar.

Pat had phoned me up when their babysitter let them down, and I agreed to fill in. They were going out for the evening, and when I came round they were dressed up to the nines.

"You lead such a glamorous life!" I exclaimed. Pat was dressed up in furs and jewellery, and I wished I knew where they were going.

Pat laughed. "Oh, Linda darlin', we're just going to see some friends at a club. Here, you make yourself comfortable and have a nice evening with the kids. Thanks for doing this. I'll sort some money out for you when we get back."

I was surprised at Pat's generosity. "You don't need to do that! You're my cousin, Pat, I'm happy to babysit for you any time. You don't need to pay me."

Pat looked surprised. "Oh, well, if you're sure, darlin'. Maybe we can organise somethin' else to say thank you." She turned to George.

"Tell you what," he smiled. "Next time we go out, why don't you come along with us. Would you like to? There's a very nice place we go to on the regular, I think you'd like it, Linda."

I looked at him with wide eyes. "I'd love to," I said earnestly. "Thank you so much, George, that would be wonderful."

He winked at me. "No problem, love, we'll let you know when we're next going."

And so, at the tender age of 19, I had my first taste of real East End nightlife. I knew Pat and George were well connected, as he did a lot of his work up in places like Mayfair, mixing with some of the most notorious names around. Neon lights blinked in the darkened windows of the club, and there was a queue stretching down the street.

A red velvet curtain was pulled back by a bouncer, and I was transported to another world. The smell of cigar smoke mixed with perfume hit me. A singer belted out a jazz number from a small spot-lit stage. The room was dark, crowded and buzzing. There was a lamp on each table casting a pink glow, while famous faces mingled with men who looked like they'd be more at home in a prison than a top-end club. Women wore diamonds around their necks. Men wore tailored suits. In short, it was heaven.

The Swinging Sixties were well and truly underway in Harold Wilson's Labour Britain, and huge change was underway across the world. America had entered the Vietnam War four years earlier, Martin Luther King was galvanising the civil rights movement, Enoch Powell was arguing against immigration, and the Beatles and Rolling Stones were vying for musical supremacy. Suddenly, London was a melting pot of hipsters, blaggers and stars – and they all seemed to be in the club that night. I was in awe of all the glamorous women and smart-suited men.

There was one man in particular who stood out as he walked through the crowds. Everyone was turning to stare at him – an impeccably-dressed, dark-haired man with a cigarette dangling from his full lips, and stylish black slicked-back hair. As he approached us, I saw his starched white shirt, his tailored navy suit with slim trousers and a thin navy tie. He looked elegant and expensive.

He shook George's hand with a smooth smile, and turned to me. "Who's this young lady, then?"

"Reg, this is my cousin Linda," glowed Pat. "Linda, say hello to Reggie Kray."

We locked eyes, and I smiled.

Well, I'd heard of the Kray twins, of course. Who hadn't? I'd grown up only a few streets away from their patch, and everyone knew they ruled everywhere east of Aldgate. The twins were feared and respected in equal measure. But until now, our worlds had been light years apart.

"Hello Reggie, I'm glad to meet you," I said.

Reggie looked me up and down, took my hand and kissed it, like a proper gent.

He smiled at Pat. "She looks very refreshing, does your Linda." I blushed. In amongst all the glammed-up women in furs and diamonds, I felt positively underdressed in my ordinary 19-year-old clothes. But Reggie instantly made me feel at ease about how I looked.

After exchanging a few more words with George, Reggie moved off again into the crowd. He exuded power and money, and it was breathtaking to meet a man like that on my first night out.

"Reg owns this club," George explained. "I've got to know him through work, and he always gives us a good time here." He laughed at my starstruck expression.

Frank wasn't happy at all when he found out I'd gone to a club without him.

"It's my choice, Frank, and my cousin invited me," I pouted.

"That's not the sort of place a girl like you should be going!" he shouted.

Frank and I were on-and-off together for around three years in total, until Mum made a discovery that changed everything and explained his evasive, aggressive behaviour.

By this point, Mum had a little boutique in Commercial Road selling clothes. A young woman came into the shop, with a newborn baby in a perambulator. She picked out a dress, and asked Mum if she could pay it off if she put £1 down as a deposit.

"What's your name and address, love?" Mum said matter-of-factly.

"Mrs Chapman," the woman replied.

Mum raised her brow, but said nothing, continuing to scribble down the girl's details. There might be many Chapmans in that part of town. It had to be a coincidence that it was Frank's surname too.

Just as the woman was about to leave, another customer came in.

"Oh hello darlin', how's your Frank? Is he alright?"

At that, my mother's ears pricked up, and she listened in to the rest of the conversation, already suspecting the worst.

"He'll be starting the coal in a few weeks." Mrs Chapman replied.

"What's he doing now then?" The friend asked.

"Oh he's on the scrap now."

At that moment, Mum knew. She knew why Frank hadn't ever taken me back to his house, why he'd been cagey about meeting his parents. He had a wife and at least one child by the looks of it.

That night, before I had a chance to take my jacket off before sitting down after a day's work, Mum grabbed my arm and instructed my dad, "Get the van, we're going out." Dad didn't dare question Mum when she was like that. "We're taking Linda to Shadwell…"

"But why, Mum, what's going on?" I said, utterly bemused.

"I'll show you. Don't argue, just come with us." In her hand, she had a dress. I was becoming more and more confused by the second.

We juddered through the streets of East London, my mother looking ahead grimly, saying nothing, and my dad just driving silently to the address she'd given him. I didn't know what to think. Was I in trouble? I racked my brains to think what I might have done to upset Mum like this.

We arrived at a block of flats, the modern type that were built after the wartime bombings destroyed many of the Victorian tenements. Mum marched the three of us up the concrete stairs, checking the numbers as she went, until at last we walked out onto a balcony strewn with washing hanging from lines that criss-crossed the pathway. We dodged grey vests, pink sagging brassieres, and nylon petticoats in various stages of drying. Children with dirty faces ran past us, calling to each other like wild animals from different floors of the building, though it was getting late. Mum walked up to one of the doors and banged on it loudly. I stood gawping at her. What was she up to?

Clutching the dress, she thrust it into the hands of the woman who opened the door. She looked about the same age as me, probably 19, with brown hair and a tired expression.

"I'm givin' you this. You don't have to pay for it because I believe your husband is goin' out with my daughter."

The woman looked at Mum, then at me, as I stared at them both.

"Frank! FRANK!" She shouted. I could hear the sound of a baby crying inside. Then my Frank, *her* Frank, appeared, poking his head round the door.

"Oh shit, I'm goin' out." He pushed past Mum and started to half walk, half run along the passage way, brushing the laundry out of his way with a practised gesture.

"Do ya know her?" screeched the woman, clearly devastated by the news. I looked down at the floor, suddenly overcome with guilt and shame. I'd been dating a married man for three years, and I hadn't realised.

"Yes, he certainly does know her, and you can tell him he won't be seein' my daughter ever again. It's time to go," Mum said, clearly satisfied at having said her piece. She motioned for Dad and me to leave. I was in shock. My first love was a total sham. Frank had a wife and child. No wonder he'd never invited me back to his.

I didn't say a single word on the way home, and that night I couldn't eat, instead lay miserably in the bedroom I shared with my sister and wept for the boy I thought I'd loved. I felt such a fool for falling for his charms and not guessing the truth. But I'd had a lucky escape, I told myself, at least I had found out in time and would never have to see him again. If only it could have been that easy.

# CHAPTER 3

# MICKEY

## 1968

I took myself off to Whitechapel market to cheer myself up after ending it with Frank, and caught sight of a pink dress with a large bow at the collar. I thought it was wonderful, and so I'd bought it, not having a clue when I'd wear it next as I had no boyfriend to impress.

Walking along, admiring the colourful clothing, the bustle of traders and sound of people going about their business always calmed me. But today the noise, the shoving as people elbowed past to get a good look at each stall, just made me feel worse. I almost walked straight into Pat and George. They were looking glamorous as usual. I wondered what had happened to the club they had taken me to, as the Kray twins had finally been arrested two months before.

"Why the scowl on that pretty face?" George said.

"Looks like you've been down the shops," Pat beamed. I tried to smile back, but I couldn't stop myself – my troubles poured out of me. I told them about the fight I'd had with Frank.

"Best off without him. Don't go buying such a lovely dress and wasting it on that idiot. That's it, you're comin' out with us tomorrow night. A pal of mine just got out of the nick after an eight-year stretch for robbin' an M&S van, and we're havin' a party for him, which *you're* comin' to!"

"Am I?" I answered.

"You are, darlin'," George said swiftly. "We've all got partners and Mickey hasn't got anybody, so you'll make up the numbers."

"I don't think I want to meet someone who's been in prison," I said, rather prudishly.

"Well, I've been in prison, does that mean you won't talk to me?" George smiled.

"No, of course not, you're lovely." I laughed. "Alright then, I'll come."

I wasn't thrilled at the prospect of meeting another man so soon after Frank – especially one that'd been banged up.

Saturday night came around and all of a sudden, I didn't feel like going out. I'd styled my long blonde hair with a false hairpiece, and was made up to the nines with false lashes and plenty of black eye make-up. Just as I was about to pull on my new mini dress with its fetching big bow, I suddenly felt tired.

"I can't be bothered to go, Mum," I said, sidling up to her on the sofa. I'd got into my dressing gown, though I still had my "face" on. In my heart, I really did feel that a man who had been in jail must be pretty horrible and ugly. I was sitting there, watching telly, when the phone rang.

"Hello?"

"Linda, it's Pat, where are ya? Why aren't ya here? Please come, George says he's really embarrassed because he's told his friend you're comin' and you've stood him up! Don't mug him off." Pat sounded upset.

"I'm not dressed, Pat, I'm so sorry, I just don't feel like it tonight. I'm missin' Frank…"

Pat snorted. "Get your dress on, I've sent a cab for you and it'll be there in a couple of minutes."

That was that. I had no choice but to run to my room and pull on the dress. I just had a moment to check my hair and grab my handbag before the cab's horn sounded outside.

"I won't be late…" I called as I banged the street door behind me.

Minutes later the taxi drew up outside a pub off Bow Common Lane. I got out, smoothed down my dress, and teetered in. As I entered the pub it seemed like the crowd of people parted, and standing there, dressed in a sharp suit with slicked black hair and glasses, was the man who would become the love of my life. I inhaled sharply. The sight of him almost stopped me in my tracks. As I approached, George appeared at my elbow and steered me over to him. Standing in front of this man, I felt my heart thumping out of my chest. I could see he liked the look of me too.

"Mickey, this is Linda, the girl I told you about. Linda, this is Mickey…" I don't remember if George hung round to make conversation, or whether we were left alone. All my focus was on this man.

"I was just sayin' to George, that any girl stayin' in on a Saturday night without a fella must be really ugly…" Mickey's voice was deep and throaty. He had liquid brown eyes and dark skin, like an Italian.

"Well, to be honest with you, I thought that a man who'd been sent to prison for eight years would be ugly too…" I replied.

Mickey and I looked at each other and smiled. We understood each other. The attraction was instant, and I knew from the way Mickey looked at me that he felt the same.

That night Mickey walked me home. Our first kiss wasn't very romantic, as my dad was asleep in the armchair in the lounge while I sat on Mickey's lap in the kitchen. I remember the feel of his stubble against my lips, which even now, so many years later, sends shivers down my spine.

"You bitch!"

Frank lunged at me, dragging my hair. I struggled for a moment as we tussled on the street outside the factory I worked in. I had walked out seconds before, completely forgetting that I was due to meet him that Monday evening. Sure enough, he was waiting for me, tooting his horn as I appeared.

Frank let go, and for a moment I thought he'd lay off me. That thought splintered as the impact of his fist hitting my face almost knocked me off my feet. The pain struck me, the world seemed to swim before my eyes and for a moment, I really did see stars, though not the kind my mother was thinking of each evening.

"Oh my God, Frank, stop! Leave me alone. I don't want to see you anymore. I've met somebody else," I said, clutching at my sore cheek, but speaking calmly. I blinked a few times, reassured that I could still see out of my left eye, but I could already feel the skin tightening, and I knew I was in for a shiner.

"No, I'm not havin' that, Linda. You have to go back out with me once you tell me how long you've been whorin' yerself out for…" Frank stepped back from me and ran his fingers through his brown ruffled hair.

"That's a horrible thing to say, Frank." He always did have a spiteful tongue. "No, I don't have to see you anymore. I'm tellin' you I met someone on Saturday night at the pub. I wasn't seein' him and you at the same time. Anyway, you're one to talk, you're still married, aren't you?" I added.

"I've realised that I want *you* Linda, and I'm goin' to 'ave you," he snarled. He stepped towards me and I instinctively shrank back, but at that moment a man wearing a dark coat and trilby hat walked past us. The factory horns were sounding around the East End as the working day ended. That seemed to bring Frank to his senses. He looked down at the cobbles as if it was the first time he'd ever seen them.

"Look, I'm sorry darlin', I don't know what came over me…" This time he was pleading with me.

"There's no goin' back from this, Frank. I don't want to see you again. I told you, after I met your *wife*," I spat the word, "that it was over. It's over. You're a married man, Frank, I won't ever go out with you again. How could you have lied to me like that? Your poor wife, and child! How d'you think they must feel seein' your fancy woman on their doorstep. You won't ever see me again, I mean it."

"I promise you I'll leave her. I don't love her, that's why I couldn't tell ya. Please believe me, Linda…" I'd shaken my head.

"You've done it now, Frank. Go and be a proper husband and leave me alone." I stormed off, leaving Frank staring after me.

When I arrived home that evening, my family crowded round me, inspecting my eye and putting cold flannels on it to try to stop the bruising. It was too late. The skin around my eye was already a florid purple, and I knew I'd have the biggest black eye the next day. My stomach turned over when I realised I was meant to be going to Mickey's mum's house, in Whitethorn Street in Bow, for tea. I hadn't believed it when Mickey invited me only a week after we'd met. Frank had never treated me anything like this. This was so different. This was how it should be at the start of a romance. I was excited and a little nervous to meet my new boyfriend's family. However, I couldn't meet them looking like *this*.

Brrring, brrring, brrring.

"'Ello, Bow 2936," a woman's voice answered.

"Hello, it's Linda Welford, is Mickey there please?"

"I'll just get him love… MICKEY! It's yer girlfriend!"

Hearing that, I almost lost my nerve and put the phone down.

"'Ello Linda, sorry about that darlin'. How are you? You still comin' over for tea? I hope you are."

My voice wavered a little as I spoke. "Sorry, Mickey, but I don't think I can come tomorrow."

"Why's that, Linda? I'm missin' ya. I want to see ya, and so does me mum," Mickey answered. He would never have dreamt of having a go at me because I was letting him down.

"Well, I can't come, because Frank punched me in the face today and by tomorrow I'll have a big black eye." I swallowed again, suddenly feeling like my throat was dry.

There was silence for a second or two, then Mickey spoke. His voice was low, dangerous almost. "A black eye. He gave you a black eye, did he? Well, don't you worry about it a moment longer. You come 'ere tomorrow and I'll sort Frank out. You promise to come?"

How could I refuse?

"Yes, I promise," I said, and hung up.

The next day, I stood outside the address Mickey had given me, one of the small terraced houses lining that part of the street. The rest was taken up with post-war blocks of flats. There were a few trees dotted along the road but it was mostly concrete. I rang the doorbell, making sure my dress was smoothed down and checking my hairpiece was intact.

A woman in her sixties opened the door. She had long grey hair twisted up in a bun, and a petite figure. She took one look at me, then hollered over her shoulder: "Michael! MICHAEL! What did ya do to this poor girl?"

I blinked before realising that she thought he had been the one to give me a shiner. Before I could say anything, Mickey's mum ushered me along the narrow corridor that led from the street door into her small kitchen.

"You'd better come in, girl."

When Mickey saw me, he jumped off his seat and came over, peering at my bruised face.

"Did you do this, Michael?" His mum had her hands on her hips and was glaring furiously at Mickey. I could see instantly that she was a proper East End mum, fierce and unafraid to say her piece, the matriarch of the family despite her diminutive size.

"Don't be stupid, Mum, I wouldn't hit a woman!"

Mickey's dad came in to see what all the fuss was about. He was a big bruiser of a man who worked down at the docks.

"Is this what prison taught you, son? Don't you know better than to hit a woman?" He too was glaring at my boyfriend. "Does she know you was a jailbird? You don't have much good taste in men," his dad added. I had to say something.

"No, no it wasn't Mickey. It was my ex. I told him I didn't want to see him anymore, and he didn't take it so well."

At that, Mickey burst out laughing, just as a young woman walked in the room. She had attractive brown shoulder-length hair and a beautiful face with high cheekbones. It was Mickey's younger sister Maureen.

"Oh Mickey, what 'ave you done? Don't tell me you've given this girl a black eye, you've only been out of prison a week!"

"It wasn't me!" roared Mickey. "But once I know where Frank lives, I'll make sure he don't do it again. You're my girl now."

"You haven't covered up that bruise very well. Come on, let me put some more make-up on it, that'll make you feel better at least."

I looked at Maureen gratefully, and let her lead me out of the kitchen and into her room. She gently patted Revlon face powder onto the bruise, tutting as she worked.

"He's really gone for it, ain't he, Linda," she said matter-of-factly.

I agreed, and we started chatting. From that moment onwards, Maureen became my best friend – and she still is today.

Later, looking a little brighter, I sat at the table eating the ham, egg and chips that had been put in front of me, wondering what Mickey really meant when he said he'd "sort it". Something told me not to ask. At first, I wouldn't tell Mickey where Frank worked, but he was very persistent and so, eventually, I gave in.

Mickey told me to come round to his the following Saturday, from where we'd go out to the pub together. My mum had insisted my dad drive me to his, sensing that there was something brewing.

She was right.

Dad and I hadn't gone far when Frank jumped out at us, brandishing a gun. He pulled open the passenger door of Dad's van, and grabbed my arm.

"You're comin' with me!" he shouted. Dad grabbed my other arm and started to pull as well.

"Charlie, don't make me shoot you," Frank spat.

I decided to take the reins. I knew that Frank would never have the guts to shoot the thing, so I turned to Dad and said, "Don't worry, it'll be ok, just go home."

This was all happening in broad daylight on Commercial Road. People were hurrying to and fro right next to my gun-toting ex. No-one seemed to notice the drama that was unfolding in this busy thoroughfare. A van tooted behind us, so I jumped out and let Frank bundle me into his car.

He drove me towards Mile End, and I knew we were heading to his yard in Burdett Road. It wasn't a nice place, this scrap metal yard, and sure enough, soon he was yanking me roughly towards the dark, damp-smelling outbuilding where he worked. Inside, there was a rough earthen floor covered in mangled bits of machinery and car doors, engine parts and other bits of metal I didn't recognise.

"You'll stay 'ere until you promise to go back to bein' my girl." He growled. I should've been afraid, but I knew that Frank only talked the talk, so I shrugged: "That won't happen, Frank."

I think he was surprised, and a bit unsettled, by how calm I was.

"You know Mickey will come for me, he knows where this yard is. Dad is probably ringing him right now," I added, just to see the look on his face. I was getting to him.

I looked around. It was a dank airless cave leading onto a forecourt filled with the same unfamiliar bits of cars and machinery.

Frank started pacing the floor. The sound was muffled inside the space, and so I couldn't hear any people or motors from the road. We were entirely alone, and yet I wasn't afraid. I wasn't even scared of him. He'd shown me what a liar and a cheat he was, and I'd lost all respect for him.

"You know my brothers will also come for you, they're probably on their way here right now."

He was staring at me, wild-eyed. Had I misread the situation? His fists clenched and unclenched.

I softened my voice. "Take me home, Frank, and we'll forget this ever happened." I knew that shouting wouldn't help.

Suddenly, he cracked. In all honesty, I thought he'd take longer. He was even weaker than I'd thought.

"Ok, ok, I'm sorry, I didn't mean no harm. Let's just forget it," he said, suddenly looking twitchy.

"That's right, Frank, we'll pretend it never happened," I replied, knowing full well that this man had it coming, either from my family, or from my boyfriend, whatever I said.

Calmly, I walked back to the car. Frank dropped me at the end of my street and I ran home, phoned up Mickey to say I was fine, then ordered a taxi to take me to his mum's.

"Get 'ere safely. I'll be out seein' Frank," Mickey said.

I didn't dare try to talk him down. If it was a member of my family who'd been kidnapped, I'd have been round there myself.

Mickey told me that he'd burst in on Frank, shouting at him that I was a young girl and I had the right to go out with whoever I wanted. There was heated talk of shooting and violence, but Mickey's friend Sammy managed to talk the pair down, saying that I might go off Mickey in a few months anyway. It did the trick and defused the situation.

One thing was for sure: Mickey had decided that I was his woman from now on. He'd told my ex Frank in no uncertain terms to stay away. I'd met my match.

# CHAPTER 4

# GANGSTER'S MOLL

## 1968-70

"I want you lookin' a million dollars tonight, love." Mickey smiled, peering round the bedroom door in the tiny flat we were renting above a launderette in Leytonstone High Road. I was standing at my mirror, putting on a pair of earrings he'd only recently bought me.

I looked over my shoulder at him. "Why? Who are we meetin' that's so special? Don't I always look good, Mickey?" I was teasing him, flicking him a glance from the side of my eye. He sidled up to me, placing his hands on my waist and nuzzling my neck. Inside I just went to mush whenever he got close to me, and tonight was no different.

"I want you lookin' beautiful, that's all, but you always do anyway."

He started kissing my neck. I batted him away, laughing, "Well, we haven't any time for *that* if you want me to get my glad rags on."

Reluctantly, Mickey let go of me, winked at me with that irresistible charm, and went to the wardrobe, picking out a brand new suit he'd just had made by his tailor in Whitechapel

Road, the heart of the Jewish East End, and a place I loved to wander round at the weekends. The Jewish shops were closed on Saturdays for the Sabbath but open on Sundays, so it made a nice change to head over there, past the hoardings painted with Silks and Woollens signs, to the little boutiques sprinkled up and down the road. Groups of unemployed men would hang about, passing the time of day. Orthodox Jewish men with their ringlets and black hats would walk earnestly. There was always something going on there.

Mickey had his suits (his "whistles and flutes", in Cockney) made by his favourite tailor. His newest whistle was grey with a white pin stripe and an expensive weave. He paired it with a lavender coloured shirt and handkerchief in his top pocket, which contrasted well with his Mediterranean looks.

"What should I wear, Mickey, is there anything in particular you like me in?" I said as I pursed my lips and applied a slick of glossy pink lipstick. I liked to wear make-up, and Mickey spoilt me, buying Guerlain and Estee Lauder. I didn't have to make do with Ponds Cold Cream, like my mum had for all these years, because my man took care of me, he bought me everything I wanted. I knew he'd been in prison, so I had my ideas about how he could afford to spoil me like this, but I was loving it. The earrings I was wearing were real diamonds. I felt very lucky to have a man who treated me so well.

Right from the start, Mickey was open with me about what he did for a living. When his pals came round to our place, they'd all pile into the kitchen-diner while I made the tea. I'd serve it up in proper china cups to three or four hard, dangerous-looking men, sitting around my expensive country cottage-style wooden table and eating the ham sandwiches I'd prepared for them. Mickey would stand over the table and unroll a large map on it. They'd spend the next half an hour scratching their chins, sipping their tea and scrutinising the streets of London, with mutters of "Let's try this place," or "That one's a possible. We should check out the post office round the corner while we're at it."

Mickey would draw his finger in a circle round a corner of the map and say, "I'll go have a look at these ones, Linda will take me." Mickey didn't drive, but I'd learnt in my late teens, so I'd take him out in the car the following day. I knew exactly what we were going out to "have a look" at.

"Park up here, Lin," he'd say when we were within striking distance of a bank or post office. We'd walk for a mile or two round the alleys, the backstreets, and Mickey was always deep in concentration, looking all around him and making a note of every hole in a fence that he spotted, or any dead end with a few cars parked up at the side of the road. Occasionally he'd mutter to himself, "This won't work – not enough outs," or "There's a good drop-off spot."

After a day or two of scouting out each location, the group would reconvene to share their discoveries. Over hours and hours of tea, weighing up the options and scrutinising each location in the minutest detail, they'd settle on one for their next job.

The other men's wives knew the boys were going out to rob banks, post offices and all sorts, but they didn't want anything to do with it. The meetings were always round our house, and I was the only woman to know the details of what they were planning in the weeks leading up to each job.

Occasionally I'd even chip in as I brought the next round of tea, and point out some possible targets I'd spotted myself. Mickey would chuckle and say, "That's my Linda, she knows exactly what she's doing."

I was curious about Mickey's work, but the main thing was that I loved him and wanted to know what he was risking each time he went out "on the pavement". I knew he'd been behind bars before, and was well aware of the risk he could end up back in the slammer if he wasn't careful. So it seemed only natural for me to make suggestions at their meetings and listen in on their plans.

I'll never forget when he came back from a job for the first time since we'd been together, and presented me with a little box. I opened it to find a gold necklace finished with a heart-shaped diamond. It had been paid for out of the spoils of a security van heist, and that day, I'd spent the whole morning pacing around my kitchen, cleaning the surfaces over and over, trying to find ways to occupy myself. My heart was in my mouth by the time there was a bang on the door three long hours after he'd left. I rushed to open it, expecting what? The police? A mortician? Mickey and two of his mates piled in, laughing, joking, high as kites on the success of their raid. They scattered money everywhere, like leaves fallen from an autumn tree, and I was giddy with happiness that he'd come home to me. The worry of those hours vanished in the celebration. Seeing all that cash was quite a splendid thing.

"We did it. They didn't see us comin', Lin," he grinned.

"Babe, I knew you could do it," I smiled, kissing him, the smell of his musky, male scent melting me inside.

"We fuckin' did it, Lin. Look, you keep the money, we're goin' for a drink. Don't wait up for us, eh love," he winked. "Why don't ya go shoppin', get yerself somethin' lovely."

I wasn't daft, I knew where the money came from, but it was all insured and no-one ever got hurt, so what was the harm in it? I was 20 years old and I'd never been on the pavement myself, so I never got to see what actually happened during their robberies. To me it was like living in a fairy tale. The money appeared on a Saturday night or a Tuesday afternoon, depending on which security vans they went after, and that was that. If I had a few hours of nerves to deal with, then so what? Mickey was charmed. He always came home to me, and that's really all that mattered.

"Wear what you want. You will anyway, and you'll look amazin'. As if you'd ever let me tell you what to do!" Mickey laughed and sauntered off to the kitchen.

The flat had been a distinctly unglamorous one-bedder above a steamy shop, and had seemed grotty to me when I first set eyes on it. But we furnished it well and transformed it into our own little palace. Mickey bought me heavy velvet curtains for the windows. We had a large L-shaped sofa, and we were one of the first people we knew to have a globe drinks bar – the sort that slid open to reveal the bottles.

We hadn't waited long before moving in. It had just felt right from the moment we met, so why wait? I loved the area, the hustle and bustle, the eateries – the pie and mash shop, the pease pudding van and the whelk stall opposite the Green Man pub. One thing was for sure: we'd never starve living there.

"Come on Lin, we 'ave to get movin', the cab's 'ere," Mickey called from the front door.

I'd slipped into a silk lavender dress with high heels and a fox-fur wrap around my shoulders. I saw the diamonds in my ears and on my necklace wink in the light as I turned to leave.

"Stop 'ere mate, thanks," he said, handing a note to the man, who tipped his cap. I looked up as Mickey helped me out.

The club we'd stopped outside of was run by a mate of Mickey's called Colin. Inside, it was dark but plush, with a DJ and a small dancefloor, as well as booths in red velvet with tables in front.

Colin greeted us warmly. "What kept you?" he smiled. "I told you to come along as soon as you came home. You've been out a few months now."

"It's great to see ya," Mickey replied. "I wasn't coming until I had a couple of new whistles made."

"Ah, of course," Colin said, turning to me. "I forgot what a peacock he was." We all burst into laughter. "You never saw anybody with such perfect prison gear. When we were inside together, his was all pressed like he was going out."

Mickey gave me a wink.

"Whatever you want tonight is on me," Colin added. He called the bar tender over to put a bottle of champagne on ice for us.

"I'll tell you exactly what I want," said Mickey, with a mischievous look. "I want the DJ to play 'I Heard It Through the Grapevine' by Marvin Gaye."

"No problem," grinned Colin. "Anything at all that you want, you just let me know."

"That's all I want," Mickey nodded. "But I want it played all night."

"You're joking," Colin goggled.

"No I ain't. Or are you going back on your word?" asked Mickey, with a wry smile.

"No, of course not," Colin replied, looking a little flustered. "Your wish is my command."

He went over to the DJ, took the mic, and pointed to us, saying, "Ladies and gentlemen, this is a good friend of mine, Mickey Calvey. He's just come out of the big house and I made a promise he could have anything he wanted."

Everyone cheered.

"Well, he wants Marvin Gaye 'I Heard It Through the Grapevine'."

They cheered again.

"The only thing is, he wants it played all night."

"Oh, leave it out," someone laughed.

"Sorry," Colin chuckled, "I made a promise."

True to Colin's word, the record came on and we danced to it a couple of times over, then went and sat with Colin and an attractive blonde lady to have a drink. After the song had played about eight times, even Mickey gave up the joke and said he'd heard enough. The DJ was relieved to play his music for the rest of the night.

Mickey told me that Colin had got nicked a little while later. I don't know what for, but it was part and parcel of life for people in that world.

"What about the post office around the corner from there?" one of the men said one day that summer, as they sat round our table with Mickey, poring over the map.

"Nah, there's only one exit and we can't risk it," Mickey replied. He was always the anchor man, the one who made sure everyone else got out of a raid. No-one ever wanted that position, because it meant they were the last to leave, holding off security while the rest made their getaway, with sirens squealing and alarms ringing. Mickey knew he would be the easiest to catch, but he also had the respect of his peers for doing the most dangerous job of all.

"There's a security van that collects from the supermarket there, we could do a hit in the mornin' and be back for lunch," one of the men added.

"Why don't you try that one?" I said, pointing to the map of South-East London spread out among the crumbs and tea cups.

"From what I can see, there are three possible exit routes, and you can park a getaway car at two of them." All four of them nodded and looked over it intently.

Mickey always listened to me. He wasn't like other men, who ignored their partners or excluded them from "men's talk". He knew I was clever in my own way, and I caught on fast. None of it seemed real to me, it felt like a game, a dangerous one, but a game nevertheless.

"Yes, we could leave Tel there," said one of the men, a large, shaven-headed bloke.

The men all nodded again, this time in agreement.

"Now that's settled, another ham and pickle, anyone?" I interjected.

"Yes please, Linda, you do make a tasty sandwich," said the bald one.

I smiled at him. Somehow, I was never afraid of these violent men who were sitting in my home. I always seemed to bring out the softer side to them.

"And don't worry about disguises, I'll get a few wigs and fake moustaches from Mum's stall tomorrow," I added, knowing I'd never tell my mum what they were for, but it was at least a small contribution to the "work" these men did for their families. I knew there was no danger of a curious stallholder asking unwanted questions. In fact, when I got the black curly wigs and black moustaches, it was quite fun watching the butch fellas all trying them on.

"Do I look like me?" A man called Terry joked as he sported his new look.

"No!" I laughed, "you look like a clown gone wrong," I snorted.

"Look at me, Lin, how do I look?" Mickey joined in. He was wearing a red wig this time, with a fake black moustache and glasses.

"Stop, you're makin' me laugh, my sides hurt." To me, they looked more comical than threatening.

When the planning was over for the afternoon, the men would drink up their tea, finish the sandwiches, stack their plates in the sink like their mothers must've told them to do when they were growing up, and very politely bid me goodbye, nodding at Mickey as they left.

Mickey would go out the afternoon before each job, without telling me where he was heading. I knew he was off to pick up the guns, but he never told me the address he was going to and it would be a different place every time. Then, finally, the day of the raid, after weeks of planning, they'd gather at my table, sawn-off shotguns in their bags, wigs and glasses covering their faces. They'd be jittery and hyperactive, desperate to get out the door, and yet they all had a little ritual to go through before leaving. Mickey would religiously take off every piece of his jewellery in order, the two rings he always wore and a gold ingot necklace, and place them on the table. Without the jewellery, he'd be less easy to identify. Each man did something similar to make himself less conspicuous. I'd pace up and down all day, waiting for them to return. The raids were a success, over and over again, and enormous piles of notes were tipped onto my kitchen table.

Timing was everything. Even a minute too soon or too late could mean the difference between missing the van, or losing the right moment to raid, landing £10,000 or nothing at all. They all knew they couldn't raid until the cash was in the hands of the security guards. Then they would have seconds to mobilise as the loot was being carried to the van. Missing those vital seconds meant disaster – weeks of planning could be lost, possibly forever. Once the money was locked inside the van, all bets were off, and the robbery lost. And it would be madness to try again without weeks more of meticulous planning and organising.

"I'd like a child, Mickey," I said, a short while after we'd moved into the flat.

"Look, Lin, you realise what I am, my lifestyle. I don't think I should have children. I'm a crook. I could be here today, and be put away tomorrow."

I looked at the man I loved. "I want us to have a baby, Mickey. I know what you are, and I know how hard your life was as a child. But we could give our baby so much more."

Mickey had told me that his early life was poor. Growing up, he didn't have a lot. His dad was a docker and his working life was fraught with danger, as well as being unpredictable and low-earning. He had had a much harder upbringing than I did. He used to make racing cars out of veg boxes and pram wheels. They had nothing. One time, while in the makeshift car, he got run over by a horse and cart. He went home and his dad went mad because he'd lost a shoe.

Mickey had looked at his dad, and saw a life of toil and hardship ahead of him. He swore not to end up like that. I understood why he'd done it. He wanted more out of life, and these were the days before social mobility, before people could work their way up, excel at school or go to university no matter where they'd been born.

In those days, if you were poor, you stayed poor. Mickey and his pals decided the only way they could change that was by seizing what wasn't theirs with both hands. So that's what he did. And I couldn't blame him for not wanting to bring a child into the world, but I was adamant. I wanted a baby, and that was that. I fell pregnant quickly.

A few months before I was due, Mickey and his friends were messing about after a few drinks one Saturday afternoon, when they picked up a discarded Hilti nail gun and started shooting it at the floorboards and walls. We had builders in at the time to redecorate the flat, which is why they'd been left lying around at the weekend. I was heavily pregnant, and stayed out of their way, but within minutes there came a loud BANG-BANG-BANG on the front door.

"Are you maniacs?" came the shout from the hallway. "Who's firing bullets through the floor? One came through a washing machine and almost hit my customer!"

"Quick, stage exit!" Mickey shouted, gesturing to his pals to leave by the back door.

"What the…?" I began to answer.

"Sort it out, Lin, we're off!" And with that, they left.

I waddled over to the door and opened it to find our landlord, spitting blood. There was only one thing to do: I burst into tears. The sight of my round belly and my running mascara silenced the man, who was a one-armed Irish bloke in his fifties.

"Don't go upsetting yourself darlin'. Don't tell me it was you firing them bullets?" he said, looking alarmed as I continued to weep loudly.

"No, it weren't me. I'm so sorry, it was my Mickey. Him and his mates had a few drinks and got silly with the Hilti gun. There weren't no bullets."

"I've had a few drinks and done silly stuff myself. I can see you're pregnant so I won't report you, love, but you'll 'ave to either buy the place or move out, because I've had enough of this nonsense."

With that, he was gone.

Mickey didn't want to buy the flat, so we decided to move out. But then, eight months into my pregnancy, something happened that put an abrupt stop to our plans, and gave me a stark reminder of what I was risking by bringing a child into this life of ours.

Mickey and the boys had gone out on a big raid they'd been planning for weeks, and I was waiting at home, pacing round and round the flat. After hours of nervously finding little jobs to distract myself with, I sat down in front of the telly to watch the news.

I froze when I heard the top story.

An attempted armed robbery had failed in the East End of London. Suspects had been arrested, and I knew instantly that my Mickey was one of them. He'd been gone too long and I had known something wasn't right.

Mickey was sent up to Southend, and pleaded not guilty. It was the first time I saw him stand in the dock. He looked just as cocky, just as confident as ever – he even threw me a wink, even though we knew he'd never get off. He'd been charged with Robbery and Conspiracy to Rob, though only the Robbery charge stuck.

My Mickey was sent down. I was devastated, though it wasn't a surprise. I'd met him when he was fresh out of an eight-year stretch, and I wasn't so naive as to think he'd never get caught. But it still hurt to know he'd have to suffer prison, and I'd have to bring our baby into the world without him there.

A tear slid down my face as the sentence was read out. I cradled my big belly, our child kicking inside me. Mickey looked at me one last time before the guard he was handcuffed to led him down from the dock and into the holding cells below. He would be taken to Wandsworth Prison that evening.

"I love you," I mouthed to him.

The high life was over – for now. I whispered to my baby that I would take care of him or her, that I would keep them safe until Daddy came home, feeling like my heart would break.

"Come on, Linda, let's get you home, and look after that baby inside you, eh," Mum said. She'd come with me to court, and rather than look for a flat, it had been decided that I'd move back home with her until the baby was born.

## CHAPTER 5

# HANDCUFFS AND WEDDING BELLS

### 1970-78

Shortly after Mickey went away, I developed toxaemia, or pre-eclampsia as it's now known. I'd gone for a routine check-up with the nurse, carrying some frozen peas I'd picked up at the shops.

The matron ran some tests and gave me a look of concern.

"You'll have to stay in, your blood pressure is high, you're very ill and it might hurt the baby," she brusquely informed me in her starched white apron and blue uniform.

"I can't stay in now. I need to get these peas to my mum before they melt!" I wailed. I couldn't go wasting money on food that would spoil.

The nurse looked at me. She knew Mickey was in jail and money was tight, so she reluctantly agreed to let me go home, hand the peas over and come straight back in.

"You must come straight back in though, Linda. You might die, and your baby might die, if you don't."

"The baby might die...?" I said.

"Yes Mrs Calvey, though I'm sure it'll be ok if you go straight home and come straight back. We need to keep an eye on you both from now on."

I'd given my name as "Mrs Calvey" to appear respectable. Eyebrows were raised in those days if you were an unmarried mum. I took the peas home, explained to Mum that I had something called toxaemia, which she hadn't heard of either, and then walked back to the hospital. It is astonishing to me today how careless I was of my health that day.

I arrived back at Mile End Hospital in Bancroft Road after dropping the peas off and packing a few essentials I'd need – or so I thought. Into my small suitcase went my make-up bag, my hairpiece and rollers, and a few flimsy nighties in shades of pale pink and peach.

I was told I had to have the baby in the next 48 hours. The baby hadn't been due for another month.

"Alright, I'll have her on August the first, that's got a good ring to it," I said, naively, thinking the baby would just pop out and I'd be resting in my fancy nightwear reading a magazine before I knew it.

They started me off with injections to induce the birth at 11am the next day, and I'd got myself all made up and ready with two plaits in my hair, thinking it would be easy.

How wrong I was.

"Ahhhhh, what's goin' on?" I yelled, my voice echoing through the labour ward. "Oh my God!"

"It's alright, Mrs Calvey, the baby's coming. Now just keep breathing like we showed you… in, out, in, out, yes that's it, good girl," the matron said.

There was a flurry of activity around me as I was moved in my bed into a birthing room.

Another contraction hit. I felt like I was losing my mind. The pain was excruciating.

"I want my mum!"

"It's ok, Mrs Calvey, the baby's almost here. One more push and it'll be born. Are you ready? Good girl, now PUSH."

I did as I was told. In a rush of blood, my baby daughter was born.

"She's so quiet. Why isn't she cryin'?" I tried to lift myself up on my elbows but found my body was so weak I could hardly move.

"Come on, little one." I heard the matron's voice. The room started to swim.

Then I saw a sight. My baby girl was being held upside down by her feet, her head dangling upside down. Then the matron slapped her.

"Don't do that!" I cried, bursting into tears.

Then the baby let out a cry that filled the room.

"She's alive. Thank God, thank God," I wept, holding my arms out to her.

"Sorry, Mrs Calvey. She has to go into an incubator. She's very small and may need help breathing."

I nodded, desperate to hold my child, but trusting the matron. It was desperately difficult not to be able to cradle my first child straight away, but I told myself that they would take good care of her and that I'd at least be able to go and see her to feed her every day.

Over the course of the next two weeks while I was kept in hospital, a steady stream of Mickey's pals came to visit me. At the time, the only man allowed at your bedside was your husband.

So, sure enough, a few days after the birth, the nurse came to see me and said, "Linda, your husband's here."

I didn't bat an eyelid, knowing full well it couldn't be Mickey, so I said, "Thanks, yes, show him in."

"Alright, Linda," said the beefy looking man with a thick neck and wide, stocky build, as he stood, nervously, at the end of my bed. He looked totally out of place in the clean, ordered environment of the maternity ward, surrounded by pregnant ladies and new mums.

"Hello Fred, it's good to see you. Did Mickey ask you to come?" I asked.

"Yes, he got a message to me, and a few of the fellas around 'ere. He wants us to make sure you're bein' looked after." Fred, who looked increasingly uncomfortable, gazed around the ward, taking in the pristine clean floors and beds with starched sheets and baby cots. There were bunches of yellow flowers given to the newly delivered mums, and a general air of peace and order. I had to fight not to giggle at the sight of him.

"It's good of you to come, tell my Mickey that I appreciate him lookin' out for me even when he's away."

"These are for you, Linda." Fred handed me a small bunch of pink dahlias.

"That's very kind of you, thank you. Matron, could we please have a vase for these?" I called out to the nurse who was passing.

"Well, I'll be off then, Linda. You take care of yerself and that baby of yours. I'll get a message to Mickey and let him know you're alright in 'ere." With that, Fred departed, and I could finally burst into fits of laughter, thinking of that tough, hard man, cowed under the serene hand of the matron and her disciplined hospital ward.

Two days later, another man came, and the nurse returned to my bedside, a look of puzzlement on her face.

"Linda your husband's come to see you again, he looks rather different today." She looked at me, her brow arching.

Unruffled, I said, "Thank you, please show him in."

On the third day, the nurse just came and sat at the end of my bed, laughing. "You'll never guess, but there's another of your 'husbands' here to see you."

Four different men came to see me over the course of my stay, all of them visiting me because they knew my Mickey was banged up and couldn't come himself. I appreciated the gesture from those hardened crooks. When I was discharged I went up to the ward every day to feed Melanie. And when Mum and Dad got back home from their August holiday, they came in with me to meet her.

The sight that greeted Mum when she went into the ward shocked her to the core. There was little Melanie, lying in her own vomit, her soiled nappy unchanged, bawling her eyes out.

My no-nonsense mum was furious. "This is how you look after a little baby?" she raged at the matron. "You take her away from her mother and leave her in a state like this? You think this is better than what her own mum could do for her?"

Mum demanded that the hospital discharge Melanie at once, and, after cleaning her up and calming her down, the three of us marched out of the hospital, my daughter finally safe in my arms.

My baby was coming home with me, and I couldn't wait to show her off to Mickey. Six weeks later, I dressed her and got ready to have our first visit as a new family.

"Come on darlin', let's get this pretty pink dress on you so you can look your best for Daddy," I cooed to my beautiful baby girl. Melanie gurgled in response. I leant over and kissed her tummy, smelling that warm, baby smell, a mixture of talc and milk.

"You're goin' to be a stunner today. Let's change that nappy and make you perfect." I undid the pin holding together the terry towelling material she was swathed in and tossed it in the bucket Mum left in the kitchen, so that she could tip the dirty ones straight into the large pot she used to boil them clean on the stove.

"Come on, beautiful, let's go and show Daddy how pretty you are," I said, adjusting the big bow I'd placed on her head.

When I got to Wandsworth Prison, both six-week-old Melanie and I were searched. I didn't like to see the screws going through her blankets, but it was unavoidable, as everyone knew that people would smuggle drugs inside by hiding them in a baby's nappies or blankets. I had to take my coat and boots off then they ran a metal detector over the length of my body.

"Find anythin'?" I quipped, and the screw shook his head, grinning, and nodded me through with a wink.

Mickey was in the visiting room, in his prison clothes. Even looking like he did, seeing him made my heart miss a beat. I sat at the table, opposite him, and passed him the bundle of blankets that was Mel. "Oh she's lovely," he said, not moving to take her.

"Go on, you won't hurt her."

"I'm scared I might drop her," Mickey replied, looking helplessly at me.

I snorted with laughter. "Course you won't. Go on, she's your daughter."

Mickey reached out and took his baby girl in his arms. My heart melted to see the look of pure joy on his face.

"'Allo darlin', I'm your daddy. I hope you haven't got the short straw by havin' me." Mickey looked up at me. "Other men in here, hard men, tough men, said to me, the minute you look at her you'll fall in love, and I have. She's the most beautiful baby I've ever seen."

I smiled, watching the love of my life hold our child. It didn't matter that we were sat in the visiting room of a prison, surrounded by other men and their families. It didn't matter that he was banged up for another three or more years. All that mattered was that we were now a family.

Mickey cleared his throat.

"Now we've got Melanie we should get married. I want her to have a proper dad. You know I love you, and I want her to be in a proper family."

I blinked, unsure what to say, my heart was so full.

"Is that your idea of a proposal, Mickey?" I joked, eventually.

"Yes," he said simply.

I could only smile my response. When I went home that day, Mum took Melanie off me, while Dad took my coat and sat me down at the kitchen table. Terry was there, Shelley and Maxine too.

"Mum, Dad, I'm goin' to marry my Mickey," was all I said.

Mum and Dad glanced at each other. Their look was one of trepidation rather than outright objection.

"We know he's a crook, love," said Mum, "but we like him and we can see he loves you."

"We know how determined you can be," Dad interjected, "and we'll support you whatever happens."

I could see in that moment how they'd struggled with the idea of me being caught up with a blagger, even one as charming and loving as my Mickey. Both my parents grew up on the right side of the law, and they'd brought us kids up to think the same way.

"Thank you, that means a lot to me. I know Mickey loves you. We're all goin' to be family now."

Mickey saw the prison chaplain and got permission from the governor for us to get married. The date was set for our wedding at Wandsworth Registry Office, and I was told we could only have two people. Mickey was good to me. He told me I could choose who came, and so I asked my parents to be there. He approved, saying that his daughter would be living with them, so it was fitting they should witness our marriage.

On the day of the wedding, I wore a cream mini dress, a fur coat, and had my hair done with flowers in it.

"Ready, love? You look lovely," Dad said in my bedroom doorway.

"Thanks Dad, yes, I'm ready."

I loved Mickey so much that I didn't mind going to a registry office near the prison in Dad's old van to meet the groom-to-be. It was hardly the most glamorous way to arrive – but as we got closer, there seemed to be some disturbance going on. Police officers were crawling over the place we were due to wed, and there was a huddle of photographers from the press.

"What's goin' on?" I said, peering out.

"I don't know, love. Oi, mate, what's goin' on here?" Dad called out to a passing police officer.

"We've got a prisoner gettin' married," the copper said, looking at me in my cream dress, and realising he was talking to the bride's party.

"But why the fuss?" Dad went on.

"It doesn't matter. Just get inside as quickly as you can," the officer replied, looking round as we got out of the car and made our way through the crowds.

"It's the bride!" said someone, and a camera flash went off in my face.

"Blimey, Dad, get me in there," I said, frightened of the crush, and the attention. Why were there press photographers at my wedding?

Once inside, another copper came over to us. "We have to search you. The baby too," he said. Dad, normally a mild-mannered man, lost it.

"What a fuckin' cheek!" he blasted. "I've never been searched in all my life, and you won't lay a hand on our Melanie."

"Dad, just let them," I whispered hastily, to try and smooth his feathers. "I want to get married today, let's just do what they're askin', please."

Dad submitted. Melanie's blankets were searched. When they'd finished, I grabbed her and held her close. I didn't like this one bit.

"What's this?" the copper asked after searching Mum's handbag.

"A pair of scissors, what d'you think they are?" replied Mum, smartly.

"What are they for?"

"Cutting things," Mum retorted. "I run a market stall selling wigs, and often I need to trim them." The officer took them off her anyway.

Once searched, we had a chance to look round at the place where Mickey would make an honest woman of me. It was grand, with a sweeping staircase leading up to the rooms where the wedding would take place.

Dad whistled. We walked up, running our fingers along the smooth balustrade, smiling at each other at last. After all, it was a wedding. Inside the room, Mickey walked in wearing the suit I'd delivered a week earlier to the prison. He saw my look of surprise when I realised he was handcuffed to a screw.

"Can't he just have one cuff on? Why must both of his hands be cuffed?" I begged. The prison officer shook his head.

"They tried to put a bag over me head, and I had a police escort around the prison van." Mickey shrugged.

I didn't know whether to laugh or cry. Our married life was starting with Mickey cuffed to a screw, while I hovered beside him, clutching a small posy of white roses. It wasn't the most romantic of ceremonies.

"I now pronounce you man and wife," the registrar said finally, and immediately the screw pulled Mickey away.

"Where's the bit where I can kiss my wife?" Mickey said, indignantly.

"Nowhere," said the guard. "Our orders are to take you straight back to prison. Don't want you trying to escape, do we?"

I looked at Mickey, puzzled. He wasn't going to do anything as stupid as that. What was the screw talking about?

"If you keep up, you can have a half-hour visit," the screw called over his shoulder as they left.

"Come on, Dad, let's get there before that bloody guard," I said. I was fuming. Instead of being greeted by confetti, there was a barrage of camera flashes as we left the building.

"Run, Dad," I yelled, and we scuttled around the corner to our parked car, the press in hot pursuit.

"Quick, let's get out of 'ere," Dad shouted above the din, starting the engine. What was going on?

A reporter knocked on the van window, shouting, "Was this an escape plan?"

Dad replied, in no uncertain terms, "No! It was a fuckin' wedding, now clear off!"

Later, I discovered that someone had anonymously rung the police to say that Mickey was going to try and escape from the registry office. A total lie, of course. Why would Mickey try to run from such a short stretch inside and risk getting caught, and being handed a longer sentence as a result? It didn't make any sense.

Back at Wandsworth, we had a 20-minute visit talking across a table. We barely had a chance to kiss, let alone do anything more, before Mickey was taken back to his cell.

Back at Mum's, my nan said, "Oh, your wedding photographer is 'ere."

"I didn't book a photographer, Nan. What would've been the point?" I said.

Then a man stepped into the lounge from the kitchen. He was wearing a brown coat, and a large camera was slung over his chest. "If you pose for me, I'll send you a free set of the copies. At least then you'll have the pictures," the man smiled.

I didn't much like the look of him, but we didn't have any other way of marking the day.

"Why not?" I said. "And make sure you get one of the baby."

Of course, we never did get those photos. Perhaps they're in the local rag's archive somewhere, but they did end up on the front of the newspaper. Marrying a crook was, apparently, a big story.

That was the day I realised my life would never be ordinary. How many wives are swamped by the press as they marry a jailbird? Not many, I assume, though I loved Mickey too much to care.

A year before Mickey was due to come home, Mum urged me to put my name on the council housing list. Meanwhile, she found a private flat four storeys up in an old Victorian tenement block called Brady Street Mansions in Whitechapel. It was as far from a mansion as you could imagine. Dirty children played in puddles in the yard that separated the blocks, washing hung at the windows, and litter lay in the streets. The whole place felt seedy and neglected. Despite first impressions, though, I was desperate for my own place. The private housing officer for the block showed us round, but said there was a long waiting list.

"I bet if I gave you £50, that waiting list would shrink," said Mum. She was right. I got the flat, and took it, even though I felt sorry for those poor people who'd been waiting.

The day I got my key, I opened the street door straight into the shabby dark lounge. The door facing me was for the small bedroom, and one on the left led to my kitchen. It wasn't much, but it was mine. My parents had bought me a three-piece suite and a bed, while I signed a hire purchase agreement at Wickhams to get us a colour television.

That winter was horrendous. I tried to make it homely, but water was pouring in through the roof and down the walls. After a few months, I couldn't stand it any longer. I called the council to complain. They sent round an officer. I had bowls placed under all the leaks, and they were all full to the brim with ice-cold dirty water.

"My God," said the officer, "I know all the tricks people play, throwing water at the walls to try and get moved to a better house, but this is a genuine case. You'll get an offer from the housing department for another place very soon, and it'll be more decent than this."

"Thank you, that means a lot. I can't bring up my daughter here, it will make her ill," I said. Those tenements were notorious for poverty and hardship, and were knocked down only a few years later.

And so I was offered my first council place, this time on the tenth floor of a council block in Brabazon Street, in Poplar. Mickey's brother Pat helped me to decorate it and make it my own.

And when Mickey was finally released, I brought him home for the first time.

"Ta-da, our beautiful new flat, and look at these views, Mickey!" I ran over to the window and pulled open the curtains, wanting to surprise him. Outside there was a summer haze over the city landscape, but you could still see for miles, across the rows and rows of rooftops.

"Stop! Shut them curtains, Lin!" Mickey yelled, diving onto the sofa.

"Shut them? But, why? Mickey what's wrong?"

My husband, the big tough armed robber, looked pale all of a sudden.

"I don't like heights! Shut them curtains!"

I moved quickly, pulled the fabric to cover the glorious views, and turned to Mickey.

"We can't live like this, with the curtains closed all the time!"

I hadn't known he was terrified of heights. There was nothing else we could do – Mickey, Melanie and I had to move again, so we swapped with my brother-in-law Terry, and went to live in his place in Oslack Road, Catford.

And soon enough, we had a second child to welcome into our home, a son who we called Neil. That was the icing on the cake for Mickey. When he held baby Neil in his arms, he said, "A son, I've got a son! This is wonderful, Lin, let's have two more children!"

This from a man who hadn't wanted kids in the first place.

"More children? Are you mad? I've got enough on my plate lookin' after you three, and Mickey, it isn't right to bring more little ones into the world because of what you do."

We both left that hanging in the air. I never berated Mickey for his work, but I also couldn't consider giving us more mouths to feed, so I put a stop to that idea. Being an armed robber wasn't exactly a steady job.

But we didn't settle in Terry's old place, and I soon had itchy feet again, spotting an advert for a new two-bed house in Laindon, Basildon. Going from a flat to our very own house felt wonderful, though we had a big garden, and I worried whether we'd be able to manage it. But my Mickey told me not to worry.

By this time, Mickey was going "out" again. He never told me where he was going this time round, but he'd be picked up by a pal at odd times of the day and they'd head to London. I could only assume he was back working on the pavement. Mickey never did learn how to drive, though he bought me a brand-new Datsun as the money started rolling in once more.

Mickey would always make me laugh when we met new people in Basildon. He was wary of being caught again after his stint in prison, and told me that the best way to avoid being sussed out was to hide in plain sight. When we met the neighbours, they'd inevitably ask the usual questions.

"So, what do you do for a living?"

Mickey would smile warmly and simply say, "Oh, I'm a bank robber."

This would send the neighbours into fits of laughter. "No, come on, what do you really do?"

Cool as ice, Mickey would chuckle with them and reply, "I'm a painter and decorator."

And that was that – they bought it every time, and didn't suspect a thing.

When Neil was still a baby, Mickey went out on a job which went very well. On his return, he and the lads zipped open their large holdall and showered Neil with notes as he lay gurgling on our bed.

"May you always have money," smiled Mickey.

"Amen to that," said one of the men.

Someone took a photo on one of the old Polaroids at the time and gave it to me. Neil had such a lovely smile on his face. Sadly, the photo had to be burned, as something like that sitting on my mantelpiece would've got Mickey 15 years inside.

Life felt good again. Mickey did the place up, decorating it and making it look lovely.

"But what about that garden? It's depressing," I said to him one day, staring out at the window at the flat grass and wooden fencing.

"Leave it to me," he replied, kissing me on the forehead, ruffling Neil's hair and heading for the door. It was around 7pm, and he was dressed head to toe in black. I saw that he'd put all of his jewellery in a kitchen drawer, his ritual before doing a job. Even though I was used to the uncertainty and the waiting, that evening I was fraught with worry as ever. He crept back into the house late in the night. I was lying awake in our room, unable to sleep while he had been out. The kids had been asleep for hours, but I just couldn't go off without knowing he was safe. As he slid into the bed, I put my arm out for him.

"You awake, babe?" He whispered.

"You know I can't sleep till you're home," I said, rolling onto my side.

"There's nothin' to worry about. I'm always extra careful these days," he said, as he drew the covers over us and we moved together.

The next morning, I opened the curtains and almost fainted with shock. My garden was filled with exotic plants, huge palm trees and colourful flowers.

"What the hell have you been up to?" I laughed, in utter astonishment. Mickey propped himself up on his pillow, yawning and smiling. "I told you I'd get you a garden, didn't I, babe."

"But they'll all die! They're tropical. It looks like Kew Gardens out there." It was hilarious. More so when he began to look so crestfallen as they inevitably started to die off.

At the time, I thought it was quite a romantic gesture – and it was so like my Mickey to get me whatever I wanted. It was that desire in him to look after me, which I absolutely adored.

In our new house, though, I missed my family. I was homesick, and so I found a house in Pembroke Road in Walthamstow that would suit my needs better. It was an absolute tip, but I knew we could make it nice and so I told Mickey it was a done deal: we were moving.

Mickey refused point-blank to go, but I told him I would be going anyway. We didn't usually argue, but we certainly did over that. And so the next day that Mickey went out to "work", I moved us over to Walthamstow while he was out. Mickey had to phone my mum to ask where her "cranky daughter" was now living, as he didn't even have the address! He soon got over it, as he knew how stubborn I could be once I'd set my heart on something.

Tough, scary-looking men soon started meeting round my kitchen table again to plan robberies. One of the new men at my table was called Charlie Lowe. Mickey had introduced us, and I knew instantly I didn't like him – and more importantly, didn't trust him.

Charlie Lowe was a big, handsome, well-dressed man, an outgoing character who was popular with the boys and the ladies. One night when he, Mickey and I were out together, I told him another friend of mine was going up to court, and that I was worried he'd be going away.

Charlie eyed me carefully. "As long as he's well prepared, Linda, he'll be fine. It's every man for himself when you're up there."

I raised an eyebrow. "What do you mean?" Blaggers who got caught together always stuck together in court – you had to know you could trust the people you worked with not to grass you up.

"You know what I mean," Charlie answered. "Once you're in the dock, it's dog eat dog."

My stomach turned, and from that moment, I was convinced Charlie was a grass. I told Mickey that I'd got a bad feeling about him – I even said it in front of Charlie himself.

"I'm sorry, Mickey, I don't trust him," I said one day when they were planning a job together at ours. Charlie was standing next to Mickey, leaning against my kitchen cabinet.

"I'm one hundred per cent, darlin'," he replied, smiling a crooked smile at me.

I looked at him for a moment, taking the measure of him. "No, Mickey, he's a wrong'un."

Mickey looked at his new pal, giving him an embarrassed smile. He obviously thought I was being totally out of order.

"My wife always speaks her mind, don't mind her."

"I do speak my mind, and I'm tellin' you, Mickey, there's somethin' not right about him," I said, before stalking off. I trusted my instincts, and later that night, I confronted my husband about what had taken place in my kitchen, and the conversation I'd had with Charlie.

"He's not to be trusted. You know I have a gut feelin' about these things. Why won't you listen to me?" It was rare for us to fight. This was one of those times.

"He's solid, I trust him and that's all that matters," Mickey had said, before slamming the door on me. There was nothing I could do but accept my husband's judgement.

Alongside Charlie was John, a key man – he could open any lock and disable alarms – and they all started doing jobs together. One day Mickey took me to a large furniture superstore and told me to pick out everything I wanted for the house. Thinking it was a joke, I pointed at the most expensive suite.

"That's lovely."

Mickey walked up and drew a white cross on the back in chalk.

"Go on," he said.

"That's gorgeous," I pointed to a table lamp, "and so's this," I said, holding up an Indian silk bedspread.

The game went on like this for an hour. Everything that I chose, Mickey marked with a chalk cross.

That Saturday night, Mickey and the lads went out. At around 9.30pm there was a knock at my door. I opened it.

"What's all this?" I exclaimed. John was holding the lamp and the bedspread.

"Where d'ya want these, love?"

I stared back at him, realising what they'd done. Everything I'd chosen was now mine.

"Oh my God, quick, put them in the bedroom! No-one's seen you, have they?" I stuck my head out of my doorway. It was a nice road lined with Victorian terraced houses, each with a little back garden and trees out front. We were in darkness: the only moving shapes were my husband and his men, as they unloaded a large van emblazoned with the name of the furniture company they'd visited.

I was taken aback. Their usual method was to steal a van or a getaway car in advance of a job: they'd change the number plates and wait for weeks before going out in it, as they had to be sure the police wouldn't be out looking for the stolen vehicle. But now here they were with the furniture company's own van.

"How did you all do it?" I laughed over cups of tea once they'd finished unloading.

"Well," Mickey began, "John got us into the store, turned off the alarm, opened the back, and we simply loaded everything you wanted into one of their own vans. That way it didn't look like a stolen one.

"We took the van back, put the alarm back on and locked it all back up. Can you imagine how confused the store manager will be arriving tomorrow morning to find his store empty but no sign of a break-in!" With that, they all collapsed into laughter. It was a clever move, I had to give them that.

A few months later, a knock on my door revealed the police. They took everything away, and Mickey and his pals were arrested again.

I had been right. Charlie was a supergrass. He'd told the Old Bill everything, about every robbery, big or small, that the group had undertaken together. There was honour amongst thieves, though. Mickey's friends decided to take the rap for the big robberies, as they were bang to rights. They denied my husband's involvement, though – and so, somehow, he walked free.

But the Charlie Lowe episode had made me more nervous than ever. And when Mickey started talking about doing "one final job", something that would earn enough for us to buy a place in Spain and live like royalty, I couldn't conceal the bad feeling that was taking root in the pit of my stomach.

It started when a man called Ronnie turned up on our doorstep. It was a Saturday night, and I was still wearing my blue silk dressing gown, but had done my hair and put my make-up on for a night out with Mickey.

"Get that, will ya?" Mickey shouted from the shower.

I went and opened the door. There was a man wearing a tracksuit, jogging on the spot on my doorstep.

"Hello, can I help you?" I said.

The man turned to me, and stopped moving instantly. He looked me up and down, and I suddenly felt a little self-conscious. I wrapped my bedroom gown tighter around me.

He held my gaze and there was a long pause before he spoke. "It's Ron to see Mickey, hope I'm not disturbin' ya?"

The man had brown hair, a square jaw and a flinty expression in his eyes. I had the feeling this was a man not to mess with, though I didn't have a clue who he was.

"Not at all." I recovered my poise quickly. "Mickey's in the shower, but I'll tell him you're here."

"Don't disturb him." Ron had a low, quiet voice. "Tell him I'll be back in a couple of days."

I stared after him as he jogged away, wondering who on earth I'd just met.

"Oh, that was Ron," said Mickey, towelling his hair dry and wearing nothing but a pair of boxer shorts as he walked through to the kitchen.

"Cover yerself up!" I laughed in mock horror, as I looked at him, admiringly.

"Like what you see, do ya?" he joked back, making me blush a little.

"Yes, I do, Mickey, you know I do," I said archly.

"So what did Ron say?"

I told him Ron would be back, and asked Mickey what his business was with him. I knew Ron was different from the usual crooks Mickey worked with. He had a reserved demeanour that exuded power. He didn't joke or flirt with me, as Mickey's pals always did – instead he'd been business-like, even though I'd met him so briefly.

"You workin' with him, then?" I said, dabbing my nose with expensive face powder.

"Yeah, that's the boss. He says he's givin' a job as a trial run. If it works out then I'll be in with a shot at the big time. This could be the last one, Lin, we could be made up after this. All I need is one big job and I could crack it, I'll never 'ave to work again. That'd be nice, wouldn't it, love?"

With that, he had sidled up to me, putting his arms around my waist.

"I've only just got dressed, Mickey, stop that or you'll ruin my lipstick," I said, breathless. I didn't want him to stop.

As promised, Ron returned on Monday morning.

"Come in, Mickey's ready for you. Can I make you some breakfast? I'm doin' Mickey some eggs on toast," I said politely to him.

"Only if ya don't mind, thank you."

His blue eyes watched me as I busied around the kitchen. I was aware of his eyes boring into the back of me, but tried to ignore it. Perhaps he was taking my measure, deciding if I was trustworthy or not? From what Mickey had said, he was a big time crook, so being distrustful came with the territory. But I couldn't help feeling that this man spelled trouble for us, and that Mickey's determination to hit the big time would have consequences.

# CHAPTER 6

# BAD FEELING

## DECEMBER 1978

"What are you doin', babe?" I asked Mickey as he sat, tipping shotgun pellets out onto the kitchen table until the cartridges were empty.

"Well, I'm goin' to stuff some wadding in the cartridges and seal them with candle wax," Mickey replied, carrying on with his work, cleaning and checking his shotgun in preparation for the raid.

The kids were watching television in the lounge, and thankfully hadn't seen what their father was up to only yards away from them. Melanie was eight years old and Neil was four, both very young and impressionable, and laughing raucously at *Tom and Jerry* cartoons. I'd taken Melanie to prison to see her dad when Mickey had been banged up before, but afterwards she'd gone into school and told her teacher she'd "gone to see Daddy and been tickled by a policeman", which, of course, meant she'd been searched. At the time, I was mortified, and as Mickey was almost at the end of his sentence, I didn't take her back. I went alone after that. In marrying a blagger, though, I knew I was condemned to a life lived like this, in fear of him being caught, with possible jail sentences to get through, though I never once thought of leaving him. Mickey and I were soulmates – it was as simple as that – and the way I saw it was that I'd made my bed and had to lie in it.

"What on earth are you doin' that for?" I replied, standing with my back to the cabinets blowing on a hot cup of tea.

"Because, my angel, there will be women and children out today, and if I go 'bang' it'll just be a bit of fluff that comes out. It'll make a noise and that'll do the job."

I raised my eyebrows.

"Listen, Lin, I really hope I don't 'ave to pull the trigger but if I do, I won't hurt a soul." He looked up at me, his brown eyes twinkling. At that, I shrugged. It sounded like common sense to me, despite how strange he looked, sitting there in our domestic setting with weapons scattered everywhere and bullets discarded on the floor.

"Alright, babe, you're out today then?" I asked, putting my tea down to start the washing up in the sink.

"Yeah, though I really don't want to go. I've never gone on the same job three times, it's a bad omen." I couldn't help but agree.

Mickey, with his pals, had tried the same robbery of a Caters supermarket security van twice already, each time on a Saturday morning in Eltham. They'd missed the van both times.

"Perhaps it isn't meant to be?" I asked, but Mickey shook his head.

"I'm in too deep with this one, Lin. This one is a trial for a much bigger job, working for much more important people. I've committed to it and I can't say no."

"But missing the same job twice already is really unlucky. Can't you do a different job for these people?" I reasoned, but Mickey was having none of it.

His face changed. A shadow passed over his features, and he looked scared, or so I thought.

"It isn't like that. You don't just pick and choose your jobs. No, I've got to do it. I can't let them down, I have no choice."

With that, he put his head down and carried on stuffing the cotton wool. I didn't dare ask who "they" were. I knew he wouldn't tell me anyway. I'd never heard of Mickey working for someone else before, and my hackles rose. Something didn't feel right. I also knew that Mickey was dead set on going out, so all I could do was reassure him that everything would be ok, and in a few short weeks we'd have the best Christmas ever.

There was something else that had made me superstitious about today's job. The day before, after Mickey had been round to collect the shotguns and brought them home, four-year-old Neil had found one of them and picked it up. Neil had gone racing out into Pembroke Road, waving the gun, shouting "bang, bang!". The first I heard of it was a neighbour who knocked on my door.

"Neil's out there with a gun, you need to do somethin'! Quick!" she exclaimed. She'd been out washing down her front step when Neil appeared, brandishing the weaponry.

"Oh my God, MICKEY! Come down 'ere. Neil's got one of your guns!" I screamed up the stairs.

I've never seen a man move as fast as Mickey did that moment. He threw himself down the stairs three at a time, and legged it into the road. Seconds later the sound of Neil wailing loudly announced their return. Mickey's face was bright red. He dragged our son into the house by his left arm, so I immediately leapt over and freed Neil, enfolding him in a hug.

"It's alright, darlin', you weren't to know that was Daddy's thing and not yours to play with," I crooned, rocking my devastated son back and to. I motioned to Mickey to take the bloody gun and hide it before he brought the Old Bill down on our heads.

That had felt like a bad start to today's venture. It was the first time the children had got directly caught up in their father's exploits, and somehow it suddenly made his "profession" seem real to me in a way it hadn't before. Later that night, as Mickey slept next to me, I lay awake, thinking back on the day's events. It was the first time I'd had doubts about our lifestyle, and I didn't like the feeling. I didn't want to look at the stark reality – I wanted to carry on, not asking any questions, and enjoying the money when it came. Until then, it had only really been Mickey who suffered the consequences of his actions, but that night I saw it affected us all, and I didn't know how to stop it. Those doubts had kept me sleepless until the early hours, so by the time Mickey was emptying out his guns the next day, I was already feeling anxious and on edge.

*Must be the lack of sleep,* I reassured myself, as I tried to keep upbeat for his sake. *Mickey will be fine, he's always fine, whatever happens out there...*

"Alright, darlin'. Do you want anythin' to eat before you go? It's cold out there, so make sure you wrap up warm." I busied myself making him a fried egg sandwich. I couldn't bear the thought of him going out, feeling the way he was, without any food inside him. I could see Mickey was going to go whether I approved or not, so all I could do was look after him a bit before he took the plunge.

At 10am he went up to our bedroom. I followed him, feeling jittery myself, and somehow unable to let him out of my sight. I watched as he donned a curly black wig from Mum's stall. Mickey could get away with wearing a wig that colour, because he looked Turkish or Greek with his dark skin. He put on his black anorak, and pulled the hood over the fake hair because he didn't want the children to get upset or worried by the sight of him in that daft wig, and he looked at me.

"I'm goin', Linda. I promise I'll be back and we'll go out and celebrate. Be ready for 7pm, Jerry and his new girlfriend are comin' round and we'll go out for some drinks."

"Alright, Mickey, I'll be ready. I'll have a roast ready for you at 5.30pm, don't forget," I called after him as he walked slowly back down the stairs. "Do a chicken," he said. Roast chicken was his favourite.

"Alright, babe." I replied, following him downstairs and glancing at his fingers to see if he had forgotten his rings, but he'd already taken off his jewellery. He had a new necklace – a gold dolphin on a chain from a recent trip to Malta – which had been the last piece to come off and be placed in a drawer in the kitchen.

Our Malta trip had been a blast. Mickey paid a cab driver to drive us round for the whole week we were there. When we passed the prison, Melanie, who had just turned seven, pointed at it and said, "Oh Daddy, look, that's your house." I could've died with embarrassment. The taxi driver replied, "Your daddy can't live there, that's for naughty people." Mickey changed the subject very swiftly, but later, when it was just the two of us, we couldn't help but laugh. Aside from that small blip, that holiday made me feel we were a normal, proper family doing normal, proper things, enjoying time together in the sunshine. But now we were back to *this* reality: Mickey sneaking out so he didn't upset the children, me worried all day in case he got nicked again, and – I won't deny it – anticipation of a big financial windfall. It was a strange and heady mix, and not one experienced by many ordinary housewives.

At the front door, Mickey picked up his bag, which contained two sawn-off shotguns, and turned to shout to the kids.

"Daddy's off now. I'll see you tomorrow."

"Bye Daddyyy!" they both shouted from the living room.

My stomach flipped over as I looked at my husband's beloved face, which was lined with worry. I could see he was deeply uneasy, and I suddenly felt panicked. I had to fight with an intense urge to grab his arm and keep him there with me.

"Look, Mickey…" I started but he interrupted before I could finish.

"I'm goin', Lin. I love you and I'll be home safe and sound this evenin'." He pulled open the front door, bringing a rush of cold air into the hallway. That must've been why I shivered.

The door closed and I felt a sudden urge to weep. I never cried. I usually looked on the bright side in life, but today was different. A second or two later there was a knock at the door. Mickey was standing there. He never took his keys because, again, it could lead the police to our door. "I've forgotten me turtles," he said. "I won't come in, just get 'em for me, won't you, love."

He waited outside while I looked for his gloves (his turtle doves, as he called them) under the stairs where all the coats, scarves and boots were kept. I fished them out and handed them to him. Melanie had seen her dad return, and was waving at him in the bay window, peering through the net curtains.

# CHAPTER 7

# ROBBERY

## SATURDAY, 9 DECEMBER 1978

*Where is he? Doesn't he know what time it is? The roast is getting cold...*

It was just before 7pm and I'd heard nothing all day from my husband. The roast dinner I'd cooked was set out on our two dinner plates, the gravy congealing in pools around the now-cold chicken.

*The roast potatoes will be soggy if he doesn't appear soon...*

I was starving hungry but I didn't like eating until my Mickey came home, so I'd waited.

Mickey would usually have appeared home by now after a raid, either with a long face and the slam of the front door behind him if he'd mistimed the job, or with a great whoop and a bag filled with nicked cash which he'd shower over the table in a grand gesture.

Either way, he always came home – so where was he?

I'd kept myself busy all day to try and quell my fears, though a nagging voice at the back of my mind kept thinking how spooked Mickey had seemed. It wasn't normal for him to go out a third time to the same job. I couldn't shake the feeling that all was not well.

I managed to get the kids to Mum's, where they stayed most weekends, and then I kept myself busy working her stall at Roman Road market while she was babysitting them. Luckily, I had a steady stream of customers, so I was forced to be bright and cheery, chatting away to Mum's regulars. I didn't have much time to worry about Mickey.

Mickey wasn't a normal dad. He was more involved than most – he used to do most of the school runs and get the children up, dressed and fed in the mornings, so that I could go out early to help Mum. But when he was working, that always took priority.

When I finished, I went and got my hair done. This was my Saturday ritual, a blissful bit of peace and quiet, flicking through one of the magazines.

Today was different though. I felt fidgety and nervous.

*Pull yourself together, Linda. It's all going to be fine. This is Mickey, he always gets out of the scrapes he lands himself in.*

I tried to believe it.

While the roast was cooking, I'd run myself a bubble bath, and made myself up with glossy lipstick and the black kohl I loved to draw heavily around my eyes. I liked to copy the looks I'd seen in *Vogue* and *Harper's Bazaar*. I chose one of the wonderful dresses Mickey had bought for me, a black sequinned number, paired with high heels, and I picked out one of the fur coats I had hanging in my wardrobe – a mink one that my husband particularly loved. I was glammed up but still there was no sign of Mickey.

I ate my dinner, as by now, I was too hungry to wait a second longer, and covered my husband's plate with tin foil so he could eat it later, once he'd explained why he was taking so long to come home.

By 7.45pm, I was cross. Mickey's pal was also late, and I still hadn't heard a thing.

Mickey would have to have used a public phone box or a friend's home telephone to call me, but soon enough a knock at the door announced Jerry, his new young girlfriend standing behind him.

"Alright, Lin, how are you, girl? You look lovely," he said, kissing my cheek as he came in.

"How do you do, come inside," I said to his rather plain-looking friend. She was dressed down in plain brown leather boots, a brown calf-length skirt and blouse with a bow at the neck. It had rather a prissy sort of effect. I later learnt that she was a school teacher. She had no idea Jerry and Mickey were crooks – which at the time I found amusing – but later part of me wished my life wasn't so entwined with blaggers and robbers. How much simpler it all would've been.

"Where is he?" Jerry said, looking round. He popped his head round the kitchen door as if he was expecting Mickey to be there.

Puzzled, I turned to him. "Well, I thought *you'd* know the answer to that! Don't tell me you haven't heard from my Mickey?"

Jerry shook his head. "Don't worry, Lin, he's probably forgotten the time and has gone out boozing with his mates to celebrate. Yeah, yeah that'll be it, babe, that's what he's up to."

I noticed that Jerry didn't say *why* he would be celebrating in front of his law-abiding girlfriend.

"Why would he do that when he knows his dinner was waiting for him, and you were coming round?" I countered. In my heart, I knew something wasn't right, but I couldn't put my finger on it.

"Listen, Lin, Mickey's fine." Jerry soothed. "He's just being a naughty boy with his pals. We'll find him in the pub somewhere. Come on, let's go and you can give him a proper tellin' off when you see him." Jerry winked at me.

"Ok," I said, pulling my mink onto my shoulders, turning off the cooker that was keeping Mickey's plate warm.

The three of us headed straight for The Needlegun in Roman Road, one of our usual haunts. It was busy with all the usual crowd of small-time crooks, some of whom raised a glass to us as we walked in. The air was thick with cigarette smoke and there was something loud playing on the jukebox.

"'Ave you seen Mickey Calvey?" Jerry shouted to the landlord over the din. I knew his wife quite well, and she looked over at me and shook her head.

"No darlin', we ain't seen him tonight. I think he was doin' a bit of work today."

"Well, tell him we're goin' down the Carpenters, will ya," Jerry said as he opened the door for me and his lady friend.

"We will, don't you worry," the landlady said.

Down at the Carpenter's Arms in Ben Jonson Road, Stepney, it was the same story. No-one had seen my Mickey.

The mystery deepened. The Carpenters was Mickey's favourite pub. It was a bit more downbeat than some of the pubs we usually went to, but he liked watching the old men play darts as he sipped his pint.

"Listen, let's go to The Albion and get ourselves settled and wait for him. He'll find us there," Jerry said, though his face told me he wasn't optimistic. The night was being wasted in cabbing between pubs on what felt like a wild goose chase.

*Where are you, Mickey? What's happened to you?* I said to myself, feeling furious now. How embarrassing it was to be out with *his* friends when he wasn't anywhere to be found!

We were friends with Ron and Sylvie, who ran the pub in Lauriston Road, Hackney – a late Victorian public house with a green façade, and three doors under a series of archways. Jerry, his friend and I made a strange little group at the bar: a crook, a crook's wife and a teacher all making small talk. I sat at the bar sipping my vodka and lime, when Sylvie came down the stairs. She baulked when she saw me, then she went to her husband and whispered something in his ear.

"Oh Linda, I'm so glad you're 'ere. Mickey just rang minutes before you got 'ere and said he's been held up and won't be back till later tonight."

Was it me, or was Sylvie deliberately not catching my eye as she spoke?

"Held up? What on earth does that mean?" I turned to Jerry who shook his head, bemusement on his face.

"Oh well, at least he's ok. Thank you, Sylvie."

Jerry knew something was up. On the pretence of "sortin' some business with the guv'nor", Jerry walked over to them. They started talking, and all three of them looked over at me.

"This is the weirdest night I've ever been on," the school teacher said to me.

There was nothing I could say to that except to agree with her.

As I looked over at the three of them huddled at the bar, urgently whispering, I saw pity on their faces as they turned to me. I felt my stomach swoop. Something had gone wrong.

"What's goin' on?" I said to Jerry, sharply, I could feel my heart racing now.

"Listen, Mickey ain't goin' to be 'ere until after the pub shuts."

The pub's goin' to shut?" I said incredulously. There were always lock-ins for the regulars at the weekend. I couldn't remember a night when we hadn't been offered one.

"What's goin' on?" I said again as I watched Ron empty the pub. Sylvie appeared at my side with a small holdall.

"Mickey's goin' to be really late, so I'm comin' home with you. I don't want you to be on your own at home tonight."

"But Sunday's your busiest day," I said. "You can't come back with me."

"It's fine. I'm comin' home with you and that's that." Sylvie turned to her husband and added, "I'm staying with Lin. When Mickey gets in I'll come home."

It was getting late and I'd had a drink, so Sylvie called a cab. I was really getting angry by this point.

"He really is somethin' else!" I huffed as we got into the taxi. "He's really embarrassed me this time."

"Don't worry about it," soothed Sylvie. Jerry and his girlfriend left, so it was just us heading back home.

When I opened the door, I shouted, "Mickey, babe, are you in?"

There was no reply. It was dark. The bar was unopened. It was obvious he hadn't been back here this evening.

"Let me fix you a drink and you can go straight to bed," Sylvie said.

I didn't sleep much that night, and only fitfully. When the phone rang at 6.30am, I was already awake. Sylvie must've been too, because she was the first to get to the receiver.

She picked the phone up.

"Hello, oh hello Terry. Yes, I'm the guv'nor's wife, yes, I know…"

*What did she know?*

The questions were already forming in my sluggish brain – the combined effect of lack of sleep and the vodka I'd drunk the night before weren't helping. I felt strange, like everything was all wrong, and I couldn't understand why.

There was a pause as Sylvie listened to the voice at the other end of the call.

"No, no she doesn't… ok.,, we'll be there." She hung up.

I looked at Sylvie. I knew I looked dishevelled. I'd slept in my make-up, but I didn't care.

"Tell me," was all I said.

"He's been arrested. We have to go to the nick," Sylvie replied, too quickly.

"Oh, for God's sake!" I exclaimed. "I'll need to pack him a bag."

"No, there's no time." Sylvie grabbed my wrist, stopping me from charging back into our bedroom to retrieve some clothes for my husband.

"We have to go now before the shift changes." Again, Sylvie wouldn't catch my eye. She meant that the police officers on duty were an alright bunch, so I understood we had to move fast to be able to speak to them.

"Oh, I see, alright then, give me a minute and I'll get dressed. Bloody Mickey, how the hell did he get himself arrested?" I muttered to myself as I changed. "I hope they're treatin' him well."

# CHAPTER 8

# THE TRUTH

## SUNDAY, 10 DECEMBER 1978

When the cab turned into Brabazon Street, I knew something was up.

"This isn't the way to the nick," I said to Sylvie, but she just shook her head and wouldn't answer.

"Why are we stopping outside Terry's block of flats?" I asked as the cab drew to a halt. I felt utterly bewildered.

Again, Sylvie just shook her head. "'Ere you go, love, there's a tip on there as well," she said to the cabbie, holding out a note.

By now, I was utterly confused. The feeling of dread I'd been holding at bay was becoming stronger and more powerful by the second. Perhaps Mickey had got hurt, and that was why no-one was telling me anything? I hadn't had a straight answer to anything yet so far. I felt panicky. My thoughts were spiralling out of control with "what-ifs".

"Can you please tell me what's wrong? Is Mickey hurt?"

The words had only just left my mouth when Sylvie interrupted me. "It's ok, darlin', follow me."

Meek as a lamb, I followed her into the lift and up to the 10th floor, our old apartment, which Mickey's brother had moved back into.

Sylvie knocked on the street door, and someone opened it. Nothing felt real any more. Once inside, we walked to the end of the corridor, off which were the doors leading to the bedrooms. We turned into the lounge. My mum was standing there.

"Hello Mum, what are you doin' 'ere?" I asked, not really thinking why she was standing in my husband's brother's flat on a Sunday morning at 6.45am. Nothing made any sense. I felt disorientated, but a part of my brain just wanted everything to be ok when it blatantly wasn't.

There was silence in the room. Was it me, or did everyone look awkward? They all turned to look at me. I felt like I was standing in a shop window, everyone gazing at me. My brother-in-law Terry walked over to me, taking my arm gently.

"Mickey's dead."

For a second, I thought he was joking. I almost laughed. Then the room swam. My head felt hot, prickly, like something terrible was in there and I wanted it to get out. I could feel my heart pounding, bang, bang, bang against my chest, but that didn't feel real either. Everything became a blur. I felt suddenly cold, and then I heard a woman screaming. Agonisingly, heartbreakingly.

"She's hysterical," I heard someone say, and I realised it was me, I was the one howling. My Mickey was dead, he was dead, and I couldn't breathe, couldn't think, couldn't feel anything anymore. I wailed and sobbed and railed at God.

"My Mickey, my Mickey, he's dead," I sobbed.

"Give her a brandy, for God's sake!"

A cold glass was thrust into my hand, breaking the spell.

"Drink this, darlin'." It was Terry's wife. I looked up at her, realising I was bent double. "Drink this, come on Lin."

Trembling, I stood upright and placed the rim to my lips, swallowing the bitter liquid. It made me cough, made me come to my senses. They were all there – Terry, Sylvie, Mum and other members of Mickey's family – all there because our beloved boy had died.

"Tell me," I ordered them, and let myself be guided to a sofa. I only wanted to know the truth of it.

"It looks like it was a trap," Terry said, his voice scratchy. "The coppers were waitin' for them. The Flyin' Squad got him as he tried to leave. They didn't get the money. They didn't get nothin' except a bullet."

Terry sat back, waiting for me to take in this information. When I felt composed enough to speak, I said, "He should never have gone back after two failed goes at that job. I told him, I told him not to go, that it was jinxed." Tears streamed down my face.

"The worst of it is, Lin, that the Old Bill need to identify his body, and it's you who has to do it this mornin'." Terry's voice cracked with emotion. He'd lost his brother that day too, and he started to sob like a child, the weight of his loss crushing him on that bleak December morning.

"Me? Why me? And why so quickly?" I felt panicked. I'd only just learnt my husband, the love of my life, was dead. It would be too cruel to have to go and see his body right now.

"I'm sorry, Lin, but he's been dead since five o'clock last evenin'. The police came to your door just after you left for the pub. They eventually found me – that was at about 11pm last night. The Old Bill came to my door and told me to contact you as Mickey had been shot dead. I told 'em I wouldn't phone you at that time of night, instead I said I'd call you early in the mornin' and get you to go over there.

"I wanted you to 'ave one last night of peace before findin' out." Terry looked away. I could tell he felt bad about me having to go and identify my dead husband's body – and I knew he'd been a real gent with me, giving me my last night's sleep for some while to come.

"Of course I'll go, Terry, and thank you for everythin' you've done, I know you've lost your brother as well as me losing my husband." I smiled at him, managing only a watery grimace, but it was an acknowledgement, at least. He'd done what he could for me, and now I had to do what I could for Mickey.

"Where do we go?" I said, standing up, downing the last dregs of the brandy, and wiping away the smudges of mascara and kohl that had run down my face. I must've looked a state, but as the only person I liked to look good in front of was now lying on a mortuary slab, I didn't care a jot.

"I'll take ya. Can't 'ave you goin' there alone," Terry said. "Just give me a minute."

Out on that empty London street, the frost lay heavy on the winter streets. It sparkled in the early morning light like diamonds, hard and cruel. It was bitterly cold but I barely noticed it. Sylvie left at the same time to get back to her pub. I squeezed her arm with gratitude, knowing that she'd known since last night, and she too had tried to protect me from the terrible truth.

Deep down, I'd known something was wrong, and my anger at Mickey last night was part of my survival mechanism, keeping me going when at heart I knew something awful must've happened. It was too late for regret. I had to pull myself together, for my children and for Mickey, and do what I needed to do. Mickey's mum had howled like a wounded animal when she was told the awful truth, that one of her sons was dead. None of us would escape from this unscathed.

Terry and I arrived at the mortuary in South London. It was as desperate a place as I'd imagined. I was dazed but determined to get through the morning until I could hide away and vent my sadness, the grief that threatened to swallow me whole.

"Where is he?" I asked the police officer who stood guard just by the mortuary entrance.

"D'you mean Mickey Calvey?" he replied. He can't have been much older than 30 – a mere boy really.

"Yes, my Mickey. Where is he, please?" I replied with as much dignity as I could muster. Even though I was standing there, in the mortuary, waiting to be led to where my dead husband lay, I still couldn't believe it was all really happening. It felt surreal, like a tragic joke, and nothing could burst the bubble I felt I was living inside.

"Come this way," the copper said. He showed us the room where Mickey was being kept. It was bare, with grey walls and linoleum on the floor. I baulked at the sight of it, even though I was only being allowed to look through the glass window, almost turning around and running away, gripped by a sudden urge to flee, to deny this was happening.

"Come on, Lin, you can do this, girl," Terry whispered.

The next thing I knew, there was an armed police officer standing next to me.

"I'm very sorry about your husband," he said. He looked older.

I stared at him blankly.

Then another man appeared, wheeling a trolley. On the trolley was a body covered by a white sheet. I swallowed. Could I do this? My world was about to crumble, but I had to stay calm so I could identify my sweetheart on that slab.

The man pulled back the cover. It was Mickey alright. I could tell, even though they weren't letting me get any closer to him. Thankfully his face was unchanged. He looked like he was sleeping, but his face was ashen grey, his body stiff as a board under those bare strip lights.

All my romantic hopes and dreams died that day. The man of my life, my soulmate and love of my life, was dead. There was no coming back from that. I burst into tears.

The man started to talk, seemingly oblivious to my distress. A document on a clipboard had been thrust into my hands as we arrived at the place where Mickey was being held, but I hadn't even glanced at it. The man talked and talked but I heard nothing until he said this.

"…I'm sorry, but your husband left us no choice. He faced the officer and said, 'It's me or you,' so he was shot through the front of his body."

"He said what?" I started as if from a nightmare. "What did you say?" At that point, the words suddenly made it through the fog of grief that had settled onto me. "Will you say that again, please?" I asked.

The man repeated it, and I interjected, "That's not true. I know that Mickey had no real bullets in his gun, just cotton wool in the cartridges, so he would never have faced up someone with a real gun and real bullets." I spoke slowly, as the cogs in my brain started to work.

I knew that this didn't sound right. Mickey was many things – reckless, charming, a crook – but he wasn't ever stupid. Why would he confront an officer carrying live bullets, with nothing but fluff to defend himself with? That would've been madness. Mickey had a cool head under fire, and on the raids. He'd proved himself over and over again. It was the reason he was always the anchor man: his pals knew that he wouldn't panic, that he would stay steady while alarm bells rang, staff screamed and sirens wailed, making sure everyone got out and away from whatever job they were doing.

There was no way he'd ever react like that. I knew it in my heart.

"Just sign the paper, will you, and we can release the body to you," the man said.

I looked over at him, barely registering him, and threw the clipboard on the floor.

"No, I won't sign the papers. Something's not right, I know it. I'm not signing anythin' until I know what really went on yesterday," I said calmly.

The man, glancing over at his armed colleague with a look of exasperation, repeated what he'd said. "Mrs Calvey, the officer had no choice but to shoot him. Mickey faced the officer and said, 'It's me or you'."

I turned on him. "That's a lie."

The man looked uncomfortable. He picked up the papers. "Sign this, Mrs Calvey, and you can go. We've done the post-mortem, so you can take him."

I scanned the pages. "It says here that my Mickey was shot through the front. Well, I think you're lying. I know he wouldn't confront a copper, so that doesn't sound right to me either. That wasn't how it happened, and I'm goin' to find out what really took place. I won't sign anything. I want a second opinion."

By now, even Terry was getting frustrated with me. He wanted to leave – I understood that. The sight of his brother on the slab must've been as upsetting for him as it was for me.

"Come on Lin, sign and we can go," Terry pleaded. But I wouldn't budge.

Something was being covered up. I knew that Mickey always laughed at my instincts, but time and time again they'd been proven right. This was one of those times – I was as sure of it as I had been of anything in my life.

"I will not sign this. We'll have our own autopsy, and that's my final word." I felt my strength begin to return, the fog in my brain clearing, if just for those few vital moments. "If I sign this, Mickey will never rest in peace. I don't believe that he was shot in the front because I know my husband. I knew my husband."

I was determined to see this through before I broke down again. Thoughts whirred through my head.

*Was Mickey shot as he tried to escape? If so, then the bullet would've gone through his back, not his front.*

*Why were they trying so hard to push me to sign their forms? Why would the police do that?*

I had no answers as I stood there, Terry beside me looking anguished, Mickey lying dead on a trolley in a South London mortuary. But I knew I'd never rest until I got to the truth of how my husband died that fateful day, only weeks before the bleakest Christmas I've ever known.

# CHAPTER 9

# FIGHT FOR JUSTICE

## DECEMBER 1978

In the criminal underworld, reputation is everything. Fronting up an armed member of the Flying Squad with only cotton wool for bullets would have been seen as insanity, even by blaggers with a questionable relationship with their rational minds. Mickey wasn't an idiot. He wasn't a coward either. He was shot because he would've been the last to make a run for it after ensuring that his mates all got away before him. It was just common sense. That was why I felt so uneasy about the police claiming that Mickey had taken the bullet in the front of his body.

To my mind there was no other explanation, knowing, as I did, Mickey's personality, how loyal he was to his pals. And I had seen him stuff the gun cartridges with padding on that dreadful day. The others must've got to the getaway car first while all hell was kicking off, and Mickey must've followed them and got shot in the process. I would've put a lot of money on that being the truth. But the real question was: if that was what really happened, then why were the police, the bastions of law and order, trying to make me sign a falsehood?

The days following Mickey's death flowed into one long, sleepless mess. I wept all day, huddled inside my blankets while Mum looked after Melanie and Neil. I'd asked Mum and Dad to swear on their lives that the kids would know nothing about this until I was ready to tell them. I told them to say that Mickey was in hospital, he'd hurt himself at work, and they weren't to worry, they'd see him again soon. The children were used to spending time at Mum's, and they liked it, as there were always loads of people round there. My youngest sibling Karen was only seven years older than Mel, so they had a good relationship. I knew they wouldn't suspect anything for a while at least, and so I concentrated on the grief swamping me. The only thing that kept me going through those days were the talks I had with my solicitor. I'd rung him as soon as I left that morgue.

"I want another autopsy done. I think they're lyin' to me. Can you help?" My voice was urgent. The man at the end of the phone paused for a second. "I'll do everything I can, Linda."

"Find the highest person in the land to do it, then no-one can dispute the findings." I put the phone down, swallowing down my tears, though this time they were mixed with anger.

He called back a few days later. "Linda, you won't believe this."

"What?"

"The mortuary people are saying they've lost Mickey's body."

"Lost the body?" I said, checking I'd heard him right.

"Yes, lost the body. It gets worse, doesn't it."

He'd had to apply to the court for a Writ of Habeas Corpus, which is normally used to bring to court crime suspects or witnesses who are generally alive. Not this time, though. Even the judge had commented that it was astonishing that he'd been asked to produce this writ to return an actual body.

The police told the court that yes, they'd lost the body, at which point the judge said they had 24 hours to find my Mickey's corpse or someone would be held responsible. Funnily enough, 24 hours later the body was "found", and the new autopsy was ordered. I hadn't been in court, so my lawyer told me all this over the telephone.

At around the same time, Mickey's brother Terry was contacted privately by a high-ranking police officer. Terry came to see me, to tell me the latest twist in the unfolding saga.

"This officer said he couldn't give me his name or rank, right, because he'd lose his job and his pension. But he said he was unhappy about what had happened, and that's why he was callin' me," Terry said.

"Apparently, Detective Sergeant Michael Banks," Terry pronounced his name with a sneer, "the officer who killed my brother, spent that afternoon in the Director General pub, opposite the town hall in Eltham. At 5pm he left, carrying his gun, just as the raid was getting underway. Can ya believe it?"

"Why would this copper tell you this? I don't get it," I said, confused.

"Lin, that's it, I don't know why, either. Anyway, he said that DS Banks jumped out when he saw Mickey and the robbers, and started shooting indiscriminately, firing every bullet in his gun in the busy street. Apparently, it was a wonder no-one else was killed, or so he said. He also said that Mickey was killed, shot through the back while clinging to the back of the getaway motor as they tried to make their escape."

I sat down heavily on my sofa.

This was all too much to take in. My intuition had been right. This was the reason they'd tried to hurry me into signing off the post-mortem.

"It's like the Flying Squad officers think they're gods, or somethin'," I said, shaking my head in disbelief.

I got straight on the phone to my solicitor, asking him to request all the information we could get from the police for the inquest. Only time would tell if that officer had been right.

Christmas had come and gone, and I still hadn't told my children that their father was dead.

"You've got to tell them, Linda," my mum said on Christmas Eve, her voice breaking a little with emotion. The children were tucked up in bed, excited about getting their stockings, but already Neil was asking where his daddy was.

"It ain't fair on them, you do understand that?" Mum sighed. This wasn't easy for her either.

"'Course I do, Mum, but I can't bear to, not till after Christmas at least. Please let's give them tomorrow, and then we can talk again, work out how we'll tell them."

We spent Christmas Day at Mum and Dad's, barely holding ourselves together. Mum confided in me that in the days after Mickey's death, hard men, crook pals of my late husband, kept arriving at her door. Many of them brought toys or presents for the children, and wept openly in front of them, so they'd known something was up. Neil was too young to understand, and he was delighted to receive present after present, thinking Christmas had come early.

"Melanie was different," said Mum. "She kept asking why those men kept appearin', and I didn't know what to say."

I knew the grief she was feeling, and the worry for my kids. I had tried to smile as they opened their presents from me and Mickey, and squealed with glee with their new toys. Their innocence broke my heart afresh.

Not long after we'd finished our sit-down Christmas dinner of roast turkey with all the trimmings cooked by Mum, we all collapsed on the lounge sofas, hoping that the children would be content with the television on and their new games. We'd watched the Queen, as was our tradition.

After it had finished, Neil turned to me and said, "Why can't we see Daddy today?"

For a moment, I was stung into silence. I didn't know what to say. I glanced over at Dad, who was sitting in the chair opposite, and he shook his head. He knew that today, of all days, wasn't the right time to tell them the kind of news that would shatter their world.

I breathed in. "Well, darlin', come and sit on Mummy's lap. There's a good boy. Daddy needs to rest and the hospitals aren't open on Christmas Day. The nurses and doctors have to have the day off to see their families, don't they." It was a blatant lie, but it was all I could think of. I'd been scared to bring up the whole idea of Mickey today, as much for my own grief as for the possibility of my children's.

Neil frowned. "That's not true. Melanie says the hospitals are open and we can go and see him." Neil looked up at me, his dear little face looking thoroughly determined.

"That ain't right, Neil, my darlin'. You just enjoy your train set. Look, your grandad wants to play with it with you." I mouthed a silent thank you to my dad, who had joined Neil by the tree to set up the train tracks. Diversion was the only way I could stop Neil's enquiring mind.

It was a week after Christmas when Mum took hold of my hand one Sunday afternoon as we all sat round the telly, and said, "It's time."

I knew instantly what she meant, and my eyes filled with tears.

"I can't," I croaked, shaking my head. It was too much for me. I don't think I was physically able to say those dreaded words.

Mum nodded. She understood me straight away.

"Then I will tell them, Linda, and I will do it now."

We held our gaze for a moment, the pain evident in both our faces. I nodded my assent. I knew that telling my children would be the hardest part of my widowhood, piling fresh grief onto my stricken feelings. I had held my grief at bay until now and my family had done the same – and now I saw the cost to them both. Mum had black circles under her eyes and a permanent worry line on her forehead. Dad looked older, somehow, greyer, even though he was still fit and healthy. It was definitely time. I didn't envy my mum's decision to be the one to share the terrible news one bit.

"Melanie, come with Nanny. I want you to come out for a drive with me," Mum said, gently but firmly.

"But why, Nanny?" asked Melanie as she looked up from her games.

"Just come with Nanny, it's ok, darlin'," Mum smiled sadly. My heart swooped down into the pit of my belly. I wanted to shout and scream my anguish, the loss of their father, our beautiful Mickey. I wanted to tell the world how unfair it was, how he was a good man who loved his wife and kids, who didn't mean to hurt anyone, who just wanted more than what he'd been given in life. But I could only sit and watch as Melanie reluctantly let Mum take her outside to tell her the worst possible thing a young girl could hear.

I felt the tears come again. They came so easily these days, and I had to dig my nails into my hand to stop them in their tracks. I swallowed hard.

"Where's Melanie gone?" Neil asked, not taking his eyes off the car he was playing with on the floor.

"Oh, just out with Nanny, I expect they'll be back in a bit and you can go out for a drive too." My lips trembled. I knelt down next to him, smelling his lovely clean boyish scent, and put my arms around him.

"Mummy, that's too tight, you're hurtin' me." He wriggled out of my embrace.

"Sorry, son, I didn't mean to, I just love you so much," I said, letting go of him and wiping away treacherous fresh tears that threatened to betray my emotions.

At that minute, the street door banged open, and I heard a wail unlike any I'd heard before. It was Melanie.

"Grandad, GRANDAD!" She screamed, running into the lounge and hurling herself into my dad's arms. She was sobbing, her face red and sweaty from crying.

"Oh, Melanie, oh darlin'," I said, coming straight over to stroke her arm as my dad rocked her on his lap like a small baby. My gorgeous girl was distraught. Her heart was broken into a thousand shards that day.

Mum came in. "Come on Neil, darlin', you and me, we're goin' for a little drive together. Melanie will be ok, I promise you, now come on little lad, come with me, handsome."

Neil looked confused, but curiosity won out. He ran over to Nanny, holding out his arms to be carried. She picked him up and the two of them went out. I don't know where Mum got the strength to tell them. She was one resilient, determined woman. I didn't question it. I didn't question why it was Mum telling my children, and not me or my dad. It seemed natural.

Melanie was hiccupping as the grief flowed through her. "It's alright, Melanie, I'll be your dad now," said her grandad.

"But I don't want another daddy," she wailed in response.

I had thought the day I was told Mickey had died was the worst day of my life. I was wrong. This was the worst, the cruellest day, seeing my children in such pain, feeling such loss.

At that moment, Mum walked back in, with Neil in her arms. He too was crying, but without the fierce intensity of Mel. He came straight to me and we sat on the sofa, me rocking him in my arms. I could see he didn't really understand what was going on. Later that night, as I tried to put my children to bed, knowing they'd always have a daddy-shaped hole in their hearts, Neil bombarded me with questions.

"Has Daddy gone to heaven?"

"Yes, I'm sure he has, sweetheart," I replied.

"Where is heaven?" Neil cocked his head to one side, staring at me intently.

"Well, it's up in the stars. Tonight there's a new star in the sky, and it's your daddy," I said, at a loss to explain something I wasn't able to fathom.

"Am I going to die? Will I go to heaven when I die? Will I see Daddy again when I'm up there? Are you going to die, Mummy?" The questions seemed endless.

"Darlin', we'll talk more in the mornin', now try and shut your eyes and go to sleep. Mummy loves you," I said, with more determination than I felt. My body felt heavy. I felt exhaustion like I'd never felt before. Part of me just wanted to curl up, back under my blankets, and wait for a long, long time until my grief had subsided. I didn't even know if that day would ever come, I'd loved my husband so dearly. I knew I couldn't fix my children's hurt. I could hear Melanie crying herself to sleep, my mum murmuring reassurance to her next door, and I prayed then for the strength to stay solid for my kids, to keep them safe from harm and get through these endless days of grief.

# CHAPTER 10

# VOWS

## 7 JANUARY 1979

"Hello, thank you for comin'."

"Hello, it's good to see you, thank you for comin'."

"Hello, Mickey would be so happy to see that you're here."

I stood by the street door, greeting the steady stream of hardened, violent crooks as they crossed the threshold to pay their last respects to my husband. Mickey was lying in his coffin in his mother's front room. I could barely hold myself together.

"'Allo Lin, I was gutted to 'ear about Mickey."

"'Allo darlin', I can't tell ya how sorry I am for your loss."

"He was a good'un, Linda, we always knew we could rely on him."

Everyone had a kind word to say about my Mickey. Men who routinely wielded sawn-off shotguns, who would think nothing of holding up a bank or a post office for cash, who would use any ruthless means necessary to come out of a shoot-out or raid alive, were in floods of tears as they stood by my husband. Their wives and girlfriends sipped tea in the kitchen, keeping their voices low as they talked, while the so-called hard men broke down sobbing as they saw their dead comrade, laid out like an emperor in his coffin.

The reaction to Mickey's death had been one of utter shock and intense grief. That day in Mickey's mum's front room, I saw men crumbling before my eyes. I think it was because they knew that what happened to Mickey could have happened to any of them. It could have been them lying in that casket. And although these crooks were always prepared for the possibility they could get nicked, they never expected one of them would be killed in a raid. The sight was too much for some to bear. I had to comfort two of Mickey's pals on the doorstep, because they couldn't bring themselves to come in and see him in the flesh.

I'd spared no expense. None of us had. Mickey's family and I got him a handcrafted light wood coffin, which was the most expensive at the time, and I'd had it lined with lavender-coloured silk – his favourite colour. Mickey's aunt had made a lavender silk cushion to rest his head on.

But I came a cropper when I'd first seen him lying in there. I'd stroked his beloved face, then reached in to cradle his head, and found to my horror that his brain was missing. My fingers simply disappeared inside his skull. I recoiled in shock, my heart racing. Crying out, I bolted from the room, flying into the kitchen, where my best friend, Mickey's sister Maureen, was making me a sweet cuppa to steady my nerves.

When she saw my white face, the shock imprinted all over it, she nodded. "I did it myself when he came home. You put your hands inside his skull, didn't ya?"

I nodded my response.

"Horrible, ain't it," she said, sadly. "When he first came back, his eyes were wide open in the morning, and twice I had to shut them, saying 'darlin', it's time for you to sleep now'," Maureen continued. "I said to him, 'Go on, love, 'ave a bit of rest. I'm goin' to shut yer eyes, I've got to, because people are comin' to see you'."

"He was always nosy," I replied, and we laughed and cried all at the same time.

"I think we need something stronger than a cuppa, don't you, Lin?" Maureen said, squeezing my arm. I was so grateful for every bit of kindness, but each time it brought fresh tears to my eyes.

"Don't you go cryin' on me, you'll spoil your mascara!" she joked, and I laughed tearily and took hold of the glass of brandy she had poured for me.

"To our Mickey. May he rest in peace forever." Maureen's voice wobbled, but she didn't crack. She was a glamorous Cockney woman, brought up to care for her own and weather life's storms. I loved her like a sister, and never more than now.

"To our Mickey. We loved him. We'll always love him."

We clinked glasses just as a knock at the door announced the first of our callers that day.

It was the day before Mickey's funeral, and the final chance for his pals to say goodbye to him before the coffin was shut and taken for burial. I knew Mickey was popular, but I had no idea how loved he had really been. People arrived throughout that day.

Maureen and her mum made endless cups of tea and rounds of sarnies, while the men drank spirits, smoked fat cigars and stood in hushed groups in the tiny lounge. Many put envelopes containing money into his coffin, with notes saying things like: "For your last fare home". Maureen and I remarked how strange it was that it was the men who became hysterical and wept at the sight of him – rarely the women. It was a gruesome reminder that the risks were real, their lives and their families' wellbeing were on the line every time they went out. No wonder it affected the hard men the most.

No Cockney ritual is as over-the-top or as poignant as the death traditions. The real Eastenders, the working classes born within the sound of Bow bells, were part of a deeply rooted culture, and there were ways of doing things that had to be followed to the letter – especially funerals. When someone died, their body was always laid out in the coffin with the lid off for people to spend time with their loved one. For us, it made the shock of their death feel more grounded in reality, and it gave us a chance to have our beloved in their home with their loved ones for one last time. Even though it was a harsh winter at the start of 1979, the undertakers had told us not to have any heating in the lounge, or the rest of the house, as it would speed up the decomposition of the body, even though Mickey had been embalmed. The undertaker told us to keep all the windows open, and it was freezing. I remember feeling cold to my bones that day as I welcomed Mickey's associates and friends. By nightfall, my feet were frozen in the black heels I had on, and I was shivering in the black two-piece suit I'd worn for the occasion.

"'Ere, put this around you," Maureen said, handing me a blanket. I couldn't wait to take off my heels and sit down. I'd been standing all day, making small talk, thanking people for coming, and I just wanted to collapse. My energy was drained and I took the cover gratefully. Maureen went to make something to eat, as we'd been too busy to grab any of the sandwiches and sausage rolls Mickey's mum had made for our guests.

I sat down at last, breathing out heavily and rubbing my legs, which were sore from standing all day. I realised the house had gone quiet. Mickey's dad was in hospital after suffering a stroke, and had no idea of the tragedy that had befallen us. His mum was in the kitchen with Maureen, and it was just me, alone with my husband.

Suddenly, I was gripped with the notion that I had something important to say to him. I stood up again, despite my aching body, and walked to the end of his coffin. I wouldn't make the same mistake again with his skull.

Earlier, I'd queried why Mickey wasn't wearing shoes, as he was dressed in all his finery, a handsome cream-coloured handmade suit from his tailor in Stepney. Mickey would buy himself a load of expensive fabric then take it in to the tailor, saying, "That's for the next one." As soon as my husband had a suit made, he'd already be trawling for new material to make another. He was like that. He was flash, he loved his expensive clothes, and he was proud of his appearance – and rightly so.

But the undertaker had told me that in order to put shoes on him, they'd have to smash his feet. I'd blanched at the thought of that.

"No-one will ever hurt him again," I'd replied, fervently, and that was that. Mickey would rest in peace in his Italian socks, his lavish suit and a lavender bow tie that I'd had made for him.

In the gloom of twilight, Mickey looked peaceful, at least. His skin, though still that distinctive olive colour, looked waxy. His hair was combed to the side as he liked, and yet, if you didn't know he was dead, you'd think he was sleeping. Part of me still didn't register that it was my husband, *my* Mickey, lying dead as stone. Even as I looked over at him, at the two lavender posies I'd placed in both his hands and the red rose I'd put on his lapel, I had to draw a breath. He was the most handsome man I'd ever set eyes on. I saw myself again – a young woman ready for love – and I saw why he'd bowled me over. If I'm honest with myself, the fact he was a blagger, acting outside of the law, stealing money and lavishing it on me, was a turn-on. I'd turned a blind eye to his "work" because I loved how racy he was, how glamorous and exciting. It was like an aphrodisiac to me. But where had it got me? Standing here, looking down at the man I loved, feeling my heart hollow out, an aching loss that would be with me for the rest of my days.

The words came from nowhere.

"Babe, I promise you I will make sure I do for our children what you died trying to do for them."

Perhaps it was the quiet of the evening, or the exhaustion threatening to engulf me, but I realised I wasn't just grieving, I wasn't just overwhelmed with sadness. No. There was anger there too, a deep, molten rage born of a working class mother, a widow left to fend for herself by the actions of a police officer proving himself with a gun. I realised how small we were, how easily crushed by the system, the authorities, the police, for God's sake. I was sure they'd lied to me about my Mickey's death.

I understood what Mickey did. I knew everything he did was for his family, for us. There was no greater shame for the men I knew and loved than failing to provide for your wife and kids. That was our measure of success or failure – not the moral codes we weren't privileged enough to live by.

Our men took what they wanted because it was the only way they could get it. No-one would ever give us a hand up in life. No-one would ever raise us above our social class. Mickey knew this, and he was angry too. He wanted to give us the high life – and he did. He did it in the only way he could, a violent and dangerous way. How else could he do it?

I saw then that Mickey was always destined to die this way, and I wanted to rip the heart out of the establishment that made it so. I'd been many things up to that point, but the sight of my man's corpse, the grief that swelled and shaped me now, gave me a fierce desire for revenge. I was a widow, a mother, a sister and housewife. I was a blagger's wife, a knowing recipient of stolen money and clothes. I'd never questioned it. I had taken what was given to me and laughed off the consequences – until now. My rage had no end, no edges. I knew it would burn as long as I had breath in my body.

I realised then that my heart had hardened. Morals weren't for people like me. We couldn't afford them. Morals were for rich people, people in glass houses with nice lives, nice jobs, nice children and fancy wives. Morals were expensive to people like us. They served to keep us down, to know our place.

Enough was enough. My heart turned to ice that day. My entire world changed forever, my life collapsed and I knew from then on I had to fight for our survival, to pick myself up from the wreckage and fend for myself and my children. All bets were off. I would fight back, and I would do it my way from now on.

My voice sounded steady, even powerful, as I ended, "I will take up your role, babe. I will provide for our children and give them the finest in life. I will take what's owing to us."

Everything had changed that day I'd stood in the mortuary. The helplessness I felt at the sight of my dead husband, the battle facing me to get to the truth of how he died. None of it should've happened – yet it had, and I would have to live with the result every single day of my life to come. The seed of my life to come was planted as I clutched Mickey's toes, looking down at his coffin, cursing this day.

# CHAPTER 11

# BLACK WIDOW

## 1979

I was determined to bury Mickey like a king – a king of the underworld of course – but a king never-the-less. I had put the word out that his funeral would take place in Canning Town on 8 January 1979, and so among the robbers, the crooks, the hard men and the villains, there was a truce. Criminals and racketeers from north, south, east and West London, and even parts of Scotland, agreed to lay down their weapons, their feuds, their hatred of each other, their violent search for territory and power, to come to the East End to see my Mickey off.

Some couldn't make it because they were already banged up. The Kray twins were jailed for life, while Mickey's friend Micky Ishmael, another notorious blagger, was inside at the time, along with their pal George Davis, a crook who had been imprisoned for 20 years. Micky Ishmael and George had gone on the pavement, targeting the Bank of Cyprus for a £54,000 raid, and the Flying Squad was lying in wait for them. Micky had tried to take an old geezer hostage, while George had tried to escape in the getaway car, but both men were caught and had got substantial prison sentences. My Mickey had grown up with Micky Ishmael, and they had been very close. I knew they were close pals of my husband, and was gutted they couldn't attend. I later heard that the screws at their prison had taken pity on them, letting them be told about Mickey's death together in a cell. Apparently, they sobbed together like small boys. It was a small drop of compassion in a vast ocean of suffering.

The day of the funeral arrived. It was freezing cold, but I barely noticed it. So many people had rung with messages of support, and all I could think about was the officer who had put my husband in his early grave. I wanted to tell him to come down, see how popular my man really was, and ask him, "How could Mickey be a bad man if he inspired this much love?" I felt better when I thought of the press photographers, who were bound to be staking out their part of the church grounds and the roads leading up to the cemetery to get the best shot – that meant that the world would see our love for a man who was so much more than just a blagger. He gave to local charities, particularly the boys' clubs for disadvantaged tearaways – something I only found out later at the inquest. He had a heart of gold, though he was a crook. He never wanted to become a docker like his father, and his father before him. He wanted more out of life. He wanted luxury. He wanted to give his children and his wife everything they wanted. Is that evil? I don't think so. But it had led to this – a wooden coffin being carried out of his mum's house and into a hearse. He was a robber and a thief, but he didn't deserve to die for it.

I watched the coffin bearers, his brothers and friends, pick him up and carry him out to the waiting vehicles. I felt as cold as the winter day, bare and frozen like the branches of the trees lining the road to the small cemetery. Maureen held my hand as we stood and watched him go, our faces haggard in the weak winter sunlight. Ten shiny black limos stood waiting for us. As I stepped into the car at the head of the entourage, I saw Mum's face peering up at me. She was a mirror of my grief.

We sat in silence as the cars moved slowly onwards – me, Mum and Maureen, like three stone statues. My mother had insisted my children didn't attend their father's funeral. "It's too much for them to bear, darlin'," she'd said, putting her hand on my arm as a gesture of reassurance, a few days before the ceremony.

I'd agonised over whether to allow Mel and Neil to go, but I trusted her judgement. I'd nodded my agreement, tears running down my face. I have never regretted that decision, but I know that it made their father's death seem less real for both of them. I wanted to protect them, so Mum and I agreed they shouldn't attend, and they stayed with their grandmother instead.

We pulled into the cemetery road, ambushed by flashing cameras and reporters shouting out questions as we disembarked. The wind was chilly. I pulled my coat tighter around my collar, and stepped towards the crowds of broken-nosed hard men standing around wearing thick coats and smoking roll-ups. It had seemed like the whole of East London was walking with our entourage as we moved slowly through the streets of Canning

Town, following the funeral director, who walked in front. I saw the passers-by through a blur of tears. I saw men taking off their caps or trilbies, women with their hair in curlers putting out their cigarettes and staring as we went past. Everyone knew it was Mickey's funeral. I remember the smell that greeted us inside the Chapel of Rest most clearly. The scent of roses hit me, and I struggled to keep my feelings under control.

The ceremony itself was a blur. The brandy Maureen had given me before we left to steady my nerves took the edge off it, and made it feel very unreal. I couldn't take my eyes off the wooden box that contained my husband. Outside, tough-looking Cockneys in black coats and black ties took a last drag of their ciggies before accompanying us to the place where Mickey's ashes remain. It was the tradition then to have words made up in flowers. I'd had a large heart made up, with "Love Your Lavender Lady" written across it in silver lettering, and one saying "Daddy" from the children. The sight of it broke my heart again, and I wondered how I would get through that terrible day. Micky Ishmael sent a wreath saying "My Pal". Some of the older villains were affronted when Maureen's boyfriend had a sign saying "The Fonze is Cool". It was a nod to Mickey's nickname amongst his fellow villains. They called him The Fonze, because he was a sharp dresser, and everyone always liked and respected him. There were whispers that it was too irreverent for a funeral, disrespectful even, and it caused quite a lot of upset. I didn't mind. I just wanted people to show their love for him, and they certainly did that.

I didn't want anyone but my nearest and dearest to witness my feelings that day, so I kept my head high and stayed away from the gaze of the press lenses. I knew I looked pale and drawn. As I'd got dressed that morning, I had felt so sad pulling on a lovely black dress that Mickey had bought me only a few weeks earlier. He'd never even seen me wearing it, and there I was, preparing to cremate him in it. The words I'd spoken to Mickey before his coffin was sealed now burned in my brain. I'd promised him I would give our children what he'd tried to give them: nice things, a nice life, an escape from the poverty he had been born into.

Mickey had been a Catholic, but the priest in the church nearest to Mickey's family had refused to hold the service. He was an armed robber, a bad man, someone who lived outside of the law and so, the priest had reasoned, he lived outside the church. We had come instead to the Church of England cemetery, where we were now gathered.

"We have entrusted our brother to God's mercy."

I threw a last look at the coffin before it moved to the cremation chamber, then turned away. I could bear it no longer. Outside, a rose tree was to be planted to commemorate the man I loved. Much later, Mickey's mother and father joined their son in that cemetery, but for now, it was over. I shook hands and kissed well-wishers, all the time wishing this day away.

I gazed at the crowd, taking in the number of people who had turned out to see Mickey off. And at the back of the crowd, slightly removed from the ceremony, I saw Ronnie, the man who had showed up at our door just a month or so before the Eltham raid. The memory of ordinary life, of cooking eggs for Mickey that Monday morning, almost left me doubled up in pain.

Ronnie seemed to be surveying the scene. A few hard men offered him muted greetings, but it seemed that for the most part he was being left alone. I marvelled that a man with his reputation, a big fish in a stinking pond of crooks, thugs and robbers, had no minders.

Ronnie's menace fascinated me. I had never been scared of these toughened criminals – I was interested in them, in how they came to be players in a dark and dangerous world, and I was wary of some of them, but I could never, hand on heart, say I was frightened of them. I didn't know it, but Ron had a reputation for being one of the toughest, fiercest ones out there. No-one ever picked a fight with him, because they'd end up dead.

At that exact moment I looked at him, Ron turned, and stared at me. Our eyes met. His were startling blue, and cold as ice. I couldn't work out what that look meant. A shiver went down my spine. I watched as Ron approached, feeling strangely like someone was walking over my grave. He came straight towards me, not stopping to greet the few who leant in to greet him. My stomach flipped with something like nerves. I knew from his meeting with Mickey that he was a gangland boss, a man to be respected around these parts. He was friends with all the big boys – Freddie Foreman, the Kray twins, the Arif brothers – but I could see already he liked to keep to the shadows, unlike Reggie and Ronnie.

"I'm sorry for your loss." He held out his hand to me. I shook it and felt my hand tremble in his embrace. I withdrew it quickly.

"Thank you for comin'. It would've meant a lot to Mickey."
My mind had gone blank with the pressure of the day, and I had
taken to repeating this over and over.

Ron looked me up and down. I could see he liked what he saw.
I have always been able to read men. Call it my feminine intuition.
I didn't know what else to say. The pause seemed to go on forever,
and it was clear Ron had no intention of moving off just yet.

By now, I was shaking people's hands or kissing their cheeks
as they left for the wake in the nearby pub the Carpenter's Arms.
The villains from North and South London left early, as there
was a bitter war raging between them. They'd paused for the
rites, but only for that.

"Can I come and see ya tomorrow?" Ron asked.

"Yes, alright, you can. I'm at my mum's," I said. I felt
confused, my head still rattling with ghosts.

Ron nodded, then walked away. I stood there, wondering if
I'd done the right thing in saying yes. Back at Mum's I fell into a
deep sleep, like I'd been drugged. Mickey haunted me all night,
and I was grateful to wake up the next morning, tear stains on
my pillow and eyes blackened by grief.

The first thing I did was go back to mine and Mickey's to
pick up some clothes. I hadn't lived there since the day he died,
preferring to stay with my parents for the children's sake, and I
felt strange walking up to the front door of my Victorian terraced
house. I put my key in the street door and clicked it open. I had
to push hard, as there was a pile of post on the floor. I shut the
door behind me, and picked it all up, feeling puzzled.

Walking into my kitchen, which smelled musty, I saw Mickey's jacket hanging over a chair, his house keys casually discarded on the work surface. My heart swooped and I felt dizzy. It was bizarre, seeing his stuff, not wanting to believe he'd really gone. At any minute, it felt like Mickey might walk in the door.

I dumped the post onto the table and put the kettle on to boil. *Must be from well-wishers…* I thought. All of the envelopes, big and small, were addressed to me by name. They looked harmless enough, but on opening the first one, a cry escaped from my lips.

"*I'm glad your husband is dead. We'll come and burn your house down…*" It was hand-written in florid red ink. I dropped it immediately, my hands shaking.

I opened another, and another, tearing them open each time to reveal a tide of hatred.

"*Why are you persecuting the police? Your husband was a robber, he didn't deserve to live.*"

"*Your children are going to be murdered for this.*"

I ran to the sink and retched, the sour taste of that brandy from the day before in my mouth.

How could people write such filth, such horror? How could they do this to a widow and two fatherless children? I carried on opening those envelopes, feeling thankful that I hadn't spent a single night there since he died. The vile messages were interspersed with a well-wisher sending condolences here and there, but they were few and far between.

There was a knock at the door. I froze.

Cautiously, I edged to the doorway. I didn't know what to expect. Was it someone hell-bent on revenge? Had my Mickey got enemies as well as friends, or were they targeting me? I opened the door, keeping it only slightly ajar and peered out.

"Thank goodness, hello, I wasn't expectin' the postman." I almost cried with relief. But he wasn't smiling back. In his hand was a large envelope.

"People round 'ere are sayin' you've had some nasty mail, and I thought it best if I opened this one in case there's somethin' funny in it."

"How do people know I've had hate mail? Who's sayin' that?" I realised that I was the centre of gossip now on my street, and many people were clearly feeling able to vent their jealousy and hatred now that Mickey was gone.

"I don't know, love, honest I don't. I just get told what's bein' said. Listen, I can't hang around 'ere for long, so d'you want me to open this?" The package was the size of a large envelope or small box. I nodded.

"Well, they've been quite creative." I peered at what he was holding in his hands: a folded-up piece of thick paper which opened up into a large picture, with a photograph of me and Mickey (cut out from a local newspaper) in the centre. Whoever had bothered to craft this had really gone to town. There were garish bits of thread leading out from the centre, attached to pictures of well-known murderers, including Myra Hindley, with that terrible smile playing on her lips and her beehive hairstyle in grainy black and white. The wording said: *"You and your husband should rot in hell with the rest of these monsters."*

"That's it. I can't take this anymore. I'll 'ave to call the council and be moved. I can't bring my kids home to this, they won't be safe." I thanked the postman, picked up a few of the worst letters and put them in my handbag. As I shut the door behind me, I knew I'd never go back there again.

Later that day, Ron appeared at Mum's doorstep. I still felt fragile after seeing the bile that had been thrown at me and my late husband, and so I was perhaps more vulnerable to kindness than I might usually be.

"Oh, hello Ron," I said, unsure what else to say.

"Hello. This is for you." Ron held out a thick roll of money. There was no small talk. No discussion of the funeral or Mickey, just a huge wad of cash.

"Thank you," I said, rather lost for words.

"There's a thousand there," he said stiltedly. "It'll help you get yerself sorted. What are you goin' to do now?" His voice was low. He was one of those men that didn't need to shout, everyone always listened because he inspired fear.

"I don't know, Ron. I know I can't live at my home anymore because people are sending horrible letters saying they'll burn the place down. I expect I'll apply to the council for a new place and try to start my life again.

Ron nodded. "When ya do, tell me, and I'll get you all-new furniture."

Again, it was a really unexpected thing to say.

"But I've got furniture, I don't need anythin', thank you," I replied.

"No, Linda, I will buy you new furniture, the best. You tell me when you move." It sounded like a command.

"Ok, I will. Thank you," I said, shutting the door and wondering why on earth a man I barely knew would go out of his way to furnish my home.

I had no idea if what Ron was doing was normal. Did bosses give widows money if their frontmen had been killed? Did they set them up with a new place as respect for the departed? I really hadn't a clue. Knowing I had two mouths to feed, and no visible source of income yet, I accepted the cash gratefully, even if the thought of being given a large sum of money left me uneasy. Could I turn down his notes? Could I tell Ron he wasn't welcome to call on me? How would he react to that? I was also a grieving widow, at my lowest point, and his kindness felt good – like I was being looked after.

Mickey's inquest took place on 15 February 1979 at Southwark Coroners' Court, with Home Office pathologist Professor James Cameron confirming that the bullet had indeed entered Mickey's body through his back and out his front. In that, at least, I was vindicated, and I knew my man could rest in peace knowing that the truth was out there.

Unfortunately, the press misreported Professor Cameron's conclusions. Cameron said that Mickey could plausibly have had his body turned, if the witnesses who said he was pointing a gun at the officer were to be believed. If he had turned, the bullet could've gone through his front. But Cameron then confirmed that the bullet had definitely gone through his back, so this couldn't be the case. Reporters, however, had jumped on the first theory, and wrote that Professor Cameron had cast doubt on my claim that Mickey would never have faced up the police officer.

DS Banks, who shot my Mickey, was there at the inquest, standing upright, bold as brass. It felt cruelly ironic that he was called Michael too. I stared at him, my rage building inside me as the police laid out their version of the day's events.

The court was told that he had been lying in wait for a suspected robbery outside Caters in Eltham following a tip-off. He'd shouted, "STOP! Armed Police!" at Mickey and his pals when they leapt on the security guards and tried to take the supermarket's day's takings. The raiders made a run for it, and two of them managed to get inside the car as it started to pull away. Mickey had been left outside, trying to open the back door as the getaway vehicle moved off. Witnesses said that it looked like Mickey had been locked out of the car. He had shouted, "Bastard, unlock the door!"

According to the police, DI Banks gave a final warning for Mickey to drop his weapon, then, as he tried to cling to the back of the moving car, he was shot, twice, falling down into the road and dying where he lay.

I was taken over by a mixture of numb grief, deep rage and utter fury. When DI Banks stood in the dock, our barrister questioned him, asking him if he knew what he was doing before the shooting.

"I don't remember," he said.

"And why wouldn't you recall what happened on the day you shot someone and killed them? Surely that would stand out in your memory?"

"I can't remember," came the reply.

"Do you recall being in the Director General pub from 3pm?"

"The reason I was in the pub was because I was part of an undercover covert operation and I was watching someone."

"For three hours in a pub, nursing half a bitter?" my barrister said, incredulously.

"Yes," was all Banks replied.

The high-ranking officer who had leaked the information to us anonymously had also alleged that Banks was breathalysed at the police station after the shooting and was found to be twice the legal limit – something we couldn't prove. He'd said there were no police cars lying in wait for Mickey and his pals – just Banks. None of this came to light in the inquest.

Despite our best efforts, the coroner, Arthur Gordon-Davis, upheld the police action after hearing Michael Banks say he feared for his life. Banks went further than that. He said that if he hadn't fired, he would definitely be dead.

I shook my head. I stared blankly in front of me, my head swimming. The coroner told the jury that Banks' actions were justified. He said that killing my husband was justified. I wanted to spit venom. It felt like there was a hissing cobra curled tightly in my belly. I thought I'd never again feel pain or fury like this. But when the coroner said that Banks should be commended for killing my husband, I couldn't hold it in a moment longer.

I marched up to the officer who had taken my man's life, and I said, calmly, "If you think you've killed a nobody who nobody cares about, then you're wrong. Come home with me, if you're brave enough, and show my kids the commendation you've got for shooting their father in the back. Coward. Murderer."

I never did discover why the police had lied that day I saw Mickey in the mortuary. I could only guess that they wanted to cover up Banks' actions, and make their officer a hero, rather than deal with the sordid truth that he'd shot a man fleeing for his life. Perhaps that didn't make such a good story for the Old Bill? It didn't seem to affect the outcome. Banks got his medal, and I got the truth. None of it changed the fact that my husband was dead and I was now alone in a harsh world.

I walked out of that coroner's court surrounded by press photographers, all trying to get a shot of Linda Calvey. I had worn nothing but black from the day I learnt my husband was killed, earning me the nickname "Black Widow".

One part of my life had died along with Mickey. That chapter, the first part where I met the man of my heart, where I bore our children, where I didn't question what Mickey did or the jobs he went on, was all over. I was changed. I was taken down to the bones of myself as a woman. I knew I'd have to fight for survival from now on. I didn't know how I would survive, but I would have to learn to live without the man who had shaped my life thus far.

It was a cold afternoon in the most desolate month of the year. Snow fell in gentle flakes as the press camera bulbs flashed. I walked through them, my head held high, not knowing how I was going to cope with everything that had happened, and knowing that I had no choice. I had to get through this savage grief and make a new life for myself and my fatherless children.

Dressed in black, with my bleached blonde hair and heavy eye make-up, I must've cut an impressive, and tragic, figure. No-one else could understand the depth of my suffering. My family and friends rallied round, took care of the kids whenever they could, sent over hot food for me, and it helped, but nothing and no-one ever comes close to healing the pain of a loved-one's parting, especially if the death seems unjustified, a brutal killing like Mickey's.

# CHAPTER 12

# CROOK'S BENEFIT

## SPRING 1979

It is tradition in London's gangland that a widow of a blagger, criminal, robber or thief is given a benefit night, to raise money to support the dead crook's family. Two occasions were being thrown for me, again showing the strength of feeling there was when Mickey died. The first benefit, only days away, was being organised by Jonny O'Shea, a pal of Mickey's, in a hall in Wapping. All the local blaggers and criminals would be there.

Ron had turned up at my door in Harpley Square, Stepney, the flat I'd been offered by the council after I told them about the hate mail. The council officer I spoke to had been shocked at the vitriol that had come my way, and I was given three offers of new places. I took the first one because it was close to my mum.

"Oh hello, Ron. Can I help you?" I said, trying to hide my surprise at seeing Ron a third time in as many days.

"Hello Linda. Look, I don't mean to intrude, but you've got a benefit comin' up, and I wanted to ask what you're goin' to wear."

He stood there, calm as anything, waiting for my response.

"I don't know, Ron. I haven't thought about it," I replied, wondering why on earth he was here again, and why he was asking such a strange question.

"You need to have something lovely, it'll be expected of ya and everybody's eyes will be on you," he continued. "I'll take you up the West End and buy you a nice outfit."

"Oh, well, alright, thank you, yes, I'd like that," I said, feeling puzzled and hoping it didn't show on my face. I didn't want him to think I was being ungrateful. It was a kind offer.

Ron nodded, turned and walked off, just like that, leaving me at my street door, blinking in the spring sunshine.

Back inside, I rang Mum straight away.

"That Ron just turned up again. He's offered to take me up to town to buy me a suit for my first benefit. Does that sound strange to you?" I asked, sipping my tea.

"No, that sounds lovely, that's very kind of him. Why, are you worried?" Mum said at the other end of the line.

"I don't know, Mum, my head's spinnin' with everythin' that's goin' on. Perhaps it's just a kind gesture and I should go?" I had a strange feeling in my gut but this time I ignored it. I knew I was a bit oversensitive, after all I was grieving, so it was good to hear Mum make light of it.

"Go on, go up the West End, it'll cheer you up."

"Ok, Mum, I'll do that," I said, smiling and putting down the receiver. A trip up town would be nice. I hadn't done anything like that since Mickey died – I'd been too overcome with sadness

– and I knew I couldn't carry on crying under my blankets forever. I had to pull myself together and carry on with life.

The next day, Ron was as good as his word. He took me to Bond Street, where he flashed his cash, spending £500 on a single pair of Italian shoes and a fitted black skirt suit for me.

When I came out of the dressing room, wearing the sky-high black heels and suit that whispered as I walked – the sound of silk, the feel of pure luxury – he looked me up and down again. He didn't say a word. He nodded and pulled out a huge roll of cash from inside his coat.

"You get yerself changed and I'll pay," was all he said.

It felt very odd knowing it wasn't Mickey out there on the shop floor, paying for my outfit like he'd done so many times before. I felt a lump in my throat and I knew I was in danger of breaking down again. I looked at myself in the mirror, a huge decorative piece, probably antique, and I saw a young woman, maybe not in the flush of her youth, but still beautiful. And yet I could see my responsibilities and worries laid heavy on me. There were bags under my eyes from the endless nights of broken rest. Every time I closed my eyes I dreamt about Mickey. I dreamt he was in the next room to me, and I couldn't quite hear him or see him, and somehow, I couldn't quite get to the room, no matter how I struggled. I would wake up, tears already streaming down my face, knowing that he wasn't there anymore – and never would be again. The bed felt too big. I missed the solid feel of Mickey beside me, his arm folded over me as we slept. I missed the smell of him, the way he whistled in the shower which used to drive me nuts. I would've given anything to hear that sound for one last time. Sighing, I hung up the beautiful clothes this stranger was buying me, and put a smile back on my face. It wouldn't do to burst into tears when this man was being so generous. £500 was a lot of money.

Ron was a gentleman that day, and dropped me back to my flat.

"Thank you, Ronnie, you've been really kind."

He nodded again. He didn't waste words. He didn't do small talk at all. He'd achieved what he'd set out to do today, and he left. Something about him confused me. He was so withdrawn compared to my Mickey, who was gregarious and charming. Ron seemed quieter, yet even then I could see that he was a man used to getting his own way. I didn't stop to think if I'd even had a choice whether to go on that trip. I'd gone at his command, or so it felt, but I'd been spoilt and treated to nice clothes, which I'll admit made me feel more like a woman again, rather than a grieving widow.

I didn't see Ron again until the night of the benefit. I was standing at the entrance to the hall, as was the custom, greeting people, shaking hands and offering my cheek to be kissed. Ron arrived. He was carrying a huge bottle of Chanel perfume.

"You look fabulous," he said, admiringly. "I don't know if it's appropriate to say that, but it's true." He handed me the perfume and went inside.

Again, I felt lost for words, barely managing a "thank you" before he moved on. I had to keep smiling, keep acknowledging the support the underworld was showing me that night. Once everyone had started buying drinks and most likely sunk a few, the raffle started.

People had donated some incredible things: a case of expensive wine, beautiful paintings, a china dinner service. The list was endless. It came to the wine and the bids started flying around the room.

Suddenly, Ron said, "A grand."

The place went momentarily quiet. The auctioneer almost choked on his beer.

"A grand, well, I don't suppose anyone will top that. The case of wine goes to Ron Cook."

Ron walked over and took out yet another huge roll of cash. He handed it over, then said, "Auction it again. I don't want the wine, rebid on it."

I couldn't believe what I was hearing. Ron had paid for something he didn't even want, and was putting it back up for auction. "Hope it goes well for you," he said as he walked past me out of that hall, leaving me staring after him.

My feelings were mixed. On one hand, I was bowled over by his generosity. On the other, I was left wondering why he would make such a gesture. What could he possibly hope to gain?

The second benefit was taking place in a pub in Romford. Again, Ron turned up at my door.

"Can I get you a nice outfit?"

"Thank you, but you already bought me one, I'll wear that," I said. I was perfectly happy with my gorgeous, unbelievably expensive outfit. It hadn't occurred to me I'd need something else.

"You can't wear the same outfit twice, it isn't right," he said, his voice soft but steely. "There'll be people there who were at the first one, so I won't let ya. I'll take you up the West End again."

"Ok, then I'll happily come with you, thank you, Ron."

Again, Ron came and took me up to Bond Street. This time he bought me a dress and a pair of heels. The bill can't have come in much lower than our last trip.

"You look wonderful, Linda," was all he said as he paid.

I was starting to enjoy myself. It wasn't every day that I got taken into town and treated, though Mickey always looked after me very well. I was starting to think kindly of Ron, and I dropped my suspicions. He always treated me like a lady. There seemed to be no expectation on his part. Again, he dropped me back to my flat and left. Again, I didn't see or hear from him until the night of the second benefit.

Standing at the pub doorway, I felt a million dollars. I felt like a queen, and wondered if the actual Queen would ever wear something as fine as I was wearing just then.

Ron came again, and did exactly the same thing, bidding on a case of booze, handing over the £1000 to the auctioneer and then leaving, saying, "Hope it all goes well for you." Unlike me, Maureen was becoming wary of Ron and his lavish, though infrequent, attentions.

"He fancies you, I know it," she said that night at the benefit.

I waved away her suggestion, but the thought took root in my mind. Was Ronnie Cook after me even though my Mickey had only been dead for four months?

"You know he's one of the big boys, don't you?" Maureen added, raising her right eyebrow and staring at me.

"Yes, I know he's the top man, Terry told me," I said, shrugging.

"He's done Brink's-Mat robberies, he's really big time. You be careful," my best friend warned.

"What does it matter to me?" I said, bleakly. "He ain't Mickey."

Maureen and I both smiled sadly.

Those benefits left me with a small fortune: £6,500, worth more than £32,000 in today's money. It was enough to keep me going for a while.

Ironically, I'd taken out a life insurance policy on Mickey a few years earlier. The insurance man used to go to Mum's and while she made tea, he'd do all the insurances and sort the money out. Originally, I'd insisted I couldn't afford to take one out for my husband, but the man had found me a deal where I paid 50p a week, and if Mickey died before the age of 60, I'd receive a £60,000 payout. One day, the man came to mine and Mickey's, because I owed him a couple of pounds. Mickey had asked what it was for, and the man replied that I'd taken out a life policy on him, one where he had to be dead before the age of 60.

Mickey reacted angrily. "You wicked cow! Cancel it!" He was furious, which surprised me.

"I was only lookin' out for the kids, but if it makes you happy, then of course I'll cancel it."

So I did. Two months later, Mickey was dead, and the man told me I would've qualified for the windfall. In fact, what he really said was, "Thank God you cancelled it, we had no clauses to get out of it, we would've had to pay you £60k." The benefit money was a great help, but with the insurance money my future would've been secured, and that of my children. Instead, I was a widow, taking the first steps into a big, bad world.

A day or two later, there was another knock at my door. I opened it to see Ron standing on my doorstep. This was becoming a habit. This time I smiled genuinely and offered for him to come inside. He shook his head.

"I'm 'ere to ask, can I take you for a meal?"

I took a deep breath in. "My Mickey's only been dead a few months. It wouldn't look right, Ron, surely you understand that."

"Well then, why don't you bring a friend along, or one of your brothers?" He didn't give up easily.

I couldn't think of an objection to that. My mind whirred, but I found myself nodding my head. "Alright, I'll bring Ricky, my youngest brother, to keep it all above board."

"What kind of food do you like?" Ron was so courteous, so smooth. He made it impossible to refuse him.

"I like Italian. Thank you," I replied. Three seconds ago, I had wanted to say no because I was worried what people would think of me, and now I was choosing the menu!

"Ok, we'll go for Italian."

When Friday night came, Ron seemed surprised that I was still dressed in black, even for a night out.

"After Mickey died, I swore that I would wear nothing but black until my birthday," I told him. "The copper on the case called me the Black Widow because of it."

Ron didn't reply. He just looked at me with that cool appraisal. I didn't know what to make of it.

After a pause, he finally spoke. "And when's that?"

"My birthday? It's in a week, Ron."

I thought nothing more of it. We had our strange dinner, and it turned into the first of many outings. He took me to a party, then he drove me up to Harrods and spent a small fortune kitting me out with another beautiful outfit, with matching heels and handbag. On my birthday, I was inundated with bouquets of roses – all sent by Ron.

I was being seduced by the persistence of this man. I was grieving and vulnerable, and his lavish attention was starting to turn my head. I can't say I fancied him – he was too reserved, too stern – but I was growing to like him.

As I got to know Ron over the months following Mickey's death, I gradually started socialising again and meeting more of his old crowd. I was soon introduced to Billy Blundell, one of Essex's most notorious gangsters, who I got on well with right from the off. He wasn't a tall man, but he exuded power and wouldn't take no for an answer. Billy invited me for a drink with some friends one Saturday, picked out a club to take us to, and ushered us past the queues outside, walking straight up to the door.

The bouncer stepped in front of him, blocking his way.

"Look behind you, mate. There's a queue."

Billy looked up at him without a hint of expression on his face. "I don't queue."

The bouncer smirked. "These people have been waiting, and you can wait like everyone else, pal."

Billy bristled. "I don't think you've quite understood me. I don't queue."

The bouncer shook his head. "I'm not letting you in unless you go to the back of that line."

Billy raised his eyebrows, as if the bouncer had failed to grasp something obvious. "Listen to me," he hissed. "I don't care how long those people have been waiting. I. Don't. Queue."

The bouncer glared back down at him. "In that case, you're not coming in."

I could see Billy boiling with rage as he turned to us, calm and icy. "I apologise for this, ladies," he said reassuringly, before turning back to the bouncer. "Here, can I ask you something, mate?"

"What?" Looming over Billy, the bouncer mockingly bent forward to hear what he had to say.

Billy launched himself forward and headbutted the bouncer squarely in the nose. Blood spurted into the air and he went reeling backwards, as the people in line behind us gasped in shock. Billy caught hold of his jacket and pulled the bouncer's head downwards until his ear was level with Billy's mouth.

"I don't queue," he spat into his ear. "You should know that. Now go and tell your manager that you've just refused Bill Blundell entry." He shoved the bouncer through the door of the club and turned to us. "Now that's sorted, let's go and find somewhere else."

Sure enough, when we arrived at the next club, Billy was shown straight in by the bouncers, no questions asked, and the owner came over to greet him.

"Mr Blundell, pleasure to see you, sir. Where'd you like to sit?"

Billy pointed to a table in a corner of the room, where a group was already sitting, drinking and laughing together.

"Right away, Mr Blundell."

I looked on, astonished, as the staff cleared the table in an instant, the drinkers getting up hurriedly and moving off as soon as they were told. We sat down to have a drink, and 15 minutes later, the owner came over to us once more.

"Mr Blundell, sorry to interrupt. There are some people to see you."

It was the bouncer from the previous club, gingerly cupping his bloodied nose, accompanied by his stern-looking manager. The manager spoke first.

"I'm so sorry, Mr Blundell. This one's new on the job. He just started yesterday and doesn't know who's who."

"I'm new to this part of town, sir," the bouncer stammered. "It was an honest mistake, I'm sorry."

Billy looked up at them with a serene smile. "It don't matter that he started yesterday," he said to the manager. "All your staff should know that there are some exceptions."

The pair nodded meekly and began to back off.

"Good thing you came in to apologise, though," said Billy. "'Cause if you hadn't, you wouldn't have had a club anymore. You'd have had a fire."

If anything, Mickey's death had brought me even closer to the top brass of the gangland scene. The men I was spending time with now commanded respect, and the kindness they showed to me was beginning to help me feel closer to normal again. Ron continued to take me out for meals with Ricky and trips to the shops, and Billy soon became a good friend too.

Six months after Mickey died, there was that familiar knock on my door.

Ron was standing there. As usual, he didn't bother with small talk.

"I want to take you out without your brother."

I hesitated, just ever so slightly. He nodded as if he understood my dilemma. My heart had been broken only a few short months previously. I liked the charming man in front of me, but I knew I wouldn't ever love him. I also knew that going out with him could be seen as a betrayal of Mickey's memory. I considered it. Six months wasn't a long time – but it wasn't six weeks either. My closest friends and family knew I'd love Mickey forever, and no man could ever take his place, including this notorious – and wealthy – top dog. It didn't really matter what I did from now on. My heart was out of bounds, but it didn't mean I couldn't enjoy myself again.

So I agreed. "Yes, Ron, I will go out with you."

"I suppose we can say we're an item. You're my girlfriend now. Oh, and by the way, get rid of your car." He said everything so matter-of-factly.

"What d'you mean, get rid of my car?" I said, shocked.

"I'll get you a new one. What car d'ya want?" Ron said, without batting an eyelid.

"Erm, well, I've always wanted a Mini," I said, cautiously, not for one moment thinking he'd return with a car.

He did, of course. A beautiful shiny brown Mini.

"On second thoughts, I'll take yours," he said, throwing me the new set of car keys. Ron never cared what make of car he drove. He didn't cruise round in a Mercedes like the others. He preferred to keep a low profile. My old car was perfect.

"You're welcome to it," I giggled, feeling in rather a daze. Perhaps life with Ron would work out after all.

# CHAPTER 13

# CAUGHT IN A WEB

## WINTER 1979

"You stupid cunt!"

It was the first time I'd ever heard Ron scream at someone. All heads turned in the pub in Bethnal Green. I almost dropped my drink in shock. I'd never seen Ron lose his temper before.

A man who was just out of prison had been celebrating with a group of pals in another part of the bar, fairly good-naturedly, when he recognised Ron and came over, swaying as he walked, clearly very drunk.

"How are ya, Ron?" he leered, standing too close to me as he tried to gain access into our small group, consisting of me, Ron and Maureen.

"Don't stand in front of her," Ron said, his expression turning rapidly from relaxed to defensive.

The man ignored him. I don't know why. He clearly knew who Ron was, but I suspect the drink was making him reckless.

"You're doin' it again." Ron was getting heated.

"It's ok, Ron, I can move," I said, shifting sideways to try and get away from this scary-looking, thick-set guy with his shaved head and tattoos.

*Please go away*, I was thinking, seeing Ron's face darken. Ron had never shown me anything but charm and consideration, but I knew that you didn't get to be a big name in the underworld without having another side to you, a more sinister, violent side. I could see he was on the verge of blowing his top. His face, usually so reserved, so in control, had turned red. His eyes were hard and they stared straight into the bloke's face.

The ambience in the pub had changed. People looked over at us and a hush descended. The place was expectant. People realised *something* was happening, and if it involved Ron Cook then you stayed out of it.

The man made an awkward attempt to move, but managed to step on my foot as he did so.

"Ow!" I couldn't help but cry out. He was a big guy and I was wearing strappy high-heeled sandals, and it hurt like hell.

"You stood on her foot, you stupid cunt!" Ron roared. The man shrugged, turned to me and said, foolishly, "She's only a tart, Ron, so what?"

If you could cut an atmosphere with a carving knife, then this was the moment. That was that. Ron stepped forward and bellowed in the man's face, "Do you know who that is?"

The man, who now looked confused and disconcerted despite the booze, shook his head and looked over at me. Maureen and

I had moved a few steps away by now, nervous about what might be coming next.

"That's Linda Calvey! How dare you call her a tart." Ron's voice was low now, and menacing.

"Oh if you say so…" The bloke was making it worse. "I knew she wasn't your wife."

With that, the pub silenced completely. It was an incredibly stupid thing to say to a notoriously private man.

I looked over at Ron. He was glaring at the man, his face incandescent with rage. Ron never spoke about his wife and family. I knew about them, I'm ashamed to say, and perhaps they knew about me too. I knew Ron divided his life between me – his mistress – and his family. That's all I knew, though. He would never speak about them, and I would never be invited anywhere, even to the court room where Ron eventually ended up, if there was any possibility we might meet. It seemed everyone else knew that any talk of Ron's family was off limits – everyone except this drunken idiot.

I didn't like being someone's mistress, but Ron had been very persistent, and he was sustaining my family, buying clothes for me and the kids, leaving £100 on my mantelpiece every weekend to help me with bills. I was a kept woman, and even now, while Ron was still being wonderful towards me, I knew it was a gilded cage, and one I didn't have a hope of finding the key to escape from. I knew already that people did what Ron told them to do – and I was no different. I wasn't sure I could leave Ron if he didn't want me to go.

"Get down on the floor and kiss her feet. Ask her to forgive you." Ron's eyes flashed, cold as steel.

"What?" The man looked back and forth between me and Ron.

"You heard me. Get on the floor and kiss her feet, then ask Linda Calvey to forgive you." Ron moved a step closer to the guy, at which point he kneeled clumsily, looked up at me, and said, "I am really sorry. I apologise. I didn't know who you were."

Standing behind him, Ron caught my eye, and shook his head, slowly.

"No, sorry, I can't accept your apology," I said. I wanted to be a million miles away from this bizarre scene.

"Try again," Ron sneered.

So, again, the bloke apologised while still on his knees. I looked over at my boyfriend, who, again, shook his head.

At this point, it was Maureen who broke the spell.

"Ron, stop being a bully, you're upsetting Linda!" Only a woman could've stepped in at that point. A man would've got his head kicked in for daring to call Ron out.

"Am I upsetting you?" Ron said, turning back to me.

"Yes, let's just forget it, please. He's said sorry and that's ok with me. Please, Ron."

Ron shrugged. "Just fuck off, and don't come near me or Linda again, d'ya hear me?" He motioned for the man to leave, which he did at an almost comically fast speed. The evening carried on, but it was a warning about Ron's character. There were many warnings in that first year.

A few weeks after we'd got together, I went on a family holiday to Majorca, using some of the benefit fund to give my children something nice to remember and share. We were sunbathing on our balcony when Mum looked up and said, "Linda, is Ron meant to be here with you?"

"No," I answered, puzzled.

"Well, if that's not him, then I don't know who it is." She pointed to a man sitting only a few feet away, sunning himself on his balcony. I peered over the concrete wall. The man wasn't far away, so it was easy to see that it was indeed my boyfriend sunbathing, just like us, on his private balcony.

"I think you're right, Mum, that's Ron. What on earth is he doin' here?" As we both looked over, Ron turned his head, took off his sunglasses and waved.

"Well, that's very odd. Did you tell him where we were stayin'?" My mum looked at me.

"I think so, I can't remember. I'll go and 'ave a word." I wandered off and Ron met me halfway.

"What a coincidence!" Ron said, beaming. "I can't believe we'd booked the same hotel and are staying only a few rooms away."

"You're right, Ron, that is a coincidence," I replied uneasily, wanting to believe him. We hadn't been together long, and he was so good to me – I didn't know why he would have followed me.

We did eventually all have a lovely holiday, but that feeling of unease never truly left me. I knew that, deep down, I didn't believe his story. I knew he'd planned it, but why?

As the months went on, I couldn't fault Ron's behaviour towards me. Every weekend was the same. Ron would take me out shopping and treated me kindly. I counted myself lucky to have attracted a man who wanted to take care of me in the way Ron did. He'd encourage me to wear whatever he'd bought for me and, at that point in our relationship, I was happy to oblige – even down to the lacy lingerie and stockings he loved.

I knew I'd never love him. Instinctively I knew that I had to keep that part of myself hidden from Ron, keep it to the weekdays when I didn't see him. I still woke up most mornings and cried. My bed felt so empty without my husband, yet I managed to square it with myself by thinking that Ron was taking care of me when I couldn't. If I felt any guilt towards my dead husband, I squashed it down.

When I moved into Harpley Square, Ron refused to let me take any of my furniture from Pembroke Road that Mickey had bought, insisting on buying new stuff for me.

"But, my furniture is all lovely, Ron, it don't need replacing," I said, trying to reason with him, all the while wishing to keep hold of it.

"Forget the cost. I'm buyin' everything. I like spoilin' ya," he said, grinning.

I gave in. If it gave him pleasure, why not? By the time Ron's men had finished, Harpley Square looked like a palace. I even had a chandelier in the lounge. Everything was the best, designer brands in sumptuous materials. I could've clapped my hands like an excited child when he showed me around the place. It had been transformed.

"Thank you so much, Ron. I don't know what to say. You're bein' so kind to me."

"It's nothin', don't think about it. I want ya to 'ave the best. You deserve it, Lin." When he said my name the way Mickey used to say it, I shivered a little.

"It's beautiful. I don't know how to thank you," I said, smiling away my unease.

"Well, I do. Bedroom, now." He took my hand and led me to the new four-poster with Egyptian cotton sheets and a thick, quilted, and clearly expensive, blanket in dusky pink thrown on top.

Ron loved eating at the same Italian place each Friday evening before we went out to the pubs and clubs, and he'd make me call them during the day to secure our table, in the name of Madam Harpley. For him, it had an erotic ring to it, and, again, I was happy to oblige. I liked the glamour. I discovered I liked wearing expensive clothes and eating quality food in the best restaurants. I was dazzled by Ron's generosity and seduced by his charm.

Quite soon after our relationship became public knowledge, people were becoming concerned for me. A few broached the subject hesitantly.

"You do know he's got a violent streak, don't ya?"

"I know. Well, it stands to reason with what he does for a livin'," I said, "but he's never shown me that side of him at all. He's the perfect gent with me."

"You don't know what you're getting into," said one friend, someone who worked for Ron and knew him as a blagger.

"That's all very well, but what can I do about it? Ron wants me, and what Ron wants he gets." I shrugged, looking down at my wrist as I nervously turned my new bracelet over an over again.

Ron loved to play high stakes on the horses, and went down to the betting shop one morning.

"Be ready at 2pm, I'll take you out for a meal," he called as he left.

I spent the morning doing myself up, pulling on beautiful lacy underwear, a gorgeous pink dress with matching heels and handbag, and a stunning Canadian wolf fur coat he'd only just bought me.

Two o'clock came and went. I'd gone to a lot of trouble making myself look nice for him, so at 2.45pm I decided to go down to the shop and see what he was up to.

As I walked in, all eyes turned to me. I must've looked like a film star walking into that betting shop, frequented by men sucking on cheap cigarettes. I saw immediately that Ron was placing a £200 bet on a single horse.

"Oh no you don't," I said, grabbing the cash. "You're supposed to be takin' me for a meal."

"Give that back, Lin, the race is about to start!" Ron said, indignantly.

"No," I snapped. "Mine, I believe." And I put the money into my purse.

"If that horse wins, you'll owe me."

I pouted a little, but stood firm. I could see the men's eyes go from me to Ron, waiting to see what would happen next. They all knew it was Ron Cook, big-time gangster, who I was goading.

"Can't believe she got away with that…" one of the geezers said, and at that point, Ron laughed.

"Ain't she marvellous!"

I was dazzled. With Ron I didn't have to worry about a thing. But that soon changed.

"I'm goin' up the market with Maureen later, d'you want me to pick anythin' up for you?" I asked Ron. I'd arranged to meet her because he was meant to be working that weekend.

"Oh, which market are ya goin' to?" Ron said over his newspaper, eating the eggs and bacon I'd just cooked for him.

"Just up Roman Road. Why? Do you need anythin'?" I said, sipping my coffee. It was a bright winter morning in 1979 and I was looking forward to seeing Maureen and having a catch-up.

"No, I don't think so. You 'ave a good time, there's some money on the side for ya. Treat yerself to somethin'." He looked me straight in the eye. He always liked to lock eyes as he spoke. It gave him authority. I nodded and smiled, thinking how sweetly possessive he was becoming of me.

Later that morning, as Maureen and I mooched around, going from stall to stall, chatting to the stallholders we recognised, my friend suddenly stopped. She grabbed my arm.

"Don't look, but I swear Ron's followin' us."

"You what?" I giggled.

"I'm not jokin', Lin. He's followin' us. Well, you."

I couldn't help it, I had to see what Maureen was going on about. I glanced to my right, and caught sight of Ron's face peering round the stall selling oversized women's lingerie.

"He's hidin' behind the big knickers!" I stifled a laugh.

"Linda, this is ridiculous. What on earth does Ron think you'll get up to at the market?" Maureen didn't find it as funny as I did. "Listen, I'm goin' to go and ask what's he's up to," she said, stoutly.

"Don't you dare, you'll only wind him up." I grabbed Maureen's arm. "Come on, let's just carry on and pretend we haven't seen him."

We shuffled forward, stopping to go into the deli to buy bread, then browsing through some dresses at another of our favourite stalls. Maureen looked behind her again.

"He's still here," she hissed. "This isn't funny, Lin, he's checkin' up on you."

"Let him. We're not up to anythin', so let's just make out we haven't noticed." I had a feeling that Ron wouldn't take kindly to Maureen fronting him up, even though he was the one acting strangely.

"Let's enjoy our day, come on, I'll buy you a cake," I said, trying to mollify my friend, but turning briefly to see if what she was saying was true.

It was. My boyfriend was still a few stalls behind us, pretending to look at something on a table of knick-knacks, clearly following me. But why?

Back at Harpley Square later that day, Ron was sitting on the sofa still apparently reading his newspaper when I arrived home.

"'Ave a good day?" he said. "Where did ya go then?"

Why did I feel like he was testing me?

"Oh well, it was nice, thank you, Ron. We went to the dress stalls and had a chat with Mrs Tranter from the flats."

"Are ya sure that's everythin' you did?" Ron was staring at me intently. I was being questioned, there was no doubt in my mind.

"Erm, well, oh yes, I stopped at the deli to buy some bits."

"So, why didn't ya tell me that?" Ron said, folding his paper up and looking at me expectantly.

"I just forgot, darlin'."

There was a slight pause, but my answer seemed to satisfy him. He smiled at last, my cue to put down my bags and head to the kitchen for a cuppa.

As the kettle boiled, I had a moment to think. Why in heaven's sake would Ron follow me so obviously? Did he really think we hadn't noticed? It was very bizarre. I decided that perhaps Ron was having a peculiar day, and it would be best not to mention it.

A few weeks later, the same thing occurred. Ron said he was working, so, again, Maureen and I decided to do a bit of shopping together. Ron asked where we were going again, and lo and behold, as we made our way round the stalls, there he was, trailing behind us, peering through the second-hand dresses, or over the cheese counter, apparently oblivious to the fact we knew he was there. Every time I went out with Maureen, he'd question me when I got in. Where had I been? Who had I spoken to?

Why had I missed out that stall from my description? Wasn't there anyone else I'd spoken to, and, if so, why hadn't I told him? I learnt to keep a mental list of everything I'd done so I wouldn't leave anything out, because if I did, he became instantly suspicious. I hadn't a clue what he thought I might be doing if I hovered in the deli too long. What did it matter if I said hello to a neighbour's husband?

Maureen thought the whole thing was ridiculous, and even though I agreed with her, I prevented her from confronting him. I had a feeling things would go badly for me if she did, even though I had no proof of that. It was becoming obvious that my "perfect" boyfriend, who lavished me with presents and money, had another, less charming side. The bed of roses I thought I'd landed in was fast becoming a bed of thorns.

# CHAPTER 14

# RING ON MY FINGER

## APRIL 1980

"Now you belong to me," Ron said as he slipped a large diamond ring onto the fourth finger – of my right hand. It was a huge solitaire on a platinum band. In short, a perfect engagement ring.

"Ron, it's so beautiful, thank you," I gasped, leaning over to kiss him before admiring it. It fitted me faultlessly, and I admit, I was bowled over by the gesture.

I knew there'd never be any wedding bells with Ron. He'd made it clear from the start that I was his girlfriend to be treated like a queen, and that the other parts of his life would be forever off-limits to me. It didn't worry me. My heart was never Ron's. It would only ever be Mickey's. So I felt nothing about that side of our arrangement, and most of the time never gave a thought to Ron's wife or kids. My life was totally separate from them, and I almost forgot about them entirely, until Ron presented me with the ring.

Before that ring went on my finger, Ron still acted the charmer with me. He'd carried on showering me with beautiful clothes and shoes, and he'd take me out every weekend, introducing me to other members of the criminal underworld. I'd met hardened robbers, hit men and blaggers, including John "Goldfinger" Fleming, who was later linked to the £26 million Brink's-Mat gold bullion robbery in 1983, and Freddie Foreman, or "Brown Bread Fred" as he was called. Freddie had served a 10-year sentence for helping Reggie Kray dispose of Jack "the Hat" McVitie's body. He was also an armed robber, and was convicted of handling proceeds from the Shoreditch security express robbery in 1983.

I was never intimidated by meeting these men. They were always scrupulously polite to me, and very sociable and charming. "Flash" Harry Hayward was another. He was a member of the Hayward family gang, which, alongside the Richardsons, ran South London. His brother Billy was a dangerous man, and involved in the infamous gangland shoot-out at Mr Smith's nightclub in Catford. In 1966, Eddie Richardson and his gang henchman "Mad" Frankie Fraser were drinking in the club, as was Billy Haward, when members of the Krays' Firm arrived. Billy sent for weapons, expecting a gun battle, which ensued in the early hours. The fight pre-empted George Cornell's death at Ronnie's hands, and Billy, along with most of the Richardson gang members, was arrested.

Another Billy, "Scatts" Tobin, was introduced to me by Ron. He ran the Thursday Gang, which was notorious for hijacking security vans, sometimes dressed as police officers. He'd been acquitted two years earlier of conspiracy to rob, and possession of firearms, in a raid on the *Daily Mirror*, claiming he bribed a high-ranking police officer in the process.

It was definitely an experience being with Ron. I knew I was leading a strange life, dabbling with the shadowy world of London's gangland, mixing with convicted criminals and gang leaders, but it was a fascinating experience. One night as Ron drove us to a pub in the East End, I asked him why he spent so much money on me. I never asked for the things he bought.

"You're my shop window," he said.

That answer was so revealing. I realised then I was more to Ron than a girlfriend. I was a symbol of his success as an armed robber and proof of him being a big man on the scene. The expensive things he gave me – the flashing diamonds on my neck and wrists, and now my finger, the luxurious furs I draped over my shoulders, the cut of the chiffon, lace and silk dresses I wore – all of this was a talisman, showing the underworld how well he was doing, how powerful he was becoming. I sensed in that answer that I too was trapped, like a fly in his web, the Black Widow entangled in her lover's tightening grip. He put his hand on my leg as he answered, one hand on the steering wheel, feeling the bump where my stockings clipped onto my suspenders.

"I can't wait to get you home to bed," he growled.

I liked his attention. Ron was always a passionate man, and he made it very clear he lusted after me. I was still a young woman, just turned 32 years old, and it felt good to be wanted. The ring, however, changed all that.

As Ron slipped the twinkling diamond onto my finger, he paused, making sure I looked into his eyes. He'd never bought me a ring before, so I knew this was something different. Something had changed between us.

"But we can't get engaged," I said, confused, even though it was going on my right hand. In my brain, it looked so like a wedding proposal that I blurted that out, foolishly.

"It isn't an engagement ring, Lin, it's a 'you belong to me' ring."

I looked back at him. His stare bored into me. I was being told something, and I knew in that moment that I'd better take heed.

"You can't ever take it off. It's on your finger, and you now belong to me."

Even though he was married, Ron was staking his claim to me.

In that second, I realised what a terrible mistake I'd made in going along with everything. I felt chilled to the bone. Ron meant every word – I could see it in the quiet determination in his eyes. More than that. It was like looking into the face of a shark about to devour me. I realised that this man, my boyfriend, was a psychopath. What everyone had been trying to tell me was true. This man owned me now. He owned me body and soul, and I would never, ever get away from him. I felt like flinging off the ring, which was now a symbol of my entrapment, and running from the room. Goodness knows what would've happened to me if I had.

That day, Ron's manner changed towards me completely. When we went out, I was now told I had to stay by his side, whereas before, I had been free to talk or chat to whomever I wanted. Now, I was told who I could speak to, where I should stand. I was a possession to be treated as he wished. He would "let" me bring Maureen on nights out, because otherwise I had no-one to speak to. He stopped me from chatting to other men, even if their wives or girlfriends were standing next to them. He told me what to wear each and every time we left the house. He would pick my outfit and lay it on the bed for me. He didn't have to order me – I could feel a menace emanating from him that hadn't been there before. Or perhaps I'd just refused to notice.

Standing in the pub, he'd say to people, "Don't talk to Linda, she's with me." Or, "Don't talk to them, you're with me and I need you at my side," or even, "She doesn't want to talk to you," and make people leave me alone. It was a bizarre about-face.

Not long afterwards, we had our first major row. I wanted to go out with Maureen and some other girls one Saturday night. Ron refused. He told me my place was with him and that was that. I couldn't understand why he felt he should control me. It was so unreasonable that I felt compelled to speak out.

"You're not fuckin' goin' out, d'ya hear me?" Ron screamed in my face. I'm not a woman easily spooked, so I didn't back down, even though my hackles were up and I knew I wouldn't win this fight.

"If I want to go out with my friends, that's my decision, Ron. You don't have a right to stop me," I shouted back. I was scared, but my sense of injustice was outweighing my usual care not to upset him.

At that moment, his face changed. Darkness came over him. He moved towards me, fast as a striking snake, and before I knew it he had his hands round my throat and had shoved me up against my kitchen wall.

"Stop, Ron, you're hurtin' me!" I was gasping for breath, trying to claw at his hands as his grip tightened.

"You need to fuckin' listen to me. I told you no, you can't fuckin' go out with your slag pals." His face was screwed up. He looked like the monster I was starting to realise he really was.

"Ron, let go of me, you're goin' to kill me if you keep goin'," I begged. For a moment, I felt a bolt of sheer panic. Was Ron going to kill me? Was he so violent that he'd lose his control and finish the job he'd started?

"Please… Please, Ron…"

Ron hesitated.

*That's it, he's goin' to murder me in my own home.*

But the horror was interrupted by my daughter Melanie. She'd chosen not to go to Nanny's that weekend, and she'd seen everything from the doorway.

"Let her go!"

She started crying, fits of sobs that seemed to bring Ron to his senses. He let go of me and turned away, running his hands through his hair. I collapsed on the floor, holding my neck, choking and gasping for air.

"Come 'ere, darlin'. I'm ok, I'm ok, shush now, Mummy's ok." I pulled my 12-year-old daughter into my arms and started to rock her like a baby.

As I did so, the front door slammed. Ron had gone out. I didn't know where he'd gone, or whether he'd be back that day, and, frankly, I didn't care. By the next day, the bruise around my neck had turned a florid purple.

To make it up to me, Ron had gone into town and bought me another piece of jewellery, but I hadn't the heart for it, and for the first time, I got no thrill whatsoever from opening the box to find yet another sparkly bracelet. Ron hadn't gone out for long – just long enough to cool down, walk back in with the key he'd had cut for himself, and pretend that nothing had happened.

"What's wrong with Mel?" he said, sitting down on the sofa and picking up the betting slips he'd discarded earlier.

I looked at him in disbelief. What on earth was Ron talking about? Why was he asking why Mel was upset when he knew damn well it was his attack on me that had caused it? That was how he was after a fight. He'd act as if he'd done nothing: if we rowed, if he hit me, or twisted my wrist until it bruised. If he held me down when I didn't want sex. If he stopped me from leaving a room by grabbing me and refusing to let go. He'd just act as if he'd done nothing wrong, and ask why I was crying. Or he'd carry on as if nothing had happened at all. Sometimes I even questioned my own sanity. *Did I make it up?*

It wasn't long before Melanie asked me one day if she could speak to me.

"Of course you can, my darlin'. What is it?" I said.

"Mum, I want to go and live with Nanny."

I looked at her, and saw what it cost her to say that. I didn't feel sad or rejected that she didn't want to live with me anymore. If anything, I was relieved she'd be away from Ron and his tempers and violence.

"Of course you can, Mel. It's only five minutes away, so I can see you every day if you want." I opened my arms and she fell into them. I hugged her. My little girl was almost a teenager. She was growing up fast, and the further away from Ron she was, the better.

Things weren't great for Neil either. Ron made it very clear from the start that he didn't like my son. I knew it was because Neil closely resembled his father, with the same olive skin and dark hair. Ron tolerated Neil, and that was as far as it went. Ron never threatened Neil in the way that he did with me, which was a good thing, but it can't have been easy for my son to have to deal with him. So most weekends he'd stay with my mum too. Anything to get him away from my bullying boyfriend.

"I won't be around next weekend. There's a weddin'." Ron didn't look up from the racing papers.

I knew immediately what Ron meant. There was a family wedding and I wasn't invited. To be honest, I was relieved to have some time away from him.

"Would you mind if I went out with Maureen then, on Saturday night?"

I knew I was trying my luck.

"Which pub are you goin' to?" Again, Ron didn't look up, so I had no idea if he was getting angry or not.

I told him the pub Maureen and I might go to, if I was allowed, without Ron.

"Ok," he said, after a long moment's hesitation.

I couldn't believe it. He'd let me go out. Excited, I rang my friend, and it was all organised.

On the Saturday of the night out, I was over at Mum's when the phone rang.

"Get that, will you?" Mum said as she washed up the dishes from lunch in the kitchen.

"Hello," I answered.

"Linda, is that you? I can't believe it, I was ringin' ya mum to find out how to get hold of ya. Haven't seen you in donkey's years." It was a man's voice at the other end of the line.

"Peter!" I exclaimed. "I thought you were in America?"

It was a very old friend, a pal of Mickey's who'd upped sticks and gone to the US, where he'd met a girl and stayed.

"Listen, Lin, I'm back for a couple of nights and I'd love to see you and Mickey."

Something caught in the back of my throat when I realised he didn't have a clue that Mickey had been killed.

"Oh, gosh. Mickey was shot, darlin'. He's dead." I couldn't think how else to break the news. "I've moved, and that's why you couldn't contact us at Pembroke Road."

"Linda! God! I'm so shocked, I can't believe it. Not Mickey. He was too full of life, weren't he?" Peter managed to say. It was obvious he was choked up.

"He was, Peter, but he's gone."

"Linda, we have to meet tonight. Tell us where you're goin' and we'll meet you there."

Without thinking about Ron's reaction, I told him. Getting ready that night, I staged a small rebellion against Ron's rule, and chose a dress I'd bought for myself – admittedly out of the money he gave me, but something I'd chosen rather than something I was told to wear. It felt good to have a moment's liberation.

Sitting in the pub, Peter was shaking his head. "It just doesn't seem real," he kept saying.

"I know, darlin'," I replied, sipping my vodka and lime. Maureen was there, chatting to Peter's girlfriend. Suddenly, we all became aware of a man standing next to our table, standing too close to us.

"Bloody hell, Ronnie Cook!" Peter exclaimed.

We all turned our heads to see Ron towering over us. I knew instantly that he'd come to check that I was where I said I'd be, and he'd seen me with another man, albeit one that was attached. Ron's face was harsh. He wasn't happy, to say the least.

"What's all this then?" He stared straight at me. "You told me you were out with Maureen tonight. You didn't tell me you were goin' with him."

All of us fell silent.

"Peter's just a friend. Don't be cross, Ron," I said, trying to smooth things over.

"I know exactly who Peter is. I'll ask you again. Why didn't you tell me who you were goin' out with?"

By now, Peter and his girlfriend were visibly uncomfortable. None of us could do anything, though. This was Ron Cook. You didn't mess with him. You didn't get into a fight with him.

"When did all this happen?" he asked again.

"Look, Ron, it's nothin'. Peter rang today. He didn't know Mickey had died, and so I told him and he wanted to hear more." My voice was steady, though my heart was racing.

"Give me all my jewellery back. Now."

"What?" I replied, confused rather than anything else.

"Take off everythin' I've given ya. Take it all off. Now. Where arc ya car keys? Good, I'll 'ave those too."

Ron was serious. I looked at Maureen, and she nodded. She looked as scared as I felt.

I divested myself of everything Ron had ever bought me: my car keys, my bracelets, earrings, necklace, fur coat, high-heeled shoes and my handbag. I tipped it all onto the table and handed him the silk purse.

"And the dress." He looked dangerous. "Did I buy it?" he asked, his head cocked to one side.

"No you didn't, Ron. I bought it." My voice wavered but I faced him up. I refused to cower under his menace.

With that, Ron turned and left.

"Oh my God, if he'd bought me this dress, he'd have made me take it off as well, in front of the whole pub," I said, looking round at my friends. I didn't know whether to laugh or cry. I realised my hands were shaking.

"Let me get you another drink," Peter said, hastily, and went to the bar. He returned with a double, saying, "Why didn't anyone tell you what a nutcase Ron is?"

"They did, Peter, but it was too late," I replied.

About 20 minutes later, Ron reappeared at the pub door. This time Maureen spoke to him. He handed her back everything he'd taken from me, though she tried to refuse, as I didn't want any of it back. All it symbolised for me now was my gilded cage.

Ron walked back in, and it was as if he was meeting us all for the first time, as if he'd never walked in and done what he'd done.

"How are ya, Peter. Good to see ya back. Let me get you all a drink… We'll 'ave our own catch-up in The Needlegun tomorrow, Peter."

Later, Ron told me the way he'd reacted was all my fault. I'd "wound him up".

"Where did ya get the dress?" he added.

"From the hoisters. Maureen bought it, but it was too big for her, so I bought it off her." The hoisters were the shoplifters who worked our area.

"Thank God for that. If I'd taken that dress off you, I'd 'ave to 'ave killed everybody in there who saw you without a dress on," Ron said matter-of-factly. His face was devoid of humour, and I realised he meant every word. I knew then, if I didn't know it before, I was with a monster.

# CHAPTER 15

# CONFESSION

## 1980-81

"Mickey's death was your fault." Ron slurred as he spoke, holding onto my wrist too tightly.

I tried to shrug him off, but his grip tightened.

We were back at Harpley Square in my bedroom after a night out drinking and meeting more of Ron's criminal acquaintances. His cold blue eyes were hazy from the whiskeys he'd been downing all evening, but he knew what he was saying, of that I was sure.

"How d'you work that out, Ron?" I replied, making sure to keep the tone of my voice even. I didn't want a blazing row, as it was late on a Saturday night and we'd been out pubbing and clubbing until the early hours. It wasn't like Ron to get drunk – he normally liked to keep control of himself – so this was a rare exception.

I couldn't begin to guess why he was in such a foul mood, as he kept all of his shady dealings from me. He wasn't like my Mickey, confiding in me, asking my opinion, respecting my take on a robbery plan. Ron was different. He kept me separate from the other parts of his life. But tonight there was something odd about the way he was behaving. My only thought was that something in his line of work had either backfired or gone horribly wrong, and that usually meant people being killed or arrested, though I'd never really know. But I knew enough about Ron now, more than a year into our relationship, to know that riling him up would only lead to misery for me, either verbally or physically. And I knew that when Ron shut that front door behind him, he stopped being the cool-headed man-about-town, and became a bully who I had to tiptoe round, making the meals he told me to cook, wearing what he told me to wear, and going to bed when he wanted. He saw me as one of his possessions, something to show off to his pals and to decorate with gems and furs. To him, I wasn't a woman with a mind of her own.

"You killed him, and d'ya want to know how ya did it, Linda?" He almost sneered those words. His breath stank of booze, though I did my best not to show my disgust as I put a smile on my face and gave him a small nod, trying not to react, trying not to light that tinderbox inside him, which one spark of anger could ignite.

"You tell me, Ron, I'm listenin'," I replied. I marvelled at how serene I sounded, as if this was a perfectly ordinary conversation between a couple. I was exhausted and wanted to sleep. My head was starting to pound, but I knew if I got this wrong then I'd get more than a bruised wrist.

"Because when I saw ya, standing at your door in your make-up with a silk dressing gown on, I fell in love with you and I had to 'ave ya."

There was silence for a second. My head spun. I knew what he was referring to: that time he knocked on our door. He and Mickey were planning the heist that got Mickey killed that day. It wasn't a day I cared to remember.

"Go on, Ron," I said quietly, all my senses alert to this man, to what he was going to say. I knew I was on the verge of hearing some kind of confession. The air seemed to still.

"I was going to get rid of Mickey, but fate did it for me."

I had to interrupt the pregnant pause that descended. "What do you mean? I don't understand." I stumbled over my words now, a sense of horror engulfing me.

Ron smiled, and the sight chilled me to the core. Then he spoke. "I was in the car at the Caters robbery. I shut the door and left him out for the gunman. Don't cry. You see, it's really your fault he's dead."

I couldn't help it. I burst into tears. Ron was telling me that the witness was right. Whoever had been in the car had pushed the lock down while Mickey was trying to get inside. By locking Mickey out, he had killed him. It might as well have been Ron firing that gun.

"You lied to me. You told me you weren't at that robbery." I'd questioned him repeatedly if he knew who'd been in the getaway car, and he'd categorically stated that he didn't know. All this time, it had been him.

I had my back to him. I was braced for his displeasure now, but I couldn't hold back. He'd confessed to helping murder my husband, and now he was planting the blame firmly on my shoulders, because Ron had wanted me so badly he was "forced" to take action. I felt utter revulsion. I turned, expecting a slap to the face – or worse. Ron was slumped back on the bed, passed out and snoring.

I sat there for a moment, thinking how easy it would be, right now, to pass a pillow over his face, to squeeze the air from his lungs, to make him pay for Mickey's death. It would be easy, over and done with in a moment, and yet something stopped me. I sighed. I knew I could never murder someone, however evil they were, however badly they treated me or mine. I was tough. I could take care of myself if I really needed to, but a murderess I most definitely was not.

Instead, I went back to my lounge, and poured myself a drink from the bar. I sat for hours, staring into the darkness, nursing the brandy, feeling crushed. How could I ever let him touch me again? Just the thought made my skin crawl. At the same time, I knew I was trapped. Ron had decided that day he first saw me that he was going to have me. I had been right. I'd never had any choice in the matter.

I hardly slept a wink. I couldn't bear to touch even an inch of Ron's body that night, so I slept on the far edge of our bed. The next day, I awoke to the sound of Ron in the shower. He was whistling tunelessly. When he came out, scrubbing his wet hair with a towel, I spoke, cautiously.

"Ron, do you remember what you told me last night?"

He paused for a second, then slid his eyes away from me. "Oh don't ya listen to me, Lin, when I'm pissed. Nothin' of any importance was said last night. If ya heard anythin' then that would be your hearin' playin' tricks on ya."

By now he was speaking from the kitchen. I heard the kettle switch flicked on, yet more of that terrible whistling, which now made my flesh crawl. He'd done it again. He'd denied what he'd said, and made out it was my problem. I knew I wasn't going mad. I knew he was lying now, just as he had lied to me when we first got together. To think that all these months, I'd been sleeping with and accepting gifts from the very man who killed my husband.

There was no escape. I saw that very clearly. I had to carry on, pretend that everything was ok, and just hope against hope that fate would intervene and Ron would come a cropper somehow. I hoped that might be a prison sentence, or losing lots of money on a raid. It wasn't a plan of action or a focused idea, just a vague longing for my own life back, far away from this non-relationship.

From that day onward, something in me changed, hardened. I realised that one day I had to get away from Ron. I just didn't know *how*.

Then things kicked off, big time.

Ron fell out with Peter Spelling, husband of my sister Maxine, and turned up one day at Mum's brandishing two handguns, demanding entry, thinking Peter was hiding from him in my mother's home. Mum told me what happened, calling me from hers. She sounded terrified. "It was awful, Linda, he was bangin' on my door, I thought he'd break it down. Then when I opened it, he just held up these two guns, one in each hand."

"Oh my God." If my strong East End mum was frightened, then he'd really gone for it.

"What did you do?" I asked.

"I refused to let him in, of course." Mum's voice was croaky as she laughed without mirth. "I said to him, 'there are babies in this house, you can't come in, take those guns away, you should be ashamed of yourself'."

That sounded like my mother.

"If that had been a man refusing Ron entry, it would've been a shoot-out, for sure," I said. "Thank goodness it was you at the door. But it sounds awful."

It was the first time Ron's violent lifestyle spilled over into family life, and from then on my parents and siblings knew what he was really like. At the time, Maxine was in hospital after giving birth, and so Mum told Dad to take Shelley over there to warn our sister what was going on.

But as Shelley was driving, she glanced in her mirror to see Ron following her in the car behind. She knew Dad would demand they stop and confront him if she let on, so instead she drove to her house, saying she had to pick up a box of things.

Shelley rang me afterwards. "Oh Linda, it was terrible. I didn't know what to do. I couldn't tell Dad, or he would've gone ballistic, and I couldn't stop, or Ron would've got us, so I had to keep drivin'. Honestly, Linda, I was frightened for my life. My hands were shakin', I had to run indoors, draggin' Dad with me, and pretend I was lookin' for a box of things to take to hospital. I locked myself in the toilet. I was panicking, Linda."

TOP Growing up in Stepney with my siblings (L to R) Vivienne, Terry, Shelley, me and Tony.
ABOVE My parents, Charlie and Eileen, who met while the bombs were falling on the East End.
LEFT On a family day out with my big brother Terry.

TOP The happiest times of my life: my Mickey with newborn Neil. LEFT Me with my beautiful Melanie at Roman Road market. ABOVE Melanie and Mickey on our wonderful holiday in Malta.

ABOVE Grieving with Mickey's brother Terry, the day before Mickey's funeral. LEFT Burning with grief and injustice after the inquest into Mickey's death. BELOW The day we buried my Mickey, the saddest day of my life. My only comfort was the outpouring of love from all the people whose lives he touched.

ABOVE Mel's wedding – a day I was truly gutted to miss because I was behind bars in Holloway. LEFT With Billy Blundell, shortly before I went away for the second time. BELOW A portrait taken of me in Holloway shortly after my murder charge.

LEFT Tying the knot with Danny in HMP Durham.
ABOVE In hindsight, my marriage to Danny was a huge
mistake, as it made us both look guilty. Here we are
enjoying happier times on a prison visit.
BELOW Mum, me and Shelley on a visiting day in
Cookham prison.

ABOVE On day release with George: my first day out of prison after 18 long years. RIGHT My beautiful sister Maxine, who died far too soon in 2016. BELOW Reunited with my sisters at Langan's restaurant.

ABOVE With my beautiful children Neil and Melanie at a charity event. LEFT Neil and his wife Mandy. BELOW Me and George, the man with whom I found happiness again after my release.

LEFT With Mickey's sister Maureen, who is my best friend to this day. ABOVE My astonishing 70th birthday cake, complete with leopard print, spiders and guns!
BELOW East End legends reunited: me with Maureen Flanagan and Freddie Foreman on Freddie's birthday.

"That's dreadful! What did you do?" I couldn't believe Ron had intimidated my family like this. I knew he was nasty, I knew how he treated me, but this was worse, somehow.

"Dad was really confused, so I had to tell him I had belly ache. I looked out of the window hoping Ron would drive off, because he was parked outside. I was in there for 20 minutes, then luckily he drove away. I feel sick talkin' about it." Shelley was clearly still shaken up.

I only found out the true story a few days later from my brother Tony. "The next day, Peter went to hospital to bring the baby and Maxine home," he said. "Peter was carrying the little one, and then Ron appeared and punched him in the face, right in front of Maxine and with the baby in his arms. It was terrible, Linda. Ron said, 'It's your lucky day. Yesterday, I'd have shot ya – I've killed 13 people and I was goin' to make you number 14. Today, you get that'."

"But why would Ron do that?" I countered, mystified.

Tony explained. Peter had been in the Ship of the Green pub a few nights previous, and there'd been two whips going – glasses left on the bar, which people put cash into for the next round of drinks. "A fight broke out, and the guv'nor threw everyone out. Peter picked up the wrong whip – the one Ron's crowd were puttin' money into. He thought it was his pals' whip, and someone grassed to Ron, saying 'Spelling's got your money'. That's all it was, an honest mistake."

It didn't matter how aggrieved my family and I were, there was no way I could confront Ron and demand that he stopped or changed his behaviour. And yet my brother-in-law had almost lost his life over a £15 whip. That's how Ron was. You couldn't go after him and confront him. One of you would end up dead.

Ron was planning on taking me to Las Vegas to watch Muhammad Ali fight in October 1980. He'd come in one Saturday with a large holdall, which he unzipped to reveal a huge stash of American dollars. Ron had done a raid on a foreign bank, and he announced that we had $4,000, and £24,000 to spend during our week in Vegas. A princely sum. Meanwhile, Ron needed somewhere to keep the dollars until we left.

"It's fine here," I offered. No-one would go looking for it in my flat, I reasoned.

Ron didn't like that idea. He wanted it kept well away from me, in case anyone got wind of it.

"There's a lady who sometimes babysits for me. She's a friend, and I know she won't ask any questions," I volunteered.

"Well, I don't want you havin' stolen money in 'ere," Ron said, so we went over to Old Bow and knocked at my friend Nita's door.

"Fuck me, not you, ya old tart," Ron swore as she opened her door.

"Oh, you, is it? I object to being called an old tart." Nita showed us in. I was bewildered until she dug out an old Polaroid picture. "I've still got a photo of you 'ere," she said to Ron.

"Oh I see, you two already know each other," I said, with eyebrows raised. They'd obviously been intimate in the past, but Ron had never said anything about it.

"Look, Neet, do me a favour. Look after this money will ya?" Ron wheedled.

Nita shrugged. "Yeah, ok, stick it in that drawer over there."

We went home and thought nothing more of it.

A few days later Nita got a spin by the police. They'd got a warrant to search the wrong address – hers – and instead of going away and rectifying their mistake, they decided to search her place anyway.

Before long they found Ron's money.

"What's this?" The copper said.

"Oh that's not mine, it's Linda Calvey's," my friend replied. She was naturally shaken by the Old Bill searching her house, and so I didn't blame her for grassing me up.

"What, Linda Calvey whose husband got shot?" an officer said.

"That's right", Nita had replied, and gave them my address.

Next thing I knew, there was a knock at the door.

"Linda Calvey?"

"Yes, that's me. Can I help you?"

"We've just searched a property in the same block, and a bag of American dollars was found," the copper said.

"How do you know?" I replied, my brain whirring as fast as it could. I had to stall them until I could think of a plausible reason why thousands of pounds worth of stolen money would've been in my possession.

"I've got them in my hand, that's how I know," the officer said smartly, and thrust the small bag in my face. I realised what

Nita must've said, and I knew that if she'd told the police who the money really belonged to, she'd have got herself in serious trouble with Ron.

"Oh, did she tell you who my husband was?" I began. A plan had formed in my mind quick as anything. I couldn't grass up Ron either, so I'd had to think of something. Being the widow of a well-known blagger had to come in useful at some point. "I found it in my husband's toolbox when I moved," I said. "It was obviously money he'd got from somewhere. He's been dead 18 months now." I looked the officer in the face without flinching.

"A likely story, Mrs Calvey," he replied.

"How often does your wife look in the toolbox?" I added, making the other officer with him snort with laughter.

"Good point," the copper said. "You'll have to come to the station and give a statement."

Later, Ron didn't take the news well.

"They'll find out where that money's from. In two days' time, they'll send in the heavy mob. You need a new story."

"No, I'll have to stick to mine, I gave a statement," I said.

"That money will be marked. They'll know it was stolen recently, and not while Mickey was alive!"

I hadn't thought of that.

Sure enough, two days later the Flying Squad arrived. Nita and I were nicked for handling stolen money. Ron had reassured me that if I got a suspended sentence and a fine, he'd pay it, but insisted I change my statement. My story just didn't stand up. I spoke to my solicitor, and told him I'd plead guilty but with mitigation.

On the day of my sentencing, I walked into the court room wearing my finest garb: a red fox fur hat, matching fur coat, and high-heeled shoes.

The screw who led me in whispered, "They'll love you in Holloway."

"I might be goin' to Hawaii," I replied, "but I'm not goin' to Holloway tonight. You just watch."

You could've heard a pin drop when I entered the dock.

I pleaded guilty. I saw the police officers say "Yes!" when they heard me.

My solicitor proceeded to tell the court what I'd instructed him to say. I was a widow of a gangster, left with two children to bring up alone, and so I'd turned to high-class prostitution to make ends meet. I'd met an American guy, and we'd gone to his hotel, where he'd asked me why I was selling my body. I'd replied that my husband, an armed robber, had been killed. The client had felt sorry for me, handing me a bag of money and telling me to treat myself and my kids. My story had touched a nerve with him, because he was obviously an armed robber himself.

Every word was a lie – except for being a widow, of course. As my lawyer spoke, I looked over at the judge and smiled a wan smile. It was like a pantomime – I was acting my part and doing it well – but even I couldn't have foreseen what happened next.

When it was my turn to speak, I told the judge that I couldn't get work anywhere because of my notoriety, and had been forced into the degrading but lucrative work. The prosecution thought they'd won. It was an open-and-shut case.

Then the judge spoke. "Mrs Calvey, I must ask you not to do this anymore. It is such a dangerous world out there. There are bad men who could do you harm. Please don't do it."

"I won't, Your Honour, I promise," I said meekly, and the judge smiled and nodded.

By this point, the prosecution barristers were glancing at each other, looks of nervous disbelief on their faces. They couldn't believe the judge had swallowed every word of my lies – and neither could I.

Both Nita and I walked out of the courtroom with suspended sentences and fines, both paid by Ron.

That meant I was free to go to America to live the life of luxury in Vegas. We stayed at Sands Hotel and Casino, went to all the shows, gambled away a small fortune, and watched the Ali fight. The atmosphere was almost sad. It was one of the last times the great boxer ever fought, and he was a shadow of his former talent, eventually retiring against Larry Holmes in the 11th round. Despite that, I felt I'd been at the ring side of history. It was a heady feeling. The problems I'd had with Ron were swept aside by presents of furs and diamonds, sharing magnums of champagne and watching him gamble like a man possessed. We spent every single cent that week. It was one of the most memorable of my life, and not at all what a girl from Ilford would ever have expected to experience in her lifetime.

# CHAPTER 16

# BANGED UP

## 1981

"I'm bringing an acquaintance round to your flat for dinner. I want you to make exactly what I'm about to tell you, nothin' more or less. Can ya do that?" Ron said, eyeing me from my kitchen doorway.

"Tell me what it is, Ron, and I'll be able to answer you." This man, I thought, whoever he was, must be privileged if Ron was inviting him home. He never let anyone come round except for my sisters or Maureen. He'd done my place up like an opulent Mayfair mansion, even though it was a council flat, and yet I never got to show it off.

"Prawn cocktail for starters, fillet steak with mushrooms, tomatoes and chips for main and strawberries and cream for dessert." Ron stared at me.

"Of course I can do that, no problem." I was unnerved by how intense he was being over such a simple meal as this.

Later that day, Ron turned up with the man. He was very good-looking, with lovely white teeth. Funny the things that stand out in my memory! He was polite, ate every scrap of the meal I'd prepared, drank the white wine I'd laid on, and thanked me afterwards.

"That's alright, darlin', Ron must really like you to invite you over. You're privileged!" I laughed.

Ron and the man, whose name I never found out, left.

"I'll pick you up at 8pm and we'll go out for a drink," Ron said, before shutting the street door. "I've left your outfit on the bed."

I went into my bedroom, and sure enough, Ron had laid out the outfit he wanted me to wear that evening.

At 8pm on the dot, Ron appeared in his car, and I got in.

"That bloke ain't joinin' us?" I enquired, as much to make conversation as anything else.

"No, he definitely won't be joinin' us." Ron snorted at his own private joke. "You look wonderful, Linda."

I thanked him and thought nothing more about the geezer who'd disappeared as quickly as he'd appeared in the first place.

Ron bought me a drink at The Needlegun on Roman Road, and then, uncharacteristically, said, "I need to do somethin' for an hour. Wait 'ere and don't talk to anyone."

Ron had never left me alone in a pub. As he left, he told me to watch the door and see who came in and out.

An hour later, he reappeared. No-one we knew had come in the pub, so we had a few drinks and then went home.

The next day, Ron told me to go and buy all the Sunday newspapers. I bought them, wondering why he was suddenly interested in news when all he ever read were the racing papers.

When I got home, he spread them all on the table and started searching through them in a kind of frenzy. He started throwing them on the floor when he'd picked through them.

"What's goin' on, Ron?" I said, bemused at his increasingly strange behaviour.

"Well, Lin, the man you cooked that meal for was in our boot when I picked you up yesterday."

I looked at him for a moment, wondering if this was some kind of sick joke.

His face was straight. Without waiting for me to speak, he carried on. "When I left ya in the pub, I dumped his body deliberately on Hackney Marshes 'cause I wanted him found. I put him in a tracksuit 'cause I wanted it to look like he'd been out joggin' and dropped dead, and I'm checkin' the papers to see if it made the news. But it ain't there." His voice was harsh.

"That's because if you dumped him last night then the papers would already have been printed," I said, pointing out the obvious as my brain worked on keeping up with this macabre and murderous twist to our Sunday morning.

I knew Ron wasn't lying. He was the kind of man who killed people and dumped their bodies. It was just strange how "normal" these kinds of events were becoming in my life with him.

The next day, the death was in the papers. It turned out he was a very high-profile man, and the police were saying he'd died from natural causes. I'd seen that poor man alive and well on Saturday, and knew that couldn't be the case.

"You killed him," I finally said, as Ron crowed over the reports. Quick as a flash, he looked up at me, his cruel eyes flashing. "No, Linda, you killed him. Perhaps you poisoned him while you made him his dinner?"

I looked back at him. It was so like Ron to shift the blame, to muddy the waters.

"No, Ron, I never poisoned him," I replied as calmly as I could, though I felt my heart start to beat faster. Was Ron going to try and pin the blame on me?

"Are ya sure about that, Lin? You might've put somethin' in the cream," he said maliciously.

I shuddered, almost questioning myself for a moment. *Oh my God, did I poison that poor man by mistake?* I hadn't, of course, but that was Ron. He twisted things until you were unsure what was true and what was a lie. Whatever had happened, I realised that what Ron had done was get me to prepare a last, perfect, meal for a man he was about to kill. It was Ron's calculating way of thinking. If he was about to get rid of someone, the least he could do was give him a send-off as good as anyone on death row. It made me shudder to think I'd been travelling in a car with a dead person stashed away. Life with Ron just got more surreal by the day.

Perhaps I was complicit because I didn't report Ron to the police. But I lived in fear of my boyfriend, and the last thing I felt able to do was grass him up. I'd have ended up on that marshland too – of that I have no doubt. A friend of mine was sitting having a quiet beer one Saturday afternoon when Ron pulled up, wound down the window and told this bloke to get in the car. He said he had business he needed him to do. Unwisely, the friend refused, saying he wanted to stay and drink his pint.

"Do me a favour, get my coat from the boot," Ron had said and, not suspecting what would come next, the man opened it up to find a dead body and a shovel. "Get in the front, you're comin' with me," Ron snapped.

The man had no choice but to obey. Ron had chosen him to help bury the body. He had a way of controlling people utterly, with threats and cruelty. And I was no different. He was a heartless bastard through and through.

*The only way I'll be free is if he's nicked soon...*

That became my mantra. I kept repeating it over and over in my head while submitting to his embraces, smiling at his conversation and wearing the clothes he picked out. He was a true psychopath. There was no escape for me. I didn't ever stand up to him now. I'd learnt not to, and I was worn down.

"D'ya like the ring my friend had made for his wife?" Ron said, not long afterwards. It was the middle of December, 1980. He opened a small velvet box. Inside was a sparkling diamond ring. "It's lovely," I said, admiringly, thinking his pal must've commissioned the ring as a Christmas present.

"Oh good, I bought it for you, but I wanted to see if ya liked it," he replied. "Put it on, then."

I slipped it onto the middle finger of my left hand and held it out, watching the light bounce off the stone.

"Oh, and I want a stockin'." Ron added.

"A what?" I said, looking up at him.

"Give me one of ya stockin's," Ron answered, suddenly sounding brusque. "I've got a bit of business, and I want to put it on my head."

I laughed at that. I went into the bedroom and picked out a black sheer stocking with a red lace top.

"You bitch!" he barked.

"D'you want it or not?" I couldn't help goad him. The thought of him going into a robbery wearing a sexy stocking was too good an opportunity to miss.

I didn't know it, but Ron was planning a Brink's-Mat robbery. That evening, as I sat watching the news, it flashed up that an armed robbery in South London had been foiled, and everyone had been arrested. Gunmen had raided a security van near a school in Dulwich. The Flying Squad had waited until the men had the money before swooping in on them.

I knew instantly it was Ron.

The robbers had been supergrassed, and police were lying in wait. There was a knock at my door. What looked like a tramp, a real down-and-out, was standing on my doorstep.

"Can I help you?" I asked, bemused.

"Where's Ron?" the man said.

"He isn't here."

"He must've been on that robbery yesterday. We were meant to do a job today, would've netted a couple of hundred grand each."

Without saying goodbye, the man slunk off. I shut my door, my brain whirring. Ron had certainly been caught, so what would that mean for me?

A couple of days later, his nephew appeared at my door. Ron was on remand at Brixton Prison, and he wanted me to go and see him. I turned up, went through the searches, and finally got to sit opposite Ron in the cheerless visitors' room. He was being held in the maximum-security part of the jail, as joyless a place as it was possible to be.

"Listen Lin, one of the co-defendants is goin' to bribe the jury to find us Not Guilty. I was goin' to do it myself, but he said he was already on it." Ron's voice was low. I had to lean over the table to hear him. "I'm goin' to be 'ere for a year cos I'm on remand, but I'll be walkin' out in a year's time. You've got to behave yerself until then." Ron stopped and stared at me. His gaze was cold.

"What d'you mean, Ron?" I asked.

"Well, you do love ya son and brother Tony, don't ya?"

"Yes, I do, Ron, and you don't need to say that," I answered, horrified.

Ron was threatening harm to my family. He was doing it to ensure that I stayed faithful to him, that I stayed scared of him, and to make sure I waited for him.

I had no choice but to visit Ron every fortnight for the next year, and woe betide me or my family if I deviated from that path. Yet again, Ron was in control of me. How stupid I'd been to imagine he wouldn't still have sway over my life if he was sent to prison.

Before Ron went away, he had introduced me to a friend of his, called Brian Thorogood. From the moment I'd met him, we had formed a mutual dislike of each other. Brian was distinctly off-hand with me, but I noticed that he was the only person who wasn't afraid to talk straight to Ron. He'd just come out of prison at the time, and had heard Ron was shacked up with me. He obviously didn't approve. When I leant forward to give him a kiss, he drew his head back, making Ron laugh.

"Isn't she wonderful, Brian?" Ron had said, chuckling.

"If you say so," he'd replied.

Brian looked like a young Bob Hoskins – the video shop owner round the corner used to call him "Long Good Friday" after the Hoskins film. He was medium height, short-haired and nice-looking, though I thought he was quite a rude man. Ron clearly liked the fact we hadn't got on, because it was Brian who Ron entrusted with keeping an eye on me, and helping me find work. Without Ron's £100 on my mantelpiece every week, life was suddenly a financial struggle again. Ron called Brian and me into prison together, and told his pal to give me a job at his haulage firm.

"Do I 'ave to?" Brian replied.

"Yes, ya do. She needs to be looked after," Ron had replied, and that was that. Under sufferance, Brian gave me work in the office, and we came to a kind of truce, as neither of us had any real choice but to follow Ron's orders.

# CHAPTER 17

# FUR COAT AND BLACK STOCKINGS

## 1981

Ron was sentenced to 16 years in prison. My heart swooped when I heard the news. Was I finally free? Whether the evidence against him was too overwhelming, or whether his contact hadn't been able to bribe the jurors, I don't know. I wasn't at court on the day of the verdict but I heard there was a torrent of abuse hurled at the judge and prosecution lawyers.

Details of the raid filtered out to me. Ron's cronies had tried to attack a Brink's-Mat security van carrying almost a million pounds outside Kingsdale Comprehensive School in Dulwich. One of the gang members had grassed up Ron and the other robbers. There was a suggestion Mr X – as the grass was known in court – had actually set up the police raid to frame one of the group that was caught. I was none the wiser. Ron never told me anything about his "business" and I didn't ever ask.

Ron called me into Brixton Prison. He was a Category A prisoner and I had to go through extensive searches, before sitting down at the same table in that dreary visiting room. I'd been to so many of those rooms. The smell of disinfectant mingled with desperation, the cheery paintings by children who'd come there to see a dad or uncle. They all merged into one, and I didn't even bother looking round as I sat myself down opposite him. Ron dispensed with small talk.

"I'm goin' to be inside for at least 10 years, but of course, you'll be waitin' for me." He was looking me full in the face.

"Of course, I will, Ron," I replied, without flinching.

What else could I say? If my son and brother's lives were on the line, as Ron had intimated they were, then I'd do anything to keep them safe. I didn't want to wait for him. When I heard he'd been given such a long sentence I felt the first real joy I'd felt since Mickey was alive. For a brief moment, I had thought I might be free of him and his control over me. But I saw now that I was trapped just as securely as Ron was.

"I thought you expected a Not Guilty verdict?" I asked.

"I did. I sat in the dock and picked out the jurors I could offer a bribe. Got someone to follow them home and offer them 10 grand if they brought in the right verdict."

There was menace in Ron's voice and I shuddered, knowing all too well how it felt being followed home by a crook and being offered money. It was all irrelevant though. Whoever Ron had entrusted with the money hadn't come through, evidently.

"So, ya will wait for me." Ron deftly turned the conversation back.

"I will, Ron."

"He's a handsome boy, he'll look good at 18."

Nothing could be clearer. Wait for Ron, or Neil wouldn't reach adulthood.

"Don't talk stupid Ron, I've told you I'll wait."

That was the end of my audience. I went back home and told Maureen what Ron had said. My best friend hated my boyfriend, and I didn't blame her. "We'll start to enjoy ourselves now that he's doin' time, don't you worry, Lin. You'll be alright."

We started going out on a Friday night, and soon Brian began to join us. He wasn't at all like the uptight, disapproving man I'd first met. I visited Ron every fortnight, and I realised I was starting to enjoy Brian's company, and look forward to our nights out together. Brian was cheerful, and everybody seemed to like him – in short, he was the exact opposite to Ron. Before long, Brian's company was sold, and even though I wasn't working for him anymore, he would pop by each Friday afternoon and give me £80 to go towards my bills.

Six months after Ron went away, the inevitable happened. One night, I invited Brian back to mine after we'd been out to the pubs, and I put a slow record on.

"Come and have a dance," I said, and we had a smooch.

"D'you know what, I can see what Ron sees in you." Brian smiled as he held me close. Brian stayed that night, and our relationship began.

Our secret was a dangerous one to keep from Ron, but I never could resist taking a risk. As I made breakfast, Brian sidled up to me and put his arms around my waist.

"I've left some money on the side, go and treat yerself. I know Ron always looked after ya."

"That's very kind of you, darlin'," I said and kissed him. It was good to feel safe in a man's arms again. All of a sudden, I felt a kind of freedom. So what if we had to hide from Ron? Brian and I could carry on as we were, pretending to my psychopath partner that everything was normal, and he wouldn't know that we were now an item. I felt a surge of happiness, so, grabbing my coat, I headed out to a gorgeous boutique on Roman Road.

"I haven't seen you for a while, Linda, how are ya?" the shop owner said as I walked in.

"I know, sorry love," I replied, "Ron is in prison."

"Sorry to hear that. Well, come in because I've got somethin' 'ere you'll like."

I grinned at her. She knew my taste, high glamour and eye-wateringly expensive. She pulled out a coat with a matching hat from the back of the shop. They were a deep maroon-coloured fur, and I was instantly smitten.

"How much are they?"

"The hat is a hundred, the coat, six hundred."

I didn't bat an eyelid. It was a sum that would run into the thousands these days, but it was normal for Ron or Mickey to spend that kind of money on me.

"I'll take them," I said, handing her the £100 that Brian had put on the mantelpiece for me. "Use that as a deposit, and I'll be back for the rest."

When I went home and told Brian what I'd done, he made a show of falling off the work surface he'd been perched upon.

"For a moment, I thought you said the coat cost £600!" he said in astonishment.

"I did, Brian. Did I do wrong?" I replied in my meekest voice.

Brian looked like he was undergoing some kind of internal battle within himself. Finally, he barked a laugh that made me sigh with relief.

"It's not your fault, you've been spoilt by Ron, and you've lost all concept of the cost of things. I'll go back with the money and get you what you want."

"Thank you, darlin'," I smiled. It was good to be treated again too.

Later that day, when Brian had left, I phoned Maureen.

"You prat!" she laughed. "Why don't I get men to do things like that for me?"

We both burst into fits of giggles at that.

"I have no idea why men buy me things, they just always have." I shook my head. It was true. I never really had to work a proper day in my life, though I also had to live a double life, lying to Ron while secretly going out with his only friend. We never flaunted our relationship. Brian wasn't a very sociable person, and so most of the time we stayed in and I'd cook for him. Whereas I loved going out and meeting people, he was just as happy sitting in front of the telly with ham, egg and chips. Often he'd drop Maureen and me down to a pub we liked on a Friday or Saturday night, then come and pick us up later. It didn't bother him that I was out without him. He wasn't controlling like Ron. The only thing he and his pal had in common was that they were both armed robbers.

Unlike Ron, I introduced Brian to all of my family, and they adored him, especially Neil and Melanie, who had moved back home with me since Ron's imprisonment. It felt like we gelled as a family, which was a nice feeling after the tumultuous years we'd all endured. Finally, we had some peace and stability, though Brian didn't stop doing raids. He would just hand over all the money he seized, barely keeping anything for himself. He was such a generous soul.

Ron's controlling behaviour didn't stop now that he was behind bars. One day, I got a call from him telling me to visit him as he was in hospital. He was under guard, but I could go and visit him in his hospital bed.

Before I could ask what was wrong with him, he said, "Lin, I want you to do exactly what I'm about to tell you to do."

"Ok Ron, what is it you want?" I replied, my curiosity piqued, though inwardly sighing at yet another demand. What now?

"I want you to dress in a red and black basque, black stockings and suspenders under your dress, and a fur coat on top. When you get to the hospital, go to the Ladies and take off your dress, keeping your coat on."

"Right." *With any luck I'll give him a heart attack*, I thought.

I did exactly what he told me to do. I turned up for visiting time, went straight to the toilets and took off my dress, packing it into my handbag. Keeping my fur coat wrapped around me, I walked up the length of the ward, my heels clicking on the floor.

Ron was sitting up in bed, with wires and bleeping machines connected up to him. He was due to have a pacemaker fitted the next afternoon.

"How are you, Ron?" I asked cautiously. Why on earth would he want me to be dressed the way I was when he was obviously sick?

Ron ignored me.

"Give me a private visit, will ya?" he said to the screw guarding him. "Shut the curtains," he commanded.

The screw looked me up and down, before obeying. From behind the thin curtains came the bleeping sound again, regular and steady.

"Open your coat," Ron said, his blue eyes staring at me, fiercely, in the gloom.

I could do nothing but obey. I pulled back my coat and revealed myself to him.

He whistled. "You'll be the death of me, Linda Calvey."

*I hope so, Ron Cook, I hope so.*

"I'm happy to oblige," I said passively, stepping closer and letting him admire me.

"You're wonderful, Linda, you're magnificent," he said, his eyes devouring me.

Just then the beeping sound went haywire. The screw called out from the other side of the curtain. "I don't know what you're doin' in there, but you have to stop 'cause your heart monitor has gone crazy!"

I whipped the coat back around me just as the prison guard threw open the curtains, glaring at me as he did so. I scurried off to put my dress back on, wondering how close I'd really come to finishing off this cruel man.

After that brush with Ron, I suddenly felt bolder. Perhaps the wires and machines made me realise Ron was mortal, just like the rest of us. Perhaps seeing that gave me the courage to do what I did next.

I don't know what it was, but the next time Brian announced he was going to get his balaclava and cosh out to do a job, I said, "I want to come with you."

"Absolutely not, Linda."

I was determined. "If you're goin' out on a job, then I want to be with you."

Brian's face softened.

"I am goin' to do it, Brian. I've got contacts still. I can get us a group together and we can go on the pavement."

I knew I'd be good at it, though who could possibly know they'd be a successful armed robber? There were too many variables, too many ways of it going wrong, but something in me clicked, and I just knew that, given half a chance, I could make a go of being a thief.

Weeks later, I invited Brian and a couple of contacts of mine to Harpley Square. One of the men was called Carl Gibney, a tall, thin man who was obsessed with the gym and modelled himself on Bruce Springsteen. He dressed just like him, in T-shirts and jeans, with long hair. I'd met him through Mickey. I knew that Carl wanted to do some robberies, but hadn't found anyone decent to do them with.

That meeting between me, Carl and Brian was more of an introduction. Brian still wasn't letting me carry a weapon or be actively involved, though he'd agreed to let me scout out possible targets. I began walking round the area, taking notes and working out escape routes and places to park possible getaway motors. I liked the thrill of it. I liked being in charge of those dangerous men who would risk their lives to steal the money. I was determined to honour my vow to Mickey, made three years ago as he lay ice cold and still in his coffin. I was about to become an armed robber.

# CHAPTER 18
# BECOMING A BLAGGER
## 1981-83

That first raid went exactly to plan. I'd spotted the target – a bank security van – and had scouted the area. The three of us had planned the rest together. Weeks of careful preparation all came down to five crucial minutes of action as Brian and Carl burst out of their hiding places, brandishing shotguns, grabbed the money as it was brought out to the van, and legged it to our getaway vehicle, where I was waiting for them.

I kept a cool head as I dropped the boys off one by one, Carl walking off to the bus stop to head home from there, Brian sauntering over to his car before heading to the garage he rented in Hackney to drop off the gear. As I got into my car and pulled out into the traffic, with police cars tearing past me up the road, I felt a thrill like never before.

It was lunchtime when I arrived home, and though I felt hungry, I knew I was too overexcited to eat. As I shut my front door behind me, I let out the burst of laughter that had been building inside me. I don't know if it was hysteria or nerves, or plain joy, but once I started I couldn't stop. I laughed and laughed, tears streaming down my face, this time for sheer happiness. I'd done it! I'd actually gone out on a raid with the fellas and Oh My God I'd loved it. The buzz of it was like nothing I'd ever experienced.

That day, my first as a blagger, I realised why Mickey had done it. It wasn't just for the money – though that was very nice. No, it was the thrill, the excitement and the risk of getting caught. It was a heady melting pot, and I knew in that moment I was hooked, and I could never turn back. I'd made my choice to embark on a life of crime, and I could never go back to being a kept woman. I could take my life into my own hands, become an armed robber and fulfil my vow to Mickey. My destiny was set.

I paced around, waiting for the boys to arrive at my place in Harpley Square, where I'd agreed to meet them an hour or two after the raid. Neil and Melanie were at Mum's as it was the weekend, and now I just had to contain myself until Brian and Carl turned up. I'd seen Mickey and his pals come back after a successful raid, and I knew now how they'd felt. They were always hyper. They bounced off the walls, shouting, joking and laughing, then they'd go and get drunk. I understood every part of their experience, so much so that I found myself pouring a large brandy to steady my nerves.

As I sipped on it, I reflected on my life with my husband – how relieved I always was when he came home safely, how little I'd really understood his life on the pavement. Well, now it was my life. It felt proper and fitting – a tribute to my murdered soulmate. I raised my glass. Tears threatened to fall again, but this time they were for sadness.

At that moment, there was a loud rap on the door. I froze. Put my brandy down, wiped away the tears and took a breath. Was it the Old Bill? Had I risked too much?

"Open up, Lin, it's us!" It was Brian's voice. I rushed over to the door and opened it. Brian and Carl walked in, both laughing, patting each other on the back. Brian was casually carrying the holdall as if he'd just got back from holiday.

"Let's 'ave a look at the money," said Carl. Brian unzipped it, and there it was. A small mountain of cash.

"Must be twenty grand in there," Carl whistled.

"At least," Brian said. He was pouring himself and Carl a large whisky each.

"Let's sort it out then," Brian said, glaring over at Carl. We all got equal shares, even though I had been waiting for them in the car. Our roles were all equally important.

Carl winked at me. "You played a blinder today, darlin'. We couldn't 'ave done it without ya."

"Thank you, darlin'," I replied.

I looked over at Brian who grinned back at me, and said, "You can keep my share, Lin. Put it towards gettin' yerself a place." I'd confided in him that my dream was to own a house. I couldn't believe that he was giving me this money towards it.

"But it's a lot of money, Brian! Are you sure?" I gasped. He really was such a sweet man.

"'Course I'm sure. You take it, Lin. A couple more jobs and you'll be able to buy yerself a nice place for the kids."

I started looking for possible houses to move into, and settled on a small two-bed place in Northumberland Avenue, Hornchurch. It backed onto a park, had a long garden and needed a lot of work. It would cost £28,000, and so I needed a small mortgage. Brian and I went to view it.

We went to pick up the keys from a man who lived over the road, confusingly also called Brian. He offered to let us in himself and show us round.

Inside the house, there were cups left on the table, as if someone had just got up and walked out.

"Yeah, it's very sad," said Brian Crowley, the neighbour. "A young couple lived 'ere, and he died. She moved out straight away and won't come back, which is why I got the key."

"How sad is that!" I exclaimed. "It's a lovely house though, safe for my children. I'd like to take it. At least then she can move on with her life if this place is sold to me."

Brian Thorogood and I quickly got friendly with Brian C. As he showed us round, he started getting curious about our lives.

"What d'ya do for a living, then?"

I laughed when I heard that.

"We're bank robbers." I expected the usual polite laugh in response.

But Brian C just gave me a curious smile, wide-eyed, and nodded his head.

"I wondered. Can I work with ya?"

It wasn't the way to let just anyone join the team, but Brian T and I agreed to talk it over with Carl and spend time checking out Brian C, to check he was solid. And soon enough, he joined me, Brian T and Carl in my kitchen, planning robberies over ham sandwiches and cups of tea.

Our next plan was to raid a post office.

"No, that one isn't viable, not enough outs," I said, pointing to the map of East London Brian T had spread out on the table. People who have brains think carefully about the number of getaway routes. You have to go in thinking you'll get caught. It's the only way to engineer a successful raid. Every risk factor has to be taken into account.

"I've seen a security van picking up cash from there," I pointed to a different branch. "There are a few ways out, down there, or you can go there, and we can park getaway cars either here or there, or maybe in both places, just in case."

The men all nodded. They knew I was fast becoming the brains of the operation – not just a woman willing to don a disguise and drive the getaway car, though I could do that too if needed.

"Ok, we'll head there and watch that one, see what times they come and go. Leave it with us," Carl said, "and can I 'ave another cuppa, if there's one goin'?"

"Of course you can, darlin'," I said, pouring him a second cup of tea. Over the next few days, Brian T, Carl and Brian C staked out the post office I'd targeted. It wasn't long before they came back to me.

"We've got the times. We think late afternoon will work best," said Brian T.

I nodded.

They didn't need me on this raid. Brian T would be first in with the sawn-off shotgun, holding up the security men as they walked out of the post office, seconds before they loaded the day's takings into the van. Carl would be the anchor man, keeping an eye on anyone trying to be a hero in there, making sure they all got out before the police arrived. Brian C would drive the getaway car.

For this raid, they had two cars stationed at two different points, one at the end of a long, thin pedestrian alley with bollards at one end, so they couldn't be chased by car. The other was stationed further away as a plan B, should their exit be blocked.

They all looked confident. It was time to send them off. I pulled out the bag in which I kept the disguises I borrowed from Mum's stall, and they donned black wigs and moustaches, keeping their balaclavas until they were in place, ready to leap out of the motor. The shotguns were kept in the same bag, buried underneath brightly coloured wigs, fake moustaches and glasses. Once they were tooled-up and ready, I wished them all luck.

Brian T would be taking the money, which meant, yet again, he would give me his share on top of mine. Later that day, as Brian and I lay in bed, a bag full of money lying inches away in a cupboard, he said, "You've got enough for that deposit now, Linda."

"Thank you, Brian," I said, my head on his chest.

In those days, you could walk into a bank with £10,000 in cash and deposit it, no questions asked. I'd banked almost double that, and mortgages were easy to get. Finally, I was ready to buy that new place on Northumberland Avenue, opposite Brian C's house. My brother Tony would take my old flat in Harpley Square.

I moved in with Brian T, and was delighted to have my own place. But soon enough I found out why the couple who owned the house before me had left it in such a hurry. Brian C revealed that the husband had killed himself because he'd found out his wife was having an affair. He hanged himself from the hatch in the ceiling directly above my bath.

"It was terrible, Linda, I had to cut him down. His body hit that bath like a slab of marble. If I hadn't have built that hatch for him, he couldn't have done it." He shook his head.

"That's it," I said to Brian T as soon we heard the truth. "I can't live here no more."

"But you've only just bought it!" he protested.

"I know, but I'll never be able to have a bath and not picture that poor man swinging over my head. No, I have to sell it. We're movin'."

I was adamant. Even though we'd had the whole place done up, I knew I couldn't live there a moment longer. I felt like death was stalking me.


As the group's getaway driver, I had all the tricks. I was taking on more and more responsibility, and I always had to be one step ahead of the police. One lapse in concentration and we could all end up banged up.

We were gradually recruiting more people into our group,

and the latest recruit was a tall black guy called Winston. He was cool-headed during raids, but became a bundle of nerves as soon as he heard a police siren.

This didn't sit well with my high-risk getaway tactics. One of my new ruses after a raid was to drive straight towards the police station, as that was the last place the coppers would expect you to head. After a raid in Hornchurch, I did exactly that, driving along with the traffic, slowly and carefully, so as not to draw any attention to ourselves. Brian was sitting in the front with me, ostentatiously holding up a copy of the *Daily Express* in front of his face, pretending to read it in the passenger seat in the most casual fashion possible. Winston was huddled in the back underneath a pile of blankets, curled up with the holdall containing the shotguns and £20,000 in cash.

As we approached Hornchurch police station, we began to hear the wail of sirens. The police had been alerted to the robbery and were setting off in pursuit.

Winston began to get nervous. "Are they onto us?" he flustered. "Is it on top?"

I murmured my reassurances to Winston and kept my eyes on the road. We were approaching a junction, and the road going off to our right led directly to the station. The sirens were quickly increasing in volume and number. I glanced to my right to see a swarm of police cars tearing up the road towards the junction.

Winston was spooked. "What's going on, Brian? We need to get away, man!" He thought we were finished.

In the middle of a heavy queue of traffic, I thought fast. The police hadn't noticed us in the getaway van and were heading straight across the junction, but I wanted to be sure the van wouldn't arouse any suspicions on their way past. I needed to make the van look as innocuous as possible. So, when the car in front of me moved forwards, I drove straight out over the junction in front of the line of police cars and blocked their way.

The police cars screeched to a halt, stopping short of the van and desperately honking their horns at me to move out of the way for them. The coppers were gesturing frantically at me as I sat in the driver's seat, playing the innocent traffic victim, helplessly looking around as if trying to work out how to get the van out of their way.

"What's going on? Is it on top?" Winston stammered once again. The sirens were right beside us now, blaring deafeningly through the van.

Brian, from behind his newspaper, chuckled to himself. "No, we're fine," he said casually. "Our lady boss is being clever, she's just holding them up."

Winston groaned.

The stranded policemen were becoming even more agitated. I turned to look at them out of the van window, pointed to the traffic blocking my way forwards, shrugged helplessly and mouthed, "Sorry!"

The police gestured wildly for me to reverse to let them through.

"I'm turning white under here!" cried Winston.

With sirens wailing all around, I slowly looked around behind me and clunked the van into reverse. Slowly and clumsily, I shunted the vehicle backwards.

"Relax, Winston," said Brian, "she's just letting them through. They'll be gone in a minute."

The police cars squeezed through the gap I'd created for them, and the grateful officers waved their thanks to me as they blazed past and disappeared up the road to our left. The officer in the first vehicle mouthed "Thank you!" as they went.

I waved cheerily back at him and mouthed, "That's alright!"

We got away with the money, and Winston became calmer as we did more jobs together. One morning, he asked to borrow my car, as he was going to meet someone in Brixton.

"I'll be gone two hours Linda, I'll bring it straight back," he assured me.

I waited and waited, keeping myself busy around the house to pass the time, but it wasn't until seven hours later that Winston showed up at my door again.

I opened the door to find him standing there, shifting from one foot to the other.

"What took you so long?" I demanded.

"Ah, well, you'll never believe it Linda..." he began. "I left the car on the street to go and meet him, and when I came back the car was gone!"

Luckily, Winston was in with the thieves in the local area, and knew exactly where to find them. He turned up at their garage to find, to his horror, that they were dismantling my car.

"You can't do that, man!" he'd shouted in desperation. "Don't you know that's the Black Widow's car!"

Winston grinned at me. "I'm tellin' you, I've never seen a bunch of crooks put a car back together more quickly than those fellas did. They were shit scared. And the car worked fine on the way back – it might not all be perfect, but it still goes alright!"

Whether it was put back together properly or not, it didn't matter, because I quickly earned enough to buy a new car. I chose a Mercedes in maroon, and took an enormous box of notes over to the garage to pay up for it. As I lifted up the box of stolen cash and tipped it out over the counter, a look of horror spread over the garage owner's face. He let out a cry and rushed round to lock the door behind me.

"My God!" he exclaimed. "You shouldn't be carrying all that cash on you! You could get robbed!"

# CHAPTER 19

# ON THE PAVEMENT

## 1983-85

The first time I held a gun, I forgot to breathe.

Somehow, through all the years I'd been around them, I'd never actually touched one myself.

My thinking was that it would be too real, make the whole robbery thing seem less of a joke, and more of a serious crime. Keeping my distance made it all seem like harmless fun, a case of "us against the law", more of a Bonnie and Clyde set-up or a Robin Hood adventure. We stole from the wealthy banks and businesses, and though we didn't freely pass it round, we considered ourselves as working class, and therefore entitled to squander rich people's money.

That all changed when I went to collect some shotguns for our next raid.

We had the guns, now we had to keep them out of sight of Neil and Melanie, who were returning from my mum's the next morning before we went out on the pavement.

I put the bag onto the table. It was heavy. I took out one of them, its shortened body fitting into my left arm as I gripped the trigger and looked down the 18-inch barrel. The end had been sawn off, because no robber can walk around with a great big long gun. You'd be arrested before you got a chance to use it. It was an odd feeling, knowing Mickey had done this, knowing Brian and the boys would carry on doing this. It felt surprisingly normal, like a tool of our trade, but it had power. Already, I knew how to stand with it, how to hold it, the effect it would have on anyone looking down the wrong end of it. I shuddered and put it back. My mind was whirring. This was normal life, and the weirdest thing about it was that it didn't feel strange.

I knew that guns were a risky business, and we all hoped we'd never be forced to use them. The dangers they brought with them were driven home when I went out with Carl and Brian on a job one afternoon. While I headed home, Brian and Carl had gone back to the garage to dump the gear. We'd agreed to meet up at mine later.

When the knock at the door came an hour or so later, I was surprised to see Carl standing there in the doorway, looking sheepish. He scratched the back of his head warily.

"Bit of an issue, actually, Linda. I accidentally shot Brian."

"What?" My heart leapt out of my chest.

"I tripped and my gun went off into his back. He's fine, but there are pellets all over him. Can you come help me get 'em out?"

Carl drove me back to Brian's garage, where I spent the next few hours delicately picking shotgun pellets out of Brian's bloodied back. They didn't do any lasting damage, but it was a severe warning for all three of us.

But not long afterwards, I decided that I would join the robberies and go out with a gun myself. It seemed like the logical next step. The first time I properly went on the pavement, it was just me and Brian. It was usually unimaginable to go out just the two of us without a driver, but this job was in such a quiet corner of London that we knew we would be ok. I wore my red wig and a balaclava, with two thick jackets to bulk up my small frame. The wool hood felt scratchy and hot against my skin. It was late evening, and Brian and I had chosen a little out-of-the-way place. I suddenly felt nervous as we packed up our gear and got in the stolen car. I'd planned many robberies, but this was different. I was going out and doing it myself. I wondered what Mickey would think of me, tooling up and preparing to carry on his legacy.

"Come on," Brian said, kindly. He could sense my hesitation. The journey passed in a blur of nerves and excitement.

"Don't you speak," Brian ordered. I nodded. My mouth was so dry I don't think I'd have managed a word anyway.

I followed close behind him. My heart was thumping, literally beating against my ribcage. I was crossing a line. From this point there was no turning back, no pretence of innocence. It was me, Brian and the guns in our hands.

"Nobody move! Give us the money. NOW!" Brian's voice boomed.

There was a brief moment of silence. Then someone, a woman, started screaming.

I stood close, holding my gun up high to make sure the staff could all see it. The woman behind the counter, who was cashing up, said something, but I couldn't make it out. I felt like a wild animal, on high alert, every sense quivering, ready for anything to happen.

Brian stuffed the money into the bag until it was full. At that point, he signalled to me it was time to go. We turned and fled. It was as simple as that.

The car was outside, though it was reckless to leave it unguarded. I jumped into the driver's seat and started the ignition, every second feeling like a million years.

"Come on, Linda, just keep hold of yerself. Let's get home."

The engine fired, I crunched into first gear and we were off. I was dizzy with the adrenalin rush, but we made it back without a single siren following us.

I couldn't believe I'd done my first raid. It was a huge buzz, a hit. The feeling of holding a loaded gun and escaping with vast amounts of money was like nothing else I'd ever experienced. I understood everything now – the lure for Mickey, the promise of easy money – it all became crystal clear.

Soon enough, we were joined by another contact of mine called Lee, and we had a solid group to choose from. The main players were still me, Brian and Carl, but we'd occasionally hire Brian C, Winston or Lee if we needed an extra man. Before I agreed to take anyone on, I had two questions to ask them.

1. Are you prepared to carry a gun?

2. Are you prepared to use it?

If the answer to either of those was no, they couldn't work with me. I already had this group of six blaggers, and we all trusted each other, so we were well set for any job.

So I was infuriated one day when the others recruited a new man without consulting me. I came home from the shops to find Brian, Carl and Lee in deep conversation. We were in the middle of planning a four-person job, and, unknown to me, Lee had asked Brian and Carl if his brother, a market trader, could come along on this job. Lee's brother was having a hard time, and was in danger of having his house repossessed, so he needed a bit of extra cash.

Brian and Carl had agreed before I knew a thing about it. They told Lee that, as it was only a four-person job, one of them would drop out to make way for Lee's brother.

I was incandescent. "That's not how it works! We need to know who this guy is, whether we can trust him! How can you go out on the pavement with a man you don't know?"

Brian and Carl apologised, but insisted they had already agreed it with Lee, so couldn't go back on it now.

I couldn't believe my ears. "Fine," I snapped, staring at them. "But if that's how you feel about it, you can do the job yourselves. I'm sitting this one out. You four can get on with it yourselves."

Then another thought occurred to me. "Is he prepared to carry a gun?"

"Yes, of course," Lee said with absolute confidence.

I steered well clear of the rest of the planning for that job, but on the day of the robbery my curiosity got the better of me. I knew the target was a security van in Hornchurch, and there was a little café opposite that I knew and liked. So I headed there to watch the action unfold from across the street. I ordered a cheese sandwich and a coffee and sat by the window.

After a while, I saw Lee's brother stationing himself in the shadows, holding a small old-fashioned shopping bag, the sort we used to hide guns in. He looked nervy and I was instantly glad I wasn't in on the job with them. I felt vindicated already. Carl was waiting in the car over the road, while Brian and Lee were poised nearby with their guns at the ready to cover Lee's brother and the cash.

As the guard came out with the money, the security van pulled up. Lee's brother leapt out, but he wasn't carrying a gun. I couldn't believe it. Was he trying to rob a bank with his bare hands? I watched, wide-eyed, as he charged towards the security guard and swung the bag up into the air. It hit the guard squarely in the side of the head, and I looked on incredulously as the guard stumbled backwards dizzily and dropped the bag. Lee's brother snatched it up and dashed back to Carl's car, and Lee and Brian leapt in as they raced off.

When I got back to my house about half an hour later, I still couldn't work out what on earth had happened. Where was the gun? If it was in that bag, what had Lee's brother been playing at? Soon enough, they all turned up at my door.

I ushered them quickly into the house, slammed the door and spun round on Lee's brother.

"What the hell happened there then?" I asked. I told them I'd been sitting in the café opposite, and had seen it all.

Lee's brother spoke up. "We got away with the money, here it is, let's split it up."

I stared fiercely at him. "Not until you explain yourself."

He looked at the ground. "I lost my nerve, I didn't want to take the gun with me. So I just left it at home and put a brick in the bag instead. I thought I could just as well take the guard out with that."

I could hardly contain my rage. I looked hard at Brian and Carl. "Now d'you see why I don't let just anyone join in?" I spat. "If something had gone wrong, this have-a-go hero would have put you all in danger."

Lee's brother sheepishly agreed, saying it was the worst experience of his life and he didn't know how any of us could do it for a living. He haughtily declared that he would never do it again. It was already clear to me that he'd certainly not be working with us again. On the plus side for him, though, he was able to get his mortgage and bills sorted, and had even made enough from the robbery to take his family on holiday to Spain for a week. So he couldn't have too much to complain about.

Ron hadn't forgotten me or my promises to him. I dreaded going to see him. He kept asking me how I was managing money-wise, and each time I told him not to fret, I was fine.

Lying to Ron wasn't usually an easy task. Despite his prison garb, his reduced circumstances, he was still a powerful man, and I had no way of knowing how far his influence stretched outside of prison. But he didn't question me any further about my financial position, and I didn't care to tell him.

I'd kept my relationship with Brian a secret, but we were living together now, and I was very aware, each time I was with Ron, that it would only take a wrong word or a clumsy lie to expose the truth about our "friendship". Ron was a possessive, controlling man. He would never have given me licence to see anyone else, especially his oldest friend. I was taking a huge gamble, but I'd found happiness with Brian and I was of the opinion that what Ron didn't know couldn't hurt him.

He also didn't know I'd bought myself a posh new home. That was another secret I had to keep. I had sold the Hornchurch house opposite Brian C, and bought a beautiful three-bedroom mock Tudor home in Squirrels Heath Road, Harold Wood. I bought it entirely with the money I'd made from robbing.

Everything was going my way. Ron was still in the dark about how I was funding my extravagant lifestyle, and who I was spending it with, and I finally had a house of my own that my children loved. Neil and Mel had settled into the local schools, and seemed happy too. We had an au pair and a gardener. They adored Brian, and he loved them back.

Funnily enough, it was Mel who almost exposed the web of deceit that I had created. Mel was 13 years old and already a bit of a livewire. One Saturday, when Neil was only 10, I asked him, "Where's your sister? I can't find her and I need to speak to her about school."

Neil looked up at me, his gorgeous brown eyes so innocent, and replied, "She gave me this, she's gone to buy toys." He held up £50, and I nearly fainted.

"She's done what, darlin'?" I repeated, thinking he was making up stories.

"She found all the money under your bed and she's gone to buy toys." The room really did swim at that point.

Mel had found the £2,000 stash of stolen money I'd hidden under my bed. I had to think fast. I was frantic with worry, and had no idea where Mel had gone.

Half an hour later, the phone rang. It was the police. 13-year-old Mel was at Romford police station. The hotel she'd booked into had naturally wondered why such a young girl would book in with lots of cash. They had called the Old Bill, though not before they'd accepted the booking and taken payment! I went straight there, my story ready in my head.

"I've been savin' for a whole year to take us on holiday," I wailed to the copper on duty, "and now it's been spent. Mel, how could you do that to me?" I pretended to break down in sobs. "It's my own fault, I should never have hidden that money."

Mel was distraught by now. "Can I at least keep the toys?" she begged as we left the station. She'd been to Hamleys with some friends, and spent a fortune on toys and games without anyone from the store saying a word to her.

"No, you can't," I said. "They're goin' to a children's hospice to teach you a lesson."

When I told Brian what had happened, he was appalled. "You can't fob her off like that, Linda. You've got to tell her where that money really came from."

I realised he was right. I'd been so worried about the police not believing me and finding out the real reason why I had so much money in cash in my house, I'd forgotten the impact my lies might have on my daughter.

That night I sat Mel and Neil down.

"This isn't easy to tell you," I started, "but that money wasn't me savin' for a holiday. It was there because your mum does what your dad used to do…"

There was silence as they both took in what I was saying.

Mel was the first to speak. "You mean, you're a bank robber?" She said the words slowly, like she was still catching up with her own thoughts.

"Yes, darlin', and what you did could've got me locked up and put in prison."

"Does Brian do it? And Carl and Brian C?" Neil said.

"Is that why you've got all them wigs?" Mel chipped in. Upstairs in a special cupboard in my wardrobe, I had a blonde afro, a long red wig, a dark brown shoulder-length one, and different pairs of glasses and scarves.

Both were giggling now. They saw it as a joke. I think we all did.

But I had to keep a straight face. "Yes it is, and yes they do," I replied.

Little Neil shrugged. "I knew already, Mum. Last week, I came in from school and Carl was playin' with a gun in the lounge. He told me not to tell ya. And you 'ave different cars out the back and Carl changes the number plates, I've seen him."

I looked at Neil, stunned. He really did know what was going on. Brian and Carl were stealing cars, changing their plates and using them as getaway cars. I'd sometimes point out a car to Brian as a likely target. One night we were coming out of Hornchurch station and there was a single car at the far end. "Go and get that one," I said to him. He walked over, got his keys out and managed to open the door, but instead of jumping in, he slammed it shut and ran back in a fluster.

"Oh my God, what's happened?" I asked, perplexed. It was a perfect target, solitary, abandoned for the night most likely.

"There's a couple havin' sex on the back seat! Quick, drive off before he gets his trousers on!"

Another time, Carl was getting a van ready for a raid, when his bank manager neighbour leant out of one of his upstairs window and called down that he'd been looking for him, because he wanted to ask a favour.

"Could you take a mattress down to the tip for me?" the bank manager asked.

Carl thought of every excuse under the sun not to do it. He tried to keep the bank manager as far away as possible from the stolen van, which still had one of its original number plates and one fake one that didn't match. But the bank manager insisted that he should come along and help Carl – it would only take a few minutes.

Carl was sweating through his shirt as he drove this man and his mattress to the dump. The van had only been stolen that day, the number plates didn't match, and it was an absolute no-go to drive around in a stolen vehicle so soon after taking it. But off they went, bank manager and bank robber side by side.

Later, the bank manager said to me, "Oh Linda, never get in a car with Carl. He drives so fast!"

Carl and I had a good laugh about it afterwards. "I had to drive at record speed," he said, "because if that number plate at the front was clocked by police, I'd have been nicked!"

Normal life had become completely abnormal, but we were too far in to realise. We stopped hiding the preparations for the robberies from the kids. Every time we went out on a raid, the men would do their good luck rituals, just like Mickey used to do. Mickey always used to keep a £10 note in his pocket to make sure he could get home – it was his "lucky note". They had found it stained in his blood in his pocket when he died. One of Brian's more peculiar rituals was to watch the film *Arthur*, and announce he was ready at the end. Carl would play Bruce Springsteen's song 'This Gun's For Hire' on an air guitar in the front room.

Even Mel's little trip didn't wake me up to the perils of the life we were leading. I was thriving on the risk, the thrill of the easy money, the robberies and the excitement. My garage was filled with props that we used on raids: workmen's clothing, hard hats, Road Closed signs, a striped hut that the utility boards used to use. I even had a temporary bus stop sign that we'd used on one job, planting it at a strategic spot on the side of the road to help our getaway. I was reckless. I was playing a dangerous game, but I felt like, at last, I was in control of my destiny.

# CHAPTER 20

# BARREL OF A GUN

## 1985

By now, I was involved in most of the raids, either as a driver or toting a gun. One of my tricks was to keep a shopping trolley in the boot of the car. When the boys came rushing out with the money, they'd throw the bag into my trolley. I'd cover it with my bag or a jacket, or a loaf of bread and some groceries. With the stolen cash hidden, I'd walk casually past the store they had raided, where all hell would be breaking loose. Shoppers would be standing around helplessly, getting in the way of the members of staff rushing around and frantically calling the police.

I'd wander up, pushing the trolley, pretending I was an innocent bystander.

"Oh My God, what's happened?" I'd ask. "Oh my God, it's a robbery, did you see anybody?" This was the perfect way to discover if anything could link us to the crime.

No one ever gave me a second look. I'd stand there looking shocked, and all the while the loot would be hidden under my large handbag. I was bold as brass. To me, that money was insured, so no-one was hurt by us taking what wasn't ours. The banks or post offices could claim that money back, and no-one got hurt. It didn't occur to me that pointing a shotgun at a counter assistant, or shoving a security guard to the floor with the end of a sawn-off gun in his face, could have a traumatic impact. It didn't occur to me that I was putting my life and my children's world at risk. I was too clever, too careful for that.

Sometimes we even had help from the public. I was the driver on one post office job that we'd been planning for a while. As we sat in the van outside the target on the outskirts of London, an old lady walked in just as we were about to jump out.

"Oh God, she looks like my nan," Carl said. "We can't go in until she's out of the way."

"We need someone to take hostage," Brian countered. "We can't wait all day for the perfect person to turn up."

"I really don't want to take her," Carl protested. He was spooked. We were determined to do this job, as we'd taken the time to plan it properly, watching it for weeks to discover when the fewest people would be there. Fewer people inside meant an easier raid.

But we were all becoming jittery now. "It'll have to be her. Just tell her you won't hurt her."

Finally, after another couple of minutes, which seemed to drag on for hours, the men pulled on their balaclavas and ran in. I sat in the car, glancing in my mirrors constantly. Eventually they crashed back out, threw open the back doors and leapt back in, which was my cue to put my foot down. The bag was full of money.

"I wish we knew where that old dear lived, to put a couple of grand through her letterbox!" Brian shouted.

"What happened in there?" I asked as we sped away.

Carl's face was screwed up with laughter. "We ran in, Brian shouted 'Give him the money or the old nanny gets it'!"

"We didn't want to frighten her, though," said Brian, "so I put my arm round her, and whispered, 'Darlin', I wouldn't hurt ya,' and d'ya know what she said?" He was grinning on the back seat like a maniac. "She said 'That's alright, boy.' Then she turned to the post office worker and demanded, 'Give these boys the money, they must be 'ard up. Why are ya only puttin' fivers in the bag? Give them the money'." Brian was nearly crying with laughter. "Can you Adam and Eve it?"

I couldn't believe it either. Sometimes, our "work" felt like an Ealing comedy. There was one post office on Ben Jonson Road that we successfully robbed three weeks running, as it came out that the cashiers had been pocketing money for themselves every time we held them up. Another time, Brian and Carl turned up to rob a South-East London security van and found some boys from North London already there, balaclavas on and guns in hand. Brian, being the gentleman he was, said, "You lads do this one." There was a code among the robbers. It was like a private members' club. They all knew and respected one another.

BANG! BANG! BANG!

"Oh my God, who's that?" I said, as my brother Tony followed me into the hall from his bedroom in the flat in Harpley

Square. I'd asked Tony if I could come to his early one Saturday morning for "discussions" with Brian and Carl. What I omitted to say was that we would be going from there to rob the post office on Globe Road. We had targeted it weeks ago and had been staking it out, looking for weaknesses, when it was busy or quiet, when the security van appeared.

Brian and Carl had set off already, and the raid would most likely be underway. I was jittery, pacing about the hallway, waiting to let them in, when the commotion started.

"Open up! Armed police!"

Nervously, I crept to the door to open it.

"FREEZE! GET DOWN!"

I was shoved back roughly, thrown to the floor by a police officer holding a shotgun. I hit my head as I fell.

"Police!"

I looked up and realised I was staring into the barrel of a gun. A tall policeman was standing over me, holding the weapon to my face, over my left eye. I felt utterly violated, and completely helpless.

"Oh my God, what are you doin'?" I screamed in real terror.

"What is this?" Tony stammered, a look of horror spreading over his face.

"POLICE! GET DOWN!"

"What for?" I shouted. Adrenaline was coursing through my veins, along with a feeling of unspeakable horror. The copper ignored me. All the excitement from the raid blew up inside me and I started to shriek uncontrollably. I was hysterical.

"Go on, shoot me, just like you shot my husband!" I screamed manically. "Or am I facing the wrong way?" Nothing was going to stop me once I'd started. I could hear Tony shouting at me to stop, to shut up, but I was beside myself. All the rage, all the hurt and grief came pouring out.

"Oh very clever, aren't you?" sneered the copper. "Just wait till you're all nicked." He turned to two of his crew. "Search the flat."

The two juniors put their guns down and headed into the bedroom. Tony's wife had also appeared at the doorway, looking as shocked as I felt.

"Stay where you are!" the officer commanded.

It wasn't long before they found what they were looking for, but I'd never before seen the bag they held up. It was huge, bulging with money and bank books. The officer who'd found it took a look inside.

"I reckon there's about seventy grand in 'ere," he whistled.

"Seventy grand?" I was confused and, by now, shaking from head to toe.

"That money's mine!" interjected Tony indignantly.

"I may not 'ave paid me tax, but those are my savin's for my wedding cruise."

We were all taken to the nick. Brian and Carl had been arrested, surrounded by armed police, at the site of the robbery, and we were all thrown into cells to await our fate.

Brian and Carl were charged with Conspiracy to Rob and Robbery, while Tony and his wife Sandra (neither of whom had anything to do with it) and I were charged with Robbery.

I barely noticed what was happening. My head was reeling and something had shifted inside me. I'd thought of gun-toting as a victimless crime, because I would never have actually shot anyone. But I now realised the sheer terror I'd inflicted upon people during all the robberies we'd committed. As I sat there in a cell that stank of urine, waiting for the appointed solicitor to visit me, I had plenty of time to think. That was the first time I'd ever thought of our crimes beyond the material riches and the emotional highs. Staring into that gun, feeling the heightened fear and terrible panic, I saw what we'd done more clearly than ever. Because we never took anything personal – only insured money from security vans and post offices – we thought that we could justify it.

I have always been someone who would run after an old nan who had dropped a £1 note. If I'd seen someone stepping out of a Rolls and dropping their wallet, I'd return their money, because that was theirs and I had no right to take it. Companies and banks had seemed different. But now the reality of our crimes was hitting home. There were people on the receiving end of our exploits. I couldn't deny it any longer, because I'd experienced it too.

There was no going back. *I will never, ever do an armed robbery again*, I vowed to myself. I didn't care that I was sitting in a cold, grey cell, on a concrete shelf that also acted as a bed, listening to Brian's shouts from down the corridor. I didn't care what happened to me, because I knew in that moment I was bang to rights. I deserved to go to prison for what I'd done. I thought of my children, and that's when I felt like collapsing. Their lives had been affected already by the death of their father, and suddenly their mum was gone too. I knew that someone would step in and take in Mel and Neil, even just for the night, until I knew what my fate would be, but it didn't stop the terrible knowledge that I'd failed them completely.

I didn't know it, but Brian and Carl were doing a deal with the police as I sat in my cell, offering to own up to other robberies and clear the books to get me a reduced sentence. Why they did that for me I'll never know. Men have always wanted to protect me or look after me. My sisters joke they are jealous of me, but it's been a fact of my life. I've always liked men. My dad called me and my sisters his Charlie's Angels, and the male sex always seem to have known that I like their company. I've lost count of the times men have offered to whisk me away, to treat me and pamper me.

I got unconditional bail – unheard of for such a serious crime and all because of my men. Brian and Carl were sent to Brixton Prison, Carl in the ordinary wing and Brian on the Category A side, and for the year leading up to our court case, I visited Brian in between my ongoing visits to Ron.

I didn't have the guts to tell Ron what had happened. I kept putting it off, telling him everything was fine, and smiling sweetly, assuring him I was still "his" each time I went. Unbelievably, he bought every word, though it was all a pack of lies.

My promises to Mickey burned on my brain. I'd done wrong over and over again. It wasn't fun or exciting any longer. It was menacing and all too real. Staring up the barrel of a gun traumatised me deeply. It gave me a taste of my own medicine. I knew I was going to prison, and I knew I had to face whatever was coming with as much dignity as I could.

Later, we discovered that it was Brian's wife who had blown our cover. She had hired a private detective, as she suspected her husband was having an affair, which, of course, he was – with me. I'd known about her as well, but I'd justified it by telling myself I was with Ron as far as things were, and Brian had a wife, so we were even and we knew neither of us would leave our partners. Me because I couldn't, him because he still loved her deep down. It turned out that the detective had watched me and Brian for several days and seen us do a raid in Hornchurch a few days earlier. He called the police straight away, and we had all been under surveillance ever since.

While I was on bail prior to our trial, I went to see Ron. He was in Frankland, a Category A men's jail in Durham. I was frightened of seeing him, and terrified of stepping inside that formidable place. I scuttled like a mouse through the searches, into the visiting room that looked much the same as all the others I'd been to in my time.

I confessed to Ron that I was in trouble. I'd been caught doing robberies with Brian, and it wasn't looking good.

Ron exploded. "That no-good cunt!" he raved. "I asked him to look after you, and he's gone and got you nicked!"

I didn't like to remind Ronnie that my first court appearance was one I'd taken in his place, when I'd taken the blame for the money he had had stored at Nita's.

On one of my visits to Brian he introduced me to a man called Danny Reece. I'd been leaving fruit and treats at reception for Brian, as prisoners on remand were allowed to have food sent in. He asked me if I would see Danny as well, as he didn't appear to have any visitors. Danny was a dangerous man. He was inside for multiple crimes, and the first time I set eyes on him in the visiting room – two screws behind me, another two walking in with Danny and Brian – I was struck by how strong he looked, and how tough. He had a shaved head, tattoos and was a stocky build with dark hair.

"Listen, I'm no charity case, ya don't 'ave to get me out of my cell," he said, looking at Brian and me.

Brian laughed at that. "Linda, he's as soft as anythin', he's just puttin' on a front for ya."

"Pleased to meet you," I said, taking off my fur coat.

Danny turned out to need particular support that year, because his eldest son was run over and killed while Danny was behind bars. He didn't know exactly where he'd been buried, but had the name of the cemetery. It was the same one where Mickey had been laid to rest. I promised him I'd put flowers on his son's grave each time I was down there, and Danny was immensely grateful for that kindness. I came to see him and Brian regularly over the course of that year leading up to my trial.

As for Brian, I owed so much to him already. He was trying to save my backside, though we both knew he could only secure leniency for me, not absolution. I would sit in the horrible visiting room, wondering if Ron would find out I was there.

It broke my heart to see Brian sitting behind that table, with screwed-down chairs and drab prison clothes. The place stank of male sweat, and Brian's face was grey.

Before I could speak, he leant across the table and spoke in a low voice. "Listen, ya know when ya go to trial, it'll come out about me and you. I will tell you now: Ron always said to me, even if you did stay with him while he was away, he would kill your son Neil when he came out. I didn't want to tell ya, but I've got to."

"Oh my God. Did he really?" I couldn't believe what I was hearing. "I thought that by visitin' Ron, I was keeping my boy safe."

Brian shook his head. The sight of it chilled me to the bone. "I've confessed to 21 armed robberies, so I'm not goin' to be around to protect ya when Ron comes out. You've got to start thinking what you're goin' to do."

At that point, the screw told us visiting time was over. I was in shock, and wanted to say more, but I was ushered away. As I looked over my shoulder, Brian was being led away, and my whole world, my protection, the loveliest, kindest man since I'd known my Mickey, couldn't help me anymore. I was alone again.

I'd been to court to support Ron on the days his family weren't there, and I'd been countless times for Mickey, but this was different. It was my turn. My case came to trial, along with Tony and Sandra, at Southwark Crown Court, a brick Brutalist building that couldn't have looked more foreboding if it tried.

Walking into the dock was surreal. Part of me didn't feel it was really happening. I glanced around the small courtroom: wooden walls at one end, a large crest decorating the wall above the judge's head, the jury at the side, the barristers directly in front of me. My defence lawyer gave me a small nod and I took my stand.

I was pleading Not Guilty, so it would go to trial. I was lying under oath this time, but I had my children to think of, there was no way I could risk being found guilty and being banged up for years. What would Neil and Mel do if I was put away?

My defence lawyer hadn't been optimistic, and I knew I didn't really have a leg to stand on. I was terrified. I told the court I had been forced to do the robbery – a story Brian and I had concocted during a visit to him at Brixton Prison during the year before our case came to trial – but I knew that once our affair became common knowledge, my story wouldn't stand up. By now I was desperate, and willing to say anything to avoid jail and keep my children by my side.

Naturally, it didn't work. Sandra was found not guilty, as was right, but Tony and I weren't so lucky. Brian had been given 21 years for multiple robberies, while Carl landed 14. Brian C got three for his part in it all. The court room had been shocked. They were long sentences in those days, and it demonstrated how severely the presiding Judge Edwards condemned our actions. As Brian passed me, being led down to start his two-decade-long stretch, I tried to make him feel better. I whispered "A mere bagatelle, you'll be able to do it standin' on your head." I wanted to cheer him up, tell him that he'd breeze through his incarceration, but when he looked at me I saw anger rise for the first time in our relationship. Later, he confessed, it was the first time he'd ever wanted to hit me.

All the men tried to play down my part in our crimes. Brian told the court he'd made me do it. Carl said the same. They were both fantastic, offering themselves up for judgement and trying to help me out of the fix we were in, but the jury saw through them and found me guilty anyway. My face froze when I heard the judgement. I stared at those people who had just condemned my children to losing their mother for years, and I just blinked. I felt nothing. Tony and I held hands as we stood there, as the judge spoke. Here was my brother, who I'd unwittingly involved in our plot by virtue of just being in his house. When the judge gave him nine years, I almost fainted. He squeezed my hand as if to tell me it was ok, he didn't blame me, but I didn't think I could ever forgive myself.

Then the judge came to me. You could have heard a pin drop in that court. The reporters were leaning over their benches, my friends and family hushed. I thought I might die, or faint, on the spot.

"I've listened to everything in this trial," he began, "and I cannot prove what I am about to say. I believe that instead of being a small cog in this operation, you were in fact, the whole machine."

I blinked again. How on earth did this man know? He was right, of course, I planned everything. Without me there would've been no robberies. Yet how could this man, this judge, possibly know?

"I believe that you, Linda Calvey, were in charge of all these men who have tried to sacrifice themselves for you."

My head was spinning in terror. I couldn't believe what I was hearing.

"If it was in my power, I'd give you 21 years. But that would be pointless, because you would win your appeal. So I have no choice but to give you the biggest sentence I can. I hope you serve all of your sentence of seven years in prison."

The court was agog. I don't think any of us had heard an eminent judge speak that way before. Mum's face was a picture of utter devastation. I looked over at her as the screw took my arm and led me away from the court room. No-one spoke. I tried to smile, but I was like ice. No other person in the police or legal services had ever made that assumption about me before.

"Fuckin' hell," breathed the female screw as she took me down. My hand left Tony's as he was led away, and I descended the steps leading me down towards prison life.

# CHAPTER 21

# MYRA

### 1985-88

In the bowels of the court sat a screw, knitting as she waited for me to arrive. She looked up at me as I descended, and gave a long, slow whistle.

"That's the biggest sentence in Holloway, and you weren't even on remand. How are you going to do it?"

I looked around, taking in the municipal walls and furniture of the court cell block, as far from my spruced-up luxurious home, with its chandelier and velvet sofas, as it was possible to be.

"I did the crime, I'll have to do the time," I said, though I was in a state of shock. I was numb, barely able to speak.

I followed the screws to the exit, where I was taken in a police van to Holloway, the place that would be my home for the next seven years. As we pulled up, I stared up at the infamous red-brick walls in utter disbelief.

"Turn yer head and pray to God," a woman in the reception area was intoning as her female companion hit her head repeatedly against the wall. The place stank of disinfectant, and I suddenly felt conspicuous in my cream-coloured silk Harrods suit. I'd given my Cartier watch, diamond necklace and rings to my solicitor back in Southwark to pass to my family, as we were only allowed religious items such as a Cross or a Star of David. But apart from the expensive clothes I was wearing, I had nothing: no money, no proper clothing, not even a toothbrush.

I'd expected to go free. My arrogance, my wilful ignorance, my stubborn pride in believing I'd somehow walk out of the courtroom home to my children, had left me totally ill-equipped. It was akin to culture shock. I was given a pair of jelly plastic shoes, a towel and flannel, with HMP stamped on one side, a bar of soap and a wrap of green powder which I bathed in, assuming it was bath salts. I was wrong: it was tooth powder. And so I started my life with a borrowed second-hand tube of cheap toothpaste and little else. It was undignified, as it was meant to be.

As the metal door was shut behind me, I stared around at the tiny cell with its grey brick walls and single bed. I had a small table, a chair, a toilet in the corner and nothing else. The air was fetid with the sweat and horror of girls shrieking and crying from their cells all night long. I didn't know it, but those cries were coming from the C1 wing. The prisoners held there should've been in a mental hospital, but due to overcrowding and cuts, they were here.

Shattered, I lay on the hard bed, my scratchy woollen prison-issue blanket covering me, waiting for morning light, hoping and praying I'd get through. That sleepless night, I had plenty of time to review my life, as the sound of girls screaming, wailing, begging and laughing manically pierced through the walls. I remembered the anguish on my mother's face in that courtroom as my sentence was handed down. She'd had no idea I was a robber, all the time assuming Brian had paid for my house and lifestyle.

When I was arrested for robbery, it was the first anyone knew what I'd been up to. The shockwaves spread through my family like a tsunami. They'd all known Mickey was a gangster, but me? They just couldn't believe it. They'd always seen me baking or ironing at home, helping Mum bring up the younger kids, wiping their bottoms, brushing their hair and making them rounds of sandwiches over the years. I was a motherly girl, protective of my family. I liked to keep them safe and away from trouble. But another side of me walked a path that most other people would run from. I didn't bat an eyelid at the sight of violence, or associating with infamous criminals, or living off stolen money. I'd kept that part of my life totally secret.

Shock and fear rolled into one. My kids' lives were in ruins – again. I'd betrayed their trust, and goodness knows what would happen to them during my long stretch. I knew they would be cared for by my family, but it wasn't the same as being home with me. They'd had so much disruption in their lives, they'd struggled with my relationship with Ron, they'd moved from place to place as I spent money, lavished them with toys and clothes, and walked straight into a trap of my own making.

One good thing – the only good thing – about my jail sentence was that it kept me safe from Ron. I had no idea how he'd react when he found out I had been with Brian. And I knew he would.

Each morning, a screw would pass my breakfast through the hatch in my door. For the first three days I would be confined to my individual cell, until they worked out what sort of prisoner I was going to be: a troublemaker, violent, or hell-bent on suicide. The first morning, I was given a single slice of cheap white bread scraped with margarine and two slices of oily streaky bacon.

"I'll die of starvation before my sentence is finished!" I joked, staring down at the meagre contents of my blue plastic plate. Later, I was given a green scouring pad, a bucket and some yellow carbolic soap.

"Your job is to clean the corridor floors," the screw, a woman in her mid-forties, said – not unkindly.

So there I was, scrubbing floors on my hands and knees, wearing my designer suit, because I was waiting for family to bring in some suitable prison garb. I was allowed three sets of clothes: one smart set with flat heels for visits, two tracksuits, and a pair of slippers. Wearing casual clothing almost killed me. I liked to look good, wear nice clothes and make myself up. I wasn't allowed face cream or make-up, and so I had to wait until the end of my first week of scrubbing floors to take my wages – all of 75 pence – to the prison shop. The only thing I could afford was a pot of Nivea and a bar of nicer soap. I was allowed to have 10 photographs in my cell, so if anyone posted me any, I had to decide which to keep and which to hand back. It was a hell of a reality check. My life, once lived entirely by my own rules, became completely regimented.

I didn't rail against it, though. I knew I had to pay for my crimes, and I was guilty. I didn't lash out or get upset, like many of the other inmates, because there wasn't any point. I accepted it, and got on with it – and discovered, to my surprise, I was much more resilient than I'd realised. My life had been addictive with its fast thrills and high risk. I'd become like a junkie, wanting more and more excitement every week. It had been like a huge high, and now I was coming crashing down.

After those three hellish days and nights in my cell, I was moved to a dorm of four. I formed a good bond with the other girls sharing the room with me, and we came up with all sorts of tricks to make our life in Holloway more bearable. We knew that the remand wing was just across the yard from us, and that prisoners on remand were allowed to have supplies sent in to them from outside – food, sweets, sometimes even wine. So we started sending out one of the girls in my dorm to ask for treats. Her name was called Bobble (she always wore a bobble hat) and she'd go out into the yard holding a bin bag, telling the guards she was just going out to pick up litter. The officers would let her out, thinking she was doing them a favour, and she'd go and walk up and down beneath the windows of the remand wing, calling out, "Anything for the convicted?" It gave us all a good laugh, along with the occasional treat from prisoners who had more privileges than us.

Over the weeks, I received letters from Tony in Maidstone prison. The letters were always opened and read by prison staff before I got them. Tony graciously forgave me for landing him in trouble for something he didn't do. He wrote that he'd met my old friend Billy Blundell in Maidstone, and talked about me a lot. Billy wasn't the most notorious name in Maidstone, though. Reggie Kray was banged up there too, and Tony wrote that he and Billy had told Reg all about me.

I was taken out every so often to see Brian and Ronnie separately. When I first made it to Brixton to see Brian, he had a stern look on his face as he took his seat in the visiting room.

"It's serious, Linda. Ron knows about us being together. It's been in all the papers, and there's no way he'll have missed it. I had to go and see the guv'nor when they convicted me."

My head spun. As long as either Ron or I were behind bars, I hoped I'd be safe, but what would I do once we were both out? "What did you say to the guv'nor?" I asked.

"I told him that Ron and me can never, ever be in the same prison. If they ever put us in together, one of us will end up dead. I know it. The guv'nor took me seriously, thank God. He says he'll make sure we're always kept apart."

I was full of trepidation the next time I was let out to visit Ron. I knew I couldn't just stop going to see him, or that would simply confirm the rumours.

Ron walked in to the visiting room with a pile of newspapers under one arm and a box of chocolates under the other.

"Look at this, that scumbag has really mugged me off," he said, throwing the newspaper down on the table. My chest tightened. "I swear I'll bury him if I can get it done. And there's every chance I can, Linda."

"What do you mean, Ron? What are you talking about?"

"I am a wealthy man and have a lot of friends in prison," he sneered. "I can send messages to everyone I know, and I will make sure Brian's a dead man."

I was terrified. Was he angry at Brian just because of our going out on the pavement together, or did he know we'd been living together?

Thankfully, his face softened, and he looked at me sympathetically. "How will you manage?" he asked. Ronnie thought life in a women's prison would be a lot harder and rougher for me than it was for him in a men's prison. "Listen, Linda, I love ya and I can't wait till we can be together again. I just want you to be alright in there. I can't forgive Brian for gettin' ya banged up."

I breathed a sigh of relief. Ronnie was still besotted with me. He hated Brian with a passion, and blamed him for everything, but I'd got away with it. I had to let Brian know that Ron would be trying to get him hurt through his contacts in Brixton, but I knew Brian was a careful man and would be able to look after himself.

"So, 'ave ya been true to me?" Ron suddenly asked.

His eyes bored into mine, though his expression was tender now. His time away had aged him. He had grey hairs amongst the brown, and his face was more lined than I remembered. But he still had that cold, hard stare.

I faced him up, stared right back, and said, "Of course I have, Ron." It was the only way to deal with him. One whiff of fear and he'd have crushed me.

"That bastard Brian has a lot to answer for. There hasn't been anything going on with him, then?"

My heart began to thump. Did he know? I looked him dead in the eye. "No Ron, of course there's nothing going on."

"You know what would 'appen if ya hadn't been true to me, Linda?" His face didn't betray a single emotion.

"No, I don't know, Ron."

"I would 'ave added ya to my list."

Ron sat back, crossing his arms, a cruel smile playing on his lips. He liked taunting me. He meant his list of people to kill, of course – the one he'd boasted of when he threatened my brother, and my son.

"Don't say things like that, Ron, there's no need."

"See what you've done to me. There's another one goin' on my list." He paused.

"Who's that then, Ron?"

"Your brother Tony."

Ron paused again to see the effect on me. I stared at him, speechless.

"When I was in Maidstone," Ron went on, "he wouldn't talk to me. Your Tony thought he was protected because he was mates with Billy Blundell. Billy thought he was bein' clever, tellin' Tony there was no need to talk to Ron Cook."

"Tony hasn't done anythin' to you," I felt compelled to say, cautiously.

"Yes, he has. Every time I wanted to know what was goin' on with you, his guard dog Blundell would come over." He paused, holding my gaze. "Brian's on my list now too."

"That's a big list, Ron," I said, knowing my poor Neil was at the top.

"I won't do anythin' in 'ere. I want to get out as quickly as possible," Ron finished.

It was clear our meeting was over. I felt shaken up. I'd contrived to forget Ron during my time with Brian, seeing my visits to him as a necessary evil, but now I was right back in the mess. Ron still had enormous power. Menace radiated from him. I'd gone all that way to prove my innocence to him, and yet again, I'd told a pack of lies designed to keep myself and my family safe.

I exhaled as he was led out, smiling up at him, trying to look like the faithful girlfriend I was pretending to be. How long would my lie convince him? I had no answer to that.

The cries from the psychiatric patients in the C1 wing continued every night. C1 was notorious. It was the secure unit with all the vulnerable girls prone to self-mutilation and suicide attempts. Many of the women incarcerated there were mentally ill, and in my opinion, should never have been in the prison system at all.

A girl in my dorm called Linda came back from work with horrific stories about C1. There was an unstable girl in there who had cut off her nipples. Another time, one of the new arrivals broke one of the china sinks in the toilets and tried to saw off her leg.

But the worst thing was that the inmates would copy each other, due to their extremely delicate mental state. When one of the girls decided to throw her cup of tea out of the cell into the corridor, she'd shout out, "I'm going to throw my cup of tea out!" at which point there would be copycat calls of "So am I!" "So am I!" from all along the row. Soon enough, one cup of boiling tea after another would come crashing out of the cells into the corridor, leaving shards of broken china and a slippery mess all the way up past the cells.

Each time, these copycat actions became more severe. Soon, the girls in C1 were throwing their dinner out of their cells – "I'm going to throw my dinner plate out!" "So am I!" – and once again there was a horrible mess to clean up afterwards.

And one day, Linda came back from work in an absolute state.

"Oh my God, Linda, oh my God," she wailed to me, "It was worse than ever today! It was awful!"

"What is it?" I asked. "What's happened?"

"One of the girls on C1," she stammered. "She shouted out that she was going to pull her eye out. Then the rest of them started shouting that they were going to pull their eyes out too!"

Linda had rushed from cell to cell, frantically trying to reassure each and every patient on the wing that the girl who'd shouted out first hadn't actually pulled her eye out, and that none of the others were doing it either.

But when she came to the cell belonging to the girl who had shouted out first, her stomach turned somersaults. There, lying on the ground outside her cell, was a lone eyeball, torn messily straight out of its socket.

The girl was lying unconscious on the floor of her cell. Distraught, Linda screamed for help. When the nurse came, she picked up the eyeball in a tissue, to stop any of the other girls seeing it and getting ideas again.

Linda put her arm out to stop her. "That tissue's dirty! You can't pick her eye up in that!"

The nurse looked at her sadly. "Oh, love. It's not like it's any good to her now, is it?"

Holloway was a bizarre place, so I was relieved when I got moved to Cookham Wood in Kent. It was there that I met Moors Murderess Myra Hindley for the first time.

"What's that for?" I asked the screw showing me round, pointing to a black and yellow strip shutting off part of the laundry.

"That's to stop people crossing into Myra's area. No-one's allowed near her. You cross that, they'll add time to your sentence."

It was one thing being in prison, another being in the same place as the sadistic child killer. She was universally hated, by inmates and screws alike. Just knowing she was there sent shivers down my spine.

I'd followed the story, her and Ian Brady's arrests in October 1965 sending shockwaves through the country. I couldn't believe I was serving time in the same place as a woman who had assisted in the murder of five children, four of whom had been sexually assaulted. They were sickening crimes, and inconceivable that a woman could have been involved in them. It was uncanny to be walking the same corridors as her, although our paths hadn't crossed – yet.

"You can work in the library," the screw said, grinning.

"But, I don't read books," I said.

"I've decided you're the best person for the library," the screw chuckled. "You start today."

The library was next to the laundry. I hadn't been working in there for more than an hour when the screw came back and told me to go and pick up my washing before the queues formed at evening break.

"Of course I will, darlin'," I said. I walked over, then stopped dead.

Someone was singing.

I peered in. There was a solitary figure bent over, scooping up clothes, singing to herself, carefree as anything.

It was Myra.

Something in me rose up. I lost my cool. Without thinking, I marched across the forbidden tape. Myra looked up to see who was coming. She had that familiar, creepy face, but with brown hair, and she looked older and smaller than her photos in the papers. My hand itched.

I slapped her hard around the face.

"You fucking bitch. How can you sing when you've killed people? Little children?"

She froze, holding her cheek, which was striped with red marks left by my fingers. She stared at me. She looked like a lost little girl, all innocent and frightened.

I stepped back, the anger in me burning out as quickly as it had flared up.

"Do that again and you'll be back in Holloway," Myra said, eventually. Her voice was a soft northern burr.

"Holloway has no fear for me."

I turned and fled back to the library, to spend the next few hours wondering what my punishment would be. Could she have me sent back to the women's prison in London?

Now I'd cooled down, I realised I'd done an incredibly stupid thing. Why had I hit her? By now she'd served 20 years in jail, and everyone knew she'd never get out. Something in me just snapped. Perhaps it was a reaction to my own confinement, my own disgrace? I didn't know. I didn't regret hitting the most evil woman in Britain, but I did wonder why I'd risked my own freedom to do it.

The next day, I was stamping a date on the inside of a book when the screw came to find me.

*Oh God, this is it.*

"Myra usually comes to the library to have her coffee break and read," the screw said, "but she didn't come yesterday."

"Right."

"Myra says, can she come in here and have her break today?" The screw was looking at me intently.

"Ah, well, of course she can if that's what she usually does," I replied.

The screw nodded as if we understood each other. The subject of Myra's slap wasn't going to be raised, and they wanted to know if Myra was safe with me.

I couldn't believe my ears. I was being asked by the most hated woman in the prison – in the entire country – if she could drink her coffee. It was as bizarre as life gets.

An hour later, Myra appeared. I had more time to study her as she sat down and opened a Maeve Binchy book, which seemed incongruous to say the least.

"Alright," she said, then ignored me as I stood mulling over the fact that I was in a prison library while Myra Hindley sipped white coffee, looking like a strange exotic creature with a flowing kaftan and her hearts-and-flowers novel.

Before she left, she came up to the counter.

"Hello, Myra," I said.

"I want you to get me books in other peoples' names, ones that don't take out books from the library. Here's what I want." She handed me a list written in her own spindly writing.

I couldn't help but shudder. The list contained the titles of violent, gory, horror books. She was asking me to compromise my position, risk being found out and sent back to Holloway, by helping her read books that were banned to her. She had a dark aura – it was a palpable presence, and I could see how everyone kept away from her. I couldn't help but wonder what it would've been like being her. How could anyone live with themselves, seeming so cold, so utterly soulless?

From then on, I kept out of her way as best I could, and was relieved when I was finally posted to East Sutton Park. From there I was released, three years after that first cell door was shut behind me.

# CHAPTER 22
# DANNY
## 1988-90

Mum and Dad came to pick me up from prison. I remember feeling as light as a feather as I stood there, waiting to step back into society. All I cared about was seeing Neil and Melanie again. I'd had drip-fed reports while I was banged up, and I knew both of my children had suffered in my absence.

Dad drove me back to my house in Beckton in Kirkham Road, which I'd bought with the money I'd put aside for when I came out. Neil was there to greet me. He'd been 11 years old when I was put away – still a baby in my eyes. He was 14 now, on the verge of becoming a young man.

"You've grown, darlin'," I said, holding out my arms to him. He submitted to my embrace, but I knew he had struggled without his mother, as had Mel.

Mel had been deeply affected by Mickey's death, perhaps because she was older, and had been troubled before I went inside. Me going away had only made the situation worse. Mel had got into drugs, and was running wild. Mel had seen first-hand how Ron treated me, and she had lived with my mum for years. But her nan had to kick her out while I was inside, as she'd become too much to cope with. I hadn't given Mel a secure, normal home after Mickey died, and I knew much of the blame for her problems lay on my shoulders. She was 15 when I went to prison, and was 18 now, a young woman who should have had her whole life ahead of her, but was taking illicit drugs to push her own emotional pain away.

"Neil, darlin', tell your mum what it was like when I was away. You never said anythin' while I was in prison, and it must've been tough for you," I said to him that first night. We were sitting on the sofa, the TV blaring out in one corner. "What happened when I was arrested?"

Neil paused for a moment, as if he was unsure whether to say anything, and I smiled to encourage him.

"Well, I went to school as normal. You said 'See ya later darlin'.' When I walked home at the end of school, I got close to the house and saw three or four police cars. Police were runnin' all over our house and there was a cordon that meant I couldn't go inside."

"Go on," I encouraged, glad that Neil could say this to me after all the time I'd been away.

"One of the coppers said, 'Are you Neil? One of your uncles is coming to pick you up.' I was like, why? The copper said, 'Your mum's been arrested and taken to the police station'."

"What happened then?" I said.

Neil looked younger than his years in that moment.

"Uncle Ricky turned up, and I went 'What's goin' on?' He said, 'I don't know, boy, we'll sort it out when we get to my house, don't ya worry.' We didn't know what was happening, then you got bailed and you came out. You looked really frightened, they must've grilled you for hours and hours because you looked really dishevelled."

I had to smile at that. "I'm sure I did, darlin'."

"You still came out and put a big smile on your face, and said 'Hello boy' to me, and you told me loads of lies. 'Don't worry Neil, I won't go to prison, I promise you'."

At that, Neil paused and looked down at his hands. "I thought you knew what you were talkin' about. And Brian as well, he was like havin' a dad around, then suddenly he was gone too…"

I let Neil's words fill the room. We were both silent for a moment as we digested what he'd said, only the television providing background noise. It wasn't just me he and Mel had missed. In one fell swoop they'd lost their father figure as well. Their whole family life had been destroyed – for the second time.

"Go on," I encouraged him, squeezing his hand, feeling choked up.

"Well, we just went from pillar to post, stayin' with relatives for a while, movin' to another uncle or aunt. The worst was in Cornwall though."

I'd sent Mel and Neil to stay with my sister Hazel in Cornwall for the week of my trial, not telling them why they were going there. Yet another mistake.

"We were runnin' about outside, then Hazel told us to come in as she had bad news. There'd been a phone call from London, then she said we shouldn't get too upset because it wasn't as bad as it seemed. That's when she said you were goin' to prison, but she said you'd got six months and you'd only serve three months. That was a lie too. Mel and I just looked at each other and burst out laughing like a pair of hyenas. I don't know what we were expectin' to hear but it didn't sound so bad. Then the phone went again. 'She got two to three years,' Hazel said. The phone went again. 'No, she got seven years.' That's when we found out. We lost our big house, Brian who was like another dad, and you."

"Darlin', you must've been so angry at me," I said, stroking his handsome face. Neil had been sent to a boarding school in Billericay, and I knew how hard it must have been for him.

"I wasn't angry, Mum, I was just really upset."

Neil's words cut through me, and for a short moment we sat in silence.

I knew I'd struggle to have a conversation like this with my daughter right now. Mel was a different fish to Neil entirely. She had been drinking and hanging out with older friends since before I was sent away. I still hadn't spoken to Mel, and I guessed I would find it harder to make my peace with her after what I'd put her through.

I wanted to get us back on our feet quickly, though. Soon after I came out, I visited my sister Shelley at her place, a Victorian terrace she'd bought in King George Avenue, Canning Town. It backed onto a park, and was right next to the local school, within spitting distance of the rest of our family. Shelley was about to move out, and as she'd done such a lovely job of doing the place up, I offered to buy it off her straight away.

Shelley agreed. Because she was moving out, she said that I could move straight in to King George Avenue while my house in Kirkham Road was being sold. Neil came to live in King George Avenue with me, while Mel stayed in Kirkham Road for the time being.

I carried on visiting Danny and Brian, as well as Ron. I became quite good friends with Danny in particular. I knew he was a hardened criminal, but he didn't frighten me. I never once felt threatened or nervous with him, though there were always screws in the room with us. We bonded over our loved ones having their graves in the same cemetery.

Most Saturdays Ron was given day release, as he was nearing the end of his time behind bars. I'd pick him up, we'd come back to the house, make love for an hour, and then I'd cook for him before driving him back to Maidstone nick.

I thought I was doing Danny a good turn by seeing him, and I had to see Ron whether I liked it or not. Things felt steady, if not great, and as the winter of 1990 approached, I was concentrating on building my relationship with Mel again. My eye had gone a bit off the ball with everything else.

It was a freezing cold November day. I'd promised Danny I'd pick him up from prison in Dorset and bring him back to London to see his family, as he had been allowed out for the weekend.

Driving along the motorway, my car heater on full blast, I thought nothing of the favour I was doing him. I'd been behind bars, and I knew what it meant to have a taste of freedom, so I was happy to collect Danny and drive him back.

"Do you still want to go to the cemetery?" I asked, as Danny lumbered his physical bulk into the car. He worked out a lot and, as a result, was thuggish-looking and intimidating. But I'd only ever seen the soft side of him.

"Yes, Linda, I want to see where my son is buried, and pay my last respects to him. Is that alright, Linda?"

I assured him it was.

After a few hours we arrived in Canning Town, where his son and my Mickey had been laid to rest.

I went into the cemetery with Danny. I walked him towards his son's resting place and showed him the gravestone. When he saw it, he started – and his shoulders seemed to droop. I saw his whole body shaking with emotion.

Danny stayed there for an hour. The bitter wind made me pull my fur around me. The trees were stark and bare against the grey sky, the gravestones jutting up, some with flowers and trinkets, some overgrown with grass and weeds. When we eventually returned to the car, his face was red and puffy, his eyes swollen from crying.

We didn't say a word until we drew up outside my house.

"Come inside, I'll drive you to your mum's later. I'll make you somethin' to eat, Danny, and you can freshen up."

"Thanks Linda, I appreciate it. You've been so kind to me."

Danny seemed to pause as he spoke. I wasn't sure why. We got out, went in, and while Danny went upstairs to wash his face,

I nipped to the local butcher and bought him a steak. It was the least I could do the state he was in.

Meanwhile, the video man had been round, and Neil had bought a couple of new films, so the boys watched *Full Metal Jacket* while I made dinner. The sound of guns and bombs blasted through from the living room.

"I'm sorry Danny," I called from the kitchen, "but I won't be able to drive you back on Monday, as Ron's gettin' out for the day."

"Oh, is he? What will ya do with him?" Danny called back.

"We'll probably just come straight back here," I said, carrying in two large plates with steak, chips and peas for Danny and Neil.

"There you go, darlin'," I said to the prisoner sitting on my sofa. "You enjoy that. When you're done, I'll drive you to your mum's."

"You're a really good friend to me," said Danny as I dropped him off. I thought nothing of it, assuming I wouldn't see him for a while.

# CHAPTER 23

# ROCKING SKULL

## NOVEMBER 1990

Monday came.

I got dressed with extra care, hoping Ron would approve of my outfit. It felt strange to think he had just a month left before he'd be back out, living with me, and it would be like the last nine years hadn't happened.

I was nervous, as I always was with him these days. Perhaps I realised just what I had to lose through my liaison with him – my family and liberty being uppermost in my mind. I was tired of being a blagger's possession. I'd been toying with the idea of going straight, setting up a shop of some kind and making my own way in the world. I was still young, only 42 years old, and I had my whole life ahead of me. There was only one person standing in my way, that person was Ron Cook.

Ron was standing outside Maidstone Prison when I pulled up. He was working in a hostel attached to the prison to reintegrate him into society. I laughed privately at that idea.

"What d'you want to do, Ron?" I said after he'd kissed me, sized up my clothes and given a small nod of the head to show he was pleased.

"Take me home, I'm only out for seven hours."

We drove back to my new house in King George Avenue. I took out my keys and opened up, asking Ron to pick up the milk on the doorstep as we stepped inside.

Ron was only just inside my kitchen when the street door crashed open with an enormous bang.

I had barely a second to turn in shock as a man dressed in black forced his way in. He had a flat cap on and his jumper was pulled up over his nose, but I could see his eyes. They were staring wildly at Ron.

I screamed. The man had a gun, and my 14-year-old son was probably in the house right now. "No!" I shrieked. "Neil!"

"GET. DOWN."

Ron turned. In a voice that was strangely calm, he said, "What's up, mate?"

The man fired.

Ron looked down at his torso in silence, an expression of mild surprise on his face. I watched in horror as blood spread slowly across his jacket. It looked like he'd taken a bullet in the chest, but he was holding his arm. He'd only been hit in the elbow, but the blood was seeping through. The smell of cordite filled the small space. I backed into the corner of the room.

Then the gunman did something surprising. He pulled his jumper down to reveal his face.

He turned to look at me.

It was Danny.

I didn't have time to shout. I gaped at Danny, who had turned back to stare intently at Ron.

My heart raced. My mouth was dry, my senses on high alert.

Danny was standing stock still, his sawn-off shotgun still pointing at Ron, who was staring back at him. Then he did the strangest thing. He smiled at me. I looked up at Danny from where I was half crouching, half standing in the corner. Danny took a deep breath.

"This one's for Mickey Calvey."

He pulled the trigger.

Instinctively, I turned my back, shielding myself as best I could from the impact. Blood splattered over my back. When I looked round, Ron's blood was decorating the wooden cupboard doors, coating the newly painted walls, the curtains I'd hung myself. The glass milk bottle had splintered into a million pieces, and shards glistened in the unholy mess Ron's body had made. The man who'd controlled me for so long had been blasted backwards onto my kitchen floor, dark red blood creeping across the tiles, bits of bone, brain and flesh clinging to the walls. A piece of Ron's skull rocked gently where it lay, upside down on the floor. His brain was exposed, and one of his eyes hung out of its socket.

He was a gruesome sight, but the worst part was the sound. As Ron's blood ran out of his butchered corpse, it hissed. It was a monstrous scene, and yet I felt nothing but relief amid the horror.

Danny turned to me.

"You'll be alright." Then he ran back out the way he came.

I didn't register the fact that Danny never knew Mickey, was nothing to do with anything Ron or Mickey were involved in. The only common denominator was me, and my stunned brain just couldn't piece anything together at that point. I was in shock.

Time seemed to slow down. I screamed again. I ran to the hallway, picked up my phone. Who was I going to ring? I dropped the receiver, reaching for the walls to steady me. I couldn't take my eyes off the carnage. I backed off, down the short corridor leading to the street door. When I reached it, I threw myself outside. My limbs felt heavy, I wanted to vomit and scream all at the same time. Ron Cook, my 56-year-old lover, a violent and cruel villain, had been murdered in my kitchen – I had to call the police.

Ever since Mickey was killed, I had hated the Old Bill. Every time I saw a cop car driving along the road, or an officer out patrolling the streets, I felt a knot in my stomach. Seeing them felt like an insult to Mickey's memory. Running for help from the police was anathema to me, but I had to do it. My brain whirred. I had to get help.

I made it onto my street, and started yelling and yelling, gripping hold of the fence to keep me upright.

"HELP ME! PLEASE! HELP ME!"

There was a policeman close by in the park. He sprinted over. The contrast between the bloodshed in my kitchen and the normality of people going about their business in the outside world hit me, and I almost fainted. I was hysterical.

The officer spoke urgently into his radio. "12.28. It's murder."

Everything became a blur. Time seemed elastic, those seconds after the shooting seemed like hours. I had no idea who was coming and going. Soon there were helicopters buzzing overhead, police sirens cutting through the air, policemen speaking in hushed, urgent tones around me. I was whisked off to the local nick, where a hot coffee was placed in my shaking hands as my house was fingerprinted from top to bottom. I tried to sip the scalding hot liquid, but my body was trembling all over, and all I could do was sit and wait for the tremors to die down.

The officers couldn't have been kinder, ringing my brother Terry and asking him to bring in another set of clothes for me, reassuring me that the killer would be found, to which I said nothing. I declined a solicitor. After all, I was a witness to a murder, not a suspect.

My face and hands were swabbed, and once I'd changed into fresh clothes, they carried out tests on the clothes I had been wearing, to check whether I'd handled a gun. They came back negative, of course. I hadn't handled a gun. They treated me properly, as an unwitting witness to a grotesque killing. All the time, my mind was whirring, trying to work out why Danny had taken it upon himself to kill Ron. Had Brian told Danny that Ron was going to kill my son? Perhaps my kindness towards Danny had been misinterpreted, and he saw killing Ron as a way of getting rid of his rival? Had Brian asked Danny to get rid of Ron for Brian's own sake, so he could get me back on his release? I had absolutely no idea, but I knew that, finally, I was free to go my own way, to live my own life at last. My son was safe. I was safe. My nightmare with Ron was over.

I signed my statement the next day.

"He burst in just after we got back to my house. He was wearing black and had an Irish accent. He might have said he was from the police, but it's all blurry, I was so shocked that I tried to hide in the corner of my kitchen, so I didn't see him properly."

"And you have no idea who it was who killed him?" the man asked.

"No. I'm sorry. Ron had many enemies, you understand…"

I stopped talking deliberately, leaving a gap I hoped the officer might fill with his own theories about the many people who might have wanted Ron dead.

Even though I knew exactly who had shot Ron, I didn't say a word. Grassing someone up was the worst of crimes in the underworld. It was dishonourable, a betrayal of the crook's code. Danny had saved my son. That meant I would never betray him. He'd been the one to take out the psychopath who had threatened to kill Neil. I would never grass up the man who did that. I had too much to thank him for. Ron Cook was a violent, controlling thug who ran serious armed robberies, profited from despair and misery, and who had killed before. There was no way I'd give Danny a life sentence for removing him from this world.

The officer looked at me. I didn't blink as I returned his gaze.

"There you go, all signed, thank you, officer."

Back at Shelley's, I found out that Neil and Mel had actually been together, sharing a ciggie a few streets away, when the police helicopters swarmed overhead. Neil would often stay over at Kirkham Road, where Mel was living, as well as at my house in King George Avenue, and he'd been there drinking and messing around when the area erupted with the sound of cop cars squealing and sirens blazing.

"We were outside smokin' a joint when these helicopters started flyin' in circles over our heads. We thought they'd come for us!" Neil said, as we sat in the safety of Kirkham Road that night. "My mate said they were flyin' over my house. That's when my phone went, and someone said, 'Look, somethin's happened.' I asked what, and he said, 'Ron's dead.' 'Fuckin' what?' I said, and he replied, 'Yeah, he was killed in your house.' That's when I knew the shit had really hit the fan."

"It's heavy stuff, Mum," Mel added.

We stared at each other.

What could I say? A man had been murdered in my home. There was nothing I could do to reassure my family, except to tell them we were lucky not to have been involved. I don't think I had really taken in the fact that Ron, an untouchable, invincible gangland boss, was dead. It didn't seem real. I had been increasingly fearful of him, for good reason, and having that weight lifted from my shoulders was a sensation I knew I would grow to like, once the trauma of witnessing the attack had dissipated.

Two weeks later, there was a knock at my door.

I opened up to find a lone policeman standing on my doorstep.

"Hello Mrs Calvey, we'd like you to come back to the station, please. There have been some developments in the investigation, and we need to talk to you again."

I frowned. "What's this really about?"

"It's nothing to worry about, Mrs Calvey," he replied. "I'm sure you'll be home again soon. But bring some clothes and overnight things, just in case."

Bemused, I gathered my stuff and went out to the car with him.

We arrived at the station.

"You're Linda Calvey, *the* Linda Calvey?" A different officer had been assigned to me from the kindly man who had taken my statement.

"Yes, I'm Linda Calvey."

"Wife of Michael Calvey, who died during an armed robbery?"

The copper's face was set hard. Gone was the concern, the support for a murder witness. The tables had turned, and I wasn't sure why.

"Linda Calvey, I'm arresting you on suspicion of the murder of Ronald Cook."

I was dumbstruck. Out of nowhere, I had gone from traumatised witness to prime suspect. I felt utterly betrayed.

I was questioned under caution in a small room at the back of Canning Town nick. This time I had the duty solicitor by my side.

"Why didn't you tell us you were the Linda Calvey who caused all that grief when your husband was shot dead?" they questioned me.

I ignored them. "You know I didn't kill Ron, because your tests all came back negative."

"Which tests were those? That's funny. None of our officers remember any tests," the officer replied, sitting back in his chair, his arms crossed in front of him.

"The ones that showed I hadn't picked up a gun," I said, impatiently.

The officer just looked back at me, shaking his head. There was a second officer with him, sitting directly opposite me.

"What's goin' on? The test results were given to me, I can swear it," I said, my head buzzing. This wasn't right. Why was he shaking his head? Where were those results? Was he denying their existence?

"Why didn't you say that Daniel Reece had been in your home? We found his fingerprints in the house. And we know he was on leave the weekend Ronald Cook was killed. Perhaps you and Daniel planned to kill him together…?"

"I've told you already that I didn't think it was important. I picked him up from Verne Prison on the Friday and took him to his son's grave. He came back to mine for dinner, then I dropped him at his mum's. I haven't seen him since." I was sticking to my story that I didn't know the murderer, even if it meant that suspicion fell upon me.

"I've told you everythin' I can remember," I continued. "Ron picked up the milk bottle, then I heard the loudest bang as the street door was kicked open. The one place you won't find Danny's fingerprints are in my bedroom. So if you think we were havin' an affair, you're wrong. Go and look. Why would I murder someone in my own house? In my kitchen? It doesn't make any sense. Who on earth would say to someone, 'Come to my house and do a killing'?"

Nothing I said made a difference. Once the police knew who I was, my reputation as the Black Widow, gangster's moll, went before me. They assumed that because I ran with wolves, I'd become one.

"You planned it all along. It was a contract killing. You paid Daniel Reece £10,000 to murder Ronald Cook." This time the officer almost snarled as he confronted me with the lies they'd concocted.

"Who says that?" I retorted.

A brief silence ensued, and the interview was terminated.

By now, I knew I was in serious trouble, but I also knew I hadn't done what I was accused of, so I was quite blasé about the whole thing. I was innocent. Justice would prevail... Wouldn't it?

I was taken from Holloway Prison to a court in Stratford, where Danny and I met with our solicitors. We'd both been charged with murder.

Danny looked gutted. "You 'ave to tell them it was me and be a witness for the prosecution, Linda."

"I can't do that, Danny. I know why you came in and did it. You saved my son, and so I can't say it was you," I replied. "If I say that, I'll be condemning you to 20 years in prison. I can't take your freedom from you. I'm sure we'll both get Not Guilty, so let's go to court and take our chances."

I was gambling our lives on the 12 good men and women who would hear our case. Our lives were in the jury's hands.

"Listen," Danny whispered to me. "I promised Brian Thorogood I'd do it. Brian knew that Ron killed Mickey, but he also told me he was frightened for you with Ron comin' out before him. He said you had a terrible life with Ron, and everyone knew what Ron was like. That's when I said I'd do it, I'd deal with Ron." Danny rubbed the back of his head absent-mindedly.

I realised, of course, that Danny had also tried to save me from the pain of losing a son, so I wouldn't go through what he had gone through after losing his own son.

"I prayed for somethin' to happen to him." My voice was low. I hadn't prayed for him to be murdered, but I couldn't deny the relief I felt when Ron died.

"Go and tell them it was me," Danny pleaded one last time.

I shook my head in response. "Never."

# CHAPTER 24

# BLACK CAP

## NOVEMBER 1991

Number One court at The Old Bailey was alive the day Danny's and my trial began. Reporters crammed into the benches on one side, notebooks in hand, lawyers darted between the prosecution and defence counsel, people lined the gallery, family members shouted encouragement.

I stepped up into the dock, and the room went silent.

"To the charge of murder, how do you plead?" Mr Justice Hidden said. The members of the jury, 12 blank-faced individuals, looked over to us. A sea of heads across the court room turned our way.

"Not Guilty."

"Not Guilty."

Danny and I stood together, the Black Widow and the alleged hitman, the real Bonnie and Clyde – or so the prosecution would have the court believe. Truth and lies. Facts and fiction, all rolled together.

With those pronouncements, our trial began. I had been driven to the court only yards from St Paul's Cathedral in a van that had been graffitied with a hangman's noose and the word "Murderess". It is still hard to explain what was going through my mind. I felt completely numb. I hadn't really expected my case to get this far, let alone to take place in the highest court in the land. The allegations of a contract killing, of me paying Danny £10,000 to kill Ron, were just so ludicrous that I'd laughed them off.

I wasn't laughing now. I was terrified, shocked, still reeling from the images of Ron's corpse ingrained in my mind. One minute, I was sure I'd be cleared. The next, I was convinced it would go the other way. My thoughts jumbled around my head. I'd practised what I would say, the description of the killer and what he said, so I wouldn't implicate the guilty man, my friend Danny Reece.

Would it be enough to keep us both out of jail? My barrister had urged me to tell the truth, to say it was Danny who fired the fatal shot, but I wouldn't consider it. What Danny had done was worth more than any possible prison sentence I could get. He'd saved my son from almost certain death. Ratting on the man who did that was out of the question. Even though standing in front of that judge and jury was one of the most terrifying experiences of my life, I knew I wouldn't waiver. I'd asked my children to keep away as I didn't want them to experience the character assassination I knew was coming.

As we drove, flashlights from press cameras popped in my face. Those images were splashed all over the national newspapers: a woman with blank terror on her face, pale-faced, with eyes open wide as if to ask, what is happening to me? The press didn't see it that way. They relished my nickname, taking the view I was a brash, bleached-blonde, cold-hearted killer.

As my van pulled into the precincts of the court, I heard shouts of "Murdering Bitch!" and all sorts of obscenities from the large crowd gathered outside. Holding my head high, I stared back at the people trying to photograph me, trying to catch a glimpse of me inside the van. The pictures that were printed of me were awful. My blonde hair looked brassy in the cold flashlight as I stared at the photographer in dumb terror.

I'd also decided not to tell the court about the true nature of my relationship with Ron. I felt it gave me the motive the prosecution was looking for. If I'd painted him as the man he was – vicious, jealous and possessive, a man I was scared of, who had said he would kill Neil for looking too much like his father – then it would've given me a reason to plan his death. By lying to the prosecution, by saying that everything was rosy and we were madly in love, what motive could I possibly have to kill the man who kept me? I had no proof of Ron's crimes towards me: how he decided everything about my life, how he called the shots, attacked me physically and manipulated me emotionally. How could I possibly bring that up now? The jury would assume I was lying, even though it was the truth. I look back and wonder whether those times were enlightened enough to understand the concept of domestic abuse, how a partner could control another down to the lingerie they wore or the people they spoke to.

No stone was left unturned as they painted a picture of my life as the wife of a notorious, dead armed robber. No part of becoming the same as Mickey, taking up the shotgun myself, was left out. I was painted as a wicked woman, an evil seductress who had Mickey, Brian, Ron and now Danny caught in my web.

I couldn't look at my family while my character was torn to shreds. Shelley was there every day. It must've been terrible for her, seeing her older sister in the dock, hearing what I'd been up to in minute detail.

Over those four weeks I gave the version I'd given the police, only leaving out the crucial fact that Danny had, in fact, killed Ron. Our forensic expert testified that I couldn't have held the gun. My arms would've needed to be eight feet long, as my back was turned at the time the second bullet was fired.

The pathologist confirmed that the gun had been angled above Ron's head when it was fired. They'd tested Danny's clothes and found the residue left when a gun is fired. They also discovered that it was a jacket I had bought only days earlier, because I felt sorry for him going on home leave without any smart clothes.

I was asked again and again: why didn't I tell the police that Danny had visited me before the shooting?

My only reply was that I hadn't thought it relevant.

Each afternoon, I was taken back to my cell in Holloway. I was confident I'd be walking out of that court room with my liberty by the end of the trial. After all, there was no evidence of the supposed contract killing, no evidence of any money changing hands, no motive as to why I'd want to kill Ron – and yet there I was, standing trial for a murder in cold blood that I hadn't committed.

It came down to who I was: the Black Widow, a woman who would stop at nothing, even murder, to get what she wanted. The court heard that Danny had fired the first shot, intending to kill Ron, but had lost his bottle, at which point I'd apparently grabbed the sawn-off shotgun and blasted away Ron's skull myself.

I'd apparently shouted "Kneel, KNEEL!" before gunning my lover down.

I'd been calling for Neil, as a neighbour testified.

After four long weeks, the jury went out to deliberate. We waited all day long inside the Old Bailey precincts. It was agonising.

On the second day, the jury came back in the afternoon to ask for a gun expert.

"If Linda Calvey was standing where she said she was when the fatal shot was fired, would she have seen what she said she saw?"

The prosecution couldn't answer this, but the police jumped in. They said that, luckily, they had a gun expert in the courtroom.

I never found out the officer's name. He stood at the bar and lied, blatantly.

"If Linda Calvey was standing where she says she was, then she would not have been able to see what she said she saw."

I'd seen a hazy puff of black smoke when that gun was fired. That was the truth, the whole truth and nothing but the truth.

The jury, satisfied, went back out.

I knew then our case was lost. 20 minutes later the verdicts were in, though it wasn't a unanimous decision.

Again, the court fell silent. I squeezed Danny's hand, and took my last breath as a free woman.

"Guilty."

"Guilty."

The room swam in front of my eyes.

The place erupted. I heard shocked voices, someone shouted something at the jury. Danny visibly sagged beside me. I looked down at my barrister, who shook his head.

A hush settled.

The judge reached to his side and placed a black cap onto his wig. My knees almost buckled beneath me.

"You have both been found guilty of the murder of Ronald Cook. There is nothing I can do but pass you directly to the Court of Appeal."

Then, to me, he said, "The only sentence I can pass on you is life, but I can give you the recommended minimum tariff of seven years."

It was an astonishingly candid speech from a High Court judge. I believe Mr Justice Hidden knew I was innocent. Why else would he say such a thing, and give me such a low sentence, when my alleged crime had been upgraded from Murder to Gangland Murder? When I'd asked my legal counsel what the difference was, he'd replied, "About 25 years."

I looked over to Danny. A single tear ran down his hard features. "This is for you, not for me," he said. Danny was given a 15-year minimum term.

My life had been destroyed in a devastating miscarriage of justice. What would happen to my children? They were there in court to see me convicted, and they were hysterical. How would they cope with this latest blow? Danny and I held hands until we were led back down, our hands breaking off as we were marched in opposite directions. In the holding area, someone had drawn an arch above the doorway, and had written *The Hall of Fame*. I knew that Dr Crippen and Reggie and Ronnie Kray had walked up those stairs and into the dock: Crippen for the murder of his wife Corrine, and the Krays for the murders of Jack McVitie and George Cornell. It made me shudder to think I had ended up in the same place, facing an almost unimaginably long jail sentence. A convicted murderer.

# CHAPTER 25

# **REGGIE**

## 1991

The great exterior gates shut slowly behind us. I was sitting inside the prison van, waiting to be unloaded at the entrance of Holloway, the vast rebuilt brick prison that housed 500 female inmates. Among those imprisoned in the past were Suffragettes Emmeline Pankhurst, Emily Davison, Mary Richardson, Ethel Smyth, Countess Markievicz and Dame Christabel Pankhurst. Those on hunger strike had been force fed within the walls of the original Victorian building, and it had also been home to women members of the Fascist movement, notably Diana Mitford, who married Sir Oswald Mosley, and lived for a time with him in a cottage inside the prison grounds. Today, it was a grim red-brick building without the imposing turreted gateway that was the prison's hallmark.

I was taken into the municipal entrance with yellow walls, where a prison guard was sitting behind a thick glass frontage. I waited as the formalities were carried out. The place stank of diesel fumes and cigarette smoke, a familiar smell to me by now. Each section of the prison was fenced in by iron barred gates painted blue, and as I was taken through, I heard each set of bars shut behind me, drawing me deeper and deeper into the formidable prison. We zigzagged through the long corridors, some made of concrete, some wooden. The walls were all the same sickly yellow, like in a hospital ward.

I stumbled on as my life collapsed with each step I took. It was very unlike me, but I didn't say a word. I was stunned into silence, literally, as the third nightmare of my life was beginning. I'd been through Mickey's death, Ron's murder, and now I was starting a life stretch. There was nothing I could say or do to make sense of it all, to change it in any way. I knew I'd have to accept my fate or I'd be crushed by the penal system. I knew this because I'd spent so long visiting people in prison: first Mickey, who had been in and out for most of our married life, from talking to Ron, Brian and Danny when they were inside – the things they'd told me about having to shut their feelings down, be a closed room so no-one could mug them off. It had sounded horrible to me, but I understood, as I never had before, that it was essential to surviving inside the brutal prison regime.

There was a part of me I knew I'd never shut down, though, and that was my anger at the system that had put me here. My hatred of the establishment burned in my chest as I was led through Holloway, towards that most feared of wings, where the inmates were in single cells rather than dorms. I would fight my conviction with every ounce of strength I possessed – of that I was sure. Most people say they didn't do whatever it was they got put into prison for, yet we all know that our prisons aren't full of innocent people. There was no point me protesting my innocence to the screws and inmates, because everyone did. It would've been a waste of breath.

"Oh Linda, I'm so upset that they found you guilty."

"I can't believe you've been banged up for it!"

"It's so shocking, Linda, I just can't believe it."

The prison guards were sympathetic, but they couldn't change the fact I was convicted for something I didn't do. Where was the justice? Where was the evidence? Had my reputation damned me so much that the jury could never have let me go free?

"Where are you takin' me?" I asked when I realised the screws weren't taking me to the wing I'd been on remand in. I'd made a good circle of friends there, and had been quite happy with my job as a cleaner, chatting to the other girls and getting on with life as I'd waited a year for my case to come to trial.

"You're goin' to C1," said the prison guard.

"C1! You're jokin', aren't you? That's a psychiatric unit!"

This was too much to cope with. C1 had a reputation of being a dumping ground for the most volatile and disturbed prisoners in the system – and they were sending me there. The unit had a punishment block where women were kept in solitary isolation. The place was a by-word for verbal assault, racism and violence between prisoners. It was nothing short of a hell-hole.

"Rules are rules. All the convicted murderers go there because we 'ave to watch you in case you try and commit suicide."

That infuriated me. "I can assure you that I won't commit suicide. I'm goin' to be fightin' for my appeal."

"Don't worry Linda, you won't be stayin', you'll get freed in a year when you can appeal, I'm sure of it."

I smiled, grateful for the optimism of the officer as she pointed to a grey metal door in front of me. We'd been through locked door after locked door to get here, our footsteps echoing on the scrubbed corridor floors, girls cat-calling from their cells as we passed. We'd walked along the glazed walkway, decorated with colourful designs by inmates, but I barely glanced at it. My world was in shreds, and it was all I could do to keep putting one foot in front of me.

I was finally introduced to the cell where I'd be spending three days alone inside. I was on solitary again, just like the first time I spent the night between these walls. The sense of irony, of deja-vu, made me sick to my stomach. A woman was moaning from a nearby cell, while another shrieked with laughter, the sound rattling down the length of the corridor. It smelled of cheap bleach and fried bacon.

"Your home for the next few nights, Linda," the screw said, ushering me inside the magnolia painted room with its familiar blue linoleum flooring. The door was locked behind me, and I took a moment to look round. It contained the same sparse items as the one I'd occupied years ago for my armed robbery conviction. There was the single bed, the toilet in the corner, a small wash basin and an empty chest of drawers. That was it. There was a small window high up the wall from which I could see the outline of a treetop, its branches bare, bitten by the winter chill.

It wasn't my first night behind bars, but it was the longest. I sat heavily on the bed, the familiar rough blankets at one end, and put my head in my hands. I had moved on from denial, thinking I'd walk free, to anger at my conviction, and now all I felt, sitting there alone, was determination to find a way to be free. I'd do anything, say anything to get myself out of that place. You can't bargain with the prison system, and yet I was determined to speak to the right people, to beg my solicitor to take action, to do anything I could to regain my freedom.

That night was the darkest of my life. I watched the light fade across the tiny slice of sky I had been given, and I could've wept in frustration and disbelief. The wheel of fortune had moved ever downwards for me. I was trapped, inconsolable and all I could think about was how Neil and Melanie would've taken the news that their mother had been found guilty of murder and taken from them yet again.

While I'd been on remand, Melanie had visited me. She'd looked brighter than she had done for months.

"Mum, I've got somethin' to tell ya," she'd said, smiling, sitting back in the chair in the drab visitors' room. The sunlight was streaming in that day.

"What is it, darlin'? Is everythin' ok?" I replied, squeezing her hand as we sat across from each other.

"Mum, I'm pregnant," Mel said, "and I'm really happy about it."

"That's wonderful, darlin', I'm so happy for you. Do you know what it is, yet?"

We'd chatted about Mel's baby, her due date, and I gave her tips about managing with a young baby, telling her to ask the family for support if she needed it, choked up inside that it wouldn't be me helping her at the birth, as my case would most likely not come up in time. I didn't let her see how I was feeling. I didn't want to spoil the moment, and she didn't let anything she must've felt out either.

I would've hated giving birth without my mum around. My parents had done everything for me when my babies came, especially when Mickey was banged up. The first time Melanie had met her father was in a prison. I found it unbearable that my first grandchild would most likely meet me for the first time in Holloway. I thought of that as the night stretched onwards until the first glimmers of bleak winter light crept across the sky, casting a grey light through the tree and into my cell.

My eyes were puffy from lack of sleep but I knew I had to get up, clean my teeth, get myself washed, and meet the day with as much dignity as I could muster. My work to be freed started today. I had to show the screws I wasn't a problem, that I was fine and could be moved back to my wing, from where I could speak to my solicitor and get the ball rolling. I had work to do.

Bullwood Hall became my next home after only weeks in the slammer. I was sad to say goodbye to the girls, but relieved to leave Holloway. Bullwood Hall was a smaller jail, half the size of the prison in North London.

The cell had painted brick walls, a slop bucket and a couple of heating pipes running up to the ceiling. It had a tiny square window, which girls would poke their heads out of to talk to each other, starched sheets, scratchy blankets and an iron bed. It looked like something out of the Victorian times.

"It looks very undignified," I said huffily, though I was laughing as well. It didn't really bother me, as I was pleased to be in Essex, closer to my family, who were all based around the Chigwell area now.

Each morning, we'd be woken up at 7.30am with a rattle on the door. A screw would pull the hatch down and say "Morning". The meals were brought in by trolley and we ate in the lobby, the only room with a television as it was such a small prison, built to be a borstal, so not really fit for use as a prison. Every morning I refused to eat the porridge. Our meals were like school dinners: lumpy mashed potato with grisly meat and a few carrots and peas, followed by jam roly-poly and custard. The place smelled permanently of boiled cabbage. We were locked in from 8pm and the lights were switched off. I didn't mind, as I've never been a reader, so I'd listen to plays on the radio – my prized, and virtually my only, possession.

From there, I worked on my appeal. I was so confident that this time justice would prevail that, the night before going to court, I gave away everything I owned to the other girls. I gave my slippers, shoes and clothing to friends who needed a new set. I gave my toiletries to girls who'd run out. I even gave my radio away to a new girl who'd come in with nothing.

This time, I told the solicitor that I wanted to say who really shot Ron.

By now, Danny was visiting me every three months, and he had chided me for not telling the prosecution the real facts. "I lost a son," he'd said. "I know what it's like to lose a boy, and that's why I had to do it. I couldn't bear the thought of you losing Neil even more tragically than my son."

Danny and I grew closer, as he was really the only person who understood my plight. He had convinced me, at last. But our legal counsel warned us that it was too late to change my tune so dramatically. They insisted that it looked like we were lying to get me freed – ironically – and so they refused to take it to the judge.

Our case was dismissed for lack of new evidence.

I was utterly devastated. I'd been moved back to Holloway in preparation for my appeal. Afterwards, bizarrely, I was told I couldn't be taken to the holding cells, so I was left to stand outside the court, handcuffed to a prison screw, as the rest of the world, city workers and students, walked by, oblivious to the fact a convicted murderess was present.

On my return, I was touched to see that everything I'd given away to the other girls had been given back to me, laid out for me on my newly made bed. Tears stung my eyes as I looked at the things I had wanted never to see again – and yet again, my cell door was locked behind me.

Worse news was in store for me on my return. After I came back from my appeal, I was called into the prison office to see the governor.

"We've had a call from the Home Office, Linda. They said that there was a mistake in your sentencing, and you should have been a Category A prisoner."

My hands began to shake. Why were they changing my status now? Were they going to send me to Durham?

"They've instructed us that you are now to be classified as a Travelling Category A prisoner. This is not something we've ever had to deal with before. What it means, Linda, is that as soon as you leave the grounds here, on a visit or a transfer, we'll have to move you immediately to Durham."

"Oh my God, I'll be in with all the nonces!" I cried. "This is so unfair, it's disgustin'. How will my family come to visit me? It's so far away from them."

At the time, Durham was a notorious men's prison with only a small section for women. I was also really worried about being locked up with women murderers, paedophiles and arsonists, and I was fuming that the Home Office had made this decision without any prior warning.

When I arrived in the far north of England, the governor Mr Smith called me to his office. He was a nice-looking, smart man in his forties, and had some words of reassurance. "The girls are all worried about meeting a gangster, armed robber and murderess," he chuckled. He seemed to be a kindly man, and I warmed to him instantly. "If I can give you one piece of advice, Linda, it's this: don't judge anybody by their crime. Just take them on face value."

"But I don't want to have anythin' to do with killers or child molesters," I said, horrified at the thought of speaking to these people.

"Well, you won't have anyone to talk to then."

It wasn't long after I settled there that I received mail.

"Linda, you've got a letter." An envelope was pushed through the hatch in my door.

"Thank you, darlin'." Getting mail was a privilege. It was always opened before we saw it, but I still relished unfolding the paper and setting the letter out to read.

This one had a prison stamp on it from Maidstone nick. I wondered who could have sent it.

Opening the letter, I scanned the unfamiliar writing and saw a name that made me burst out laughing.

"Reggie Kray, I can't believe you've written me a letter! After all this time."

He was offering me advice. I remembered that my brother Tony and my friend Billy Blundell had told him all about me when they were all serving time together in Maidstone. As a long-serving prisoner, Reggie certainly knew what was what.

"Dear Linda, I was so sorry to hear what happened to you. It may seem like you'll never get out but you will. Just be brave."

It wasn't a long letter – and I never kept it, much to my regret – but at the heart of it was his sincere regrets for my conviction. He had kind words to say, and signed off by saying, "I'd like to ask if I can call you."

I wrote back saying he could. At Durham, we were allowed incoming calls only. A week later, the call was scheduled.

"'Allo, Reg Kray 'ere." His voice was familiar, still softly spoken, though with a proper Cockney accent.

"Hello, Linda Calvey here."

At that point, Reg burst out laughing. "There ain't many people who do that, who answer and say yer full name."

I'd only said it like that because he did. It sounded amusing to me, and I played along with it. We got on really well.

"How are ya copin'?" Reg asked. He was solicitous, and seemed genuinely concerned about my wellbeing. "I've been in Durham. We may 'ave been in the same cell. Just think of that." He chuckled as we talked.

I told him my appeal had been quashed and I was facing the full life term.

"Can I call ya regular, like?" he said at the end.

"'Course you can, Reg. That'd be nice," I replied. I wasn't scared of him at all. His reputation among hard men was vicious, but to me he was always a gentleman.

A few days after that first call, I was peering out of my cell window when I saw a screw carrying a huge basket of white roses.

"I wonder who those are for?" I said to my two new friends, young women called Ella O'Dwyer and Martina Anderson. Both were IRA bombers, and had been sentenced to life at the Old Bailey in 1986 for planning attacks. Ella had been 26 years old, and Martina just 23.

"Linda, this is for you," the screw holding the basket said.

I gaped at the spray of flowers, remembering that during one of my conversations with Reg, I'd mentioned that I love white flowers.

"We don't normally allow a big basket, as people hide drugs in the oasis, but as it's you, Linda," she grinned.

The card on them simply said, "To Linda Calvey, from Reggie Kray."

# CHAPTER 26
# PRISON WEDDING
## 1994-95

"Show us yer tits!" called one shaven-headed inmate, leering out of his tiny window.

"You dirty slags!"

"Whores!"

"Oh my God, have a little decorum," I laughed back at them.

Ella and Martina were jogging around the perimeter of the tiny exercise yard while I soaked up the available sunshine on a bench smeared with spit and probably worse. The two IRA girls were very attractive, with slim figures. Both had long hair: Ella was blonde, while Martina was a brunette with curls. Every time they appeared they got a mixture of wolf whistles and abuse.

Myra Hindley had arrived from Cookham Wood, where I'd first met her, causing a stir throughout the prison. It was fitting that she was incarcerated in the same place as Ian Brady. Brady had been kept here from 1966 to the 70s, when he was moved to Wormwood Scrubs.

Myra was out in the yard with us, though by this time she was a very sick woman. She suffered from brittle bones and osteoporosis, so usually just sat on the ground, keeping herself to herself. The Rule 43 men – the nonces, child molesters, who were kept separate for their own protection – always used the yard before us girls, and they left it in a terrible state, scrawling obscenities and leaving unmentionable fluids in the areas we had to sit in. We'd complained to Mr Brown and he moved them to a different exercise yard. We often got horrible things shouted at us. Many of the women were child killers, or had done very nasty crimes, and it was an affront to the male criminals. Somehow the fact these murderers were women seemed to shock people more than if they were men. I hadn't even realised women could be paedophiles before coming here.

The prison itself was very old. The cells were originally slop-out, but toilets had recently been installed in the women's wing, dividing cells into two, with a toilet either side for the neighbouring prisoner. We were allowed our own furnishings, so Shelley had brought me in my pretty pink silk and lace bedding, pink silk curtains for the window and some ornamental picture frames with photographs of my newest grandchildren. Melanie had another child by now, and so photos of their cherubic faces lit up my room, which looked like a gypsy caravan, swathed in my beautiful throws and cushions. Mr Smith allowed us to wear our own clothes and even jewellery, so I wore a necklace Mickey had bought me all those years ago. The governor was a very humane man, and stuck to his firm belief that we were still people, even though the girls in his charge had done terrible things.

"Fuckin' bitches!"

I looked over at the man who had shouted the latest indecency.

"You should wash your mouth out," I said as I ran round the yard with Ella and Martina. I'd decided to get fit too.

One of the guards rushed out into the yard.

"Everyone come in now!"

Suddenly, we heard an almighty *CRACK*, *CRACK*, and Myra let out a scream of pain.

I stopped immediately and looked over at her. I couldn't see what was wrong at first, as her kaftan was covering her legs. I could see she'd tried to get up when the guard called everyone in, but something had stopped her.

"Everybody in!" the screw shouted. We sprinted over to the door, leaving Myra outside on her own.

"It's ok, we've called you an ambulance," the guard said.

Unbeknown to us, one of the girls who had stayed behind in her cell had taken an overdose while the rest of us were out in the yard. Myra, in her brittle condition, had broken two bones in her leg as she had tried to get up.

When the ambulance came, they couldn't take both prisoners to the hospital, so the overdose was given priority. Myra had to wait for most of the rest of the day, in that yard, by herself as the men spat abuse and bile at her. No-one even bothered to guard her, as they knew she couldn't lift herself off the floor. She was clearly in agony, but no-one really had any sympathy with her. How could you?

Meanwhile, my chats to Reggie were taking place twice a week like clockwork. Once a month I'd get a bouquet of white flowers from him too, and often he'd send his drawings for us to auction to raise money for various causes, including a young boy with a terminal illness.

"'Allo, it's Reggie Kray."

"Hello Reggie, it's Linda Calvey."

"Listen, Linda." Reggie paused, and I held the telephone receiver closer to my ear. Suddenly, he sounded a little shy. "I keep thinkin' of ya and I think we'd do well together. I'd like to 'ave somebody in my life."

I didn't know what to say. "Go on, Reggie."

"If you'd like to get married, I'd be quite happy to do so." Reggie had such a polite way of talking.

I giggled. "I don't think it's a good idea, do you, Reg? If I went and said I was goin' to marry Reggie Kray, my chances of comin' home would be considerably reduced."

Reggie coughed. He sounded a bit embarrassed, and I didn't want to hurt his feelings.

"If you were home, and I was home," I continued, "I'd probably say yes. But we're both in prison, and this isn't the real world." I hoped I hadn't upset him.

"You're right, Linda, forget what I said," replied Reggie.

We began to talk about other things, and Reggie began to sound strained. "Listen, Linda. I'm worried about Ron. People think he's havin' a cushy ride at Rampton, but it's 'orrible in there. There's nothin' I can do to help. I keep puttin' in to go and see him, but they keep refusin' me. I've got to get home so I can fight to free my poor Ron."

By then, Reggie had served 27 years at Her Majesty's pleasure. It seemed obvious to me that he'd never get out, but I didn't say that.

"If I thought of all the people who've done horrendous crimes and 'ave come in, done time then gone home, I'd go mad. I've got to keep my focus on getting out of 'ere. Ron's really ill, ya know."

"I hope you do get to see him, Reg, I really do."

Only weeks later, Reggie's prison governor refused to let him see Ronnie, as they said he wasn't ill enough to warrant a visit. Very soon afterwards, on 17 March 1995, an inmate broke the news that Ronnie's death had been announced on the radio. Reggie was beside himself with grief and anger at the system that had denied him a last chance to see his twin before he died. I felt for him. I wouldn't have wished that on anyone.

The big news in the prison was that mass murderer Rose West would be joining us. She'd just been convicted of murder and sexual abuse, though she'd denied her part in her husband Fred's sickening killing spree, saying he'd put her up to it. We were all curious to see what this serial killer was like.

When I first saw her, I was shocked at how frumpy she looked – like an ageing maiden aunt, not the salacious, sex-driven bitch the papers had painted her as. Her large glasses made her eyes boggle out of her head, and she wore old-fashioned cardigans and tweed skirts. She and Myra became friends immediately, as most people kept away from them both.

One day they were sitting on the landing at a little table with a red-and-white checked cloth, when a screw sidled up to me, saying, "I bet you'd like a camera to take a picture of that."

I nodded. Rose and Myra were eating together, chatting away as if they'd known each other for ages. Myra was wearing a brightly coloured kaftan, flowing around her, and had violently dyed red hair, while Rose looked like a small, oversized librarian opposite her. Myra smoked and so she always smelled of ciggies, and her voice, once a soft northern burr, was now gruff and throaty.

Only a few weeks after Rose arrived, their bizarre friendship ended as quickly as it began. One day they didn't sit together, and I never saw them speak after that. Former prostitute Rose had become a target for the resident arsonists. Her cell was set on fire. Rose's budgie ended up covered in black soot and was expected to die. The poor creature was given to a screw to wash and try to revive, but Rose was hysterical. She raged and wept, thrashing her arms against her cell walls, then took to her bed for two days. I couldn't help but wonder where her perspective was, how she could feel all that for a simple bird when she'd killed humans, murdered 10 people in cold blood, including her eight-year-old stepdaughter Charmaine, and torturing the rest.

I felt utter disgust for her, as did most of the girls, but their spite took an evil turn. It was visiting day, and I'd popped to the workrooms to say hello. This was the place where the girls made cushions to sell, or painted pictures to help themselves cope with life inside. Rose had asked for two stuffed elephants to be made, as her visitor had young twin babies. The guard had asked me to fetch them and bring them up for Rose to hand out. When I picked up one of the toys, I almost dropped it in shock.

"Oh God, there are pins in this!"

"Yes, Linda, don't hold them too tightly, some pins may have fallen in there…" The girl who had made them winked at me.

I was horrified. "You can't do that to two babies! It's bad enough that they'll carry the name 'West', let alone get hurt like that. I won't say who did it, but I'm goin' to tell the screw that I think they need re-stuffing."

I showed the guard what the girls had done. The stuffing was filled with sharp pins.

"They need to be taken out carefully, and the toys re-stuffed," I said.

I was so happy I did that. Later, I caught a glimpse of the two babies sucking on the ears of the animals, and gave a sigh of relief. The girl who had made the elephants came to find me that evening.

"I'm so sorry, Linda, thanks for stoppin' me hurtin' those babies."

Danny's visits continued every three months, as they had done for years now. We'd grown close, but not in an intimate sense. Despite this, Danny proposed.

I think we both felt we were in the same situation, and it was his way of making things up to me, but really, the whole idea of getting married was crazy.

Crazy or not, Danny and I put in to the governor asking to get wed, and he agreed. The girls in my wing were beside themselves, lining up to be bridesmaids, planning the big day with more glee than me or the groom. Danny was at top security Whitemoor Prison in Cambridgeshire, and so he would stay in the male cells during the times he came over. Martina offered me her wedding dress, as did Ronnie Kray's widow, Kate, who I was in contact with by now, and the date was set: 1 December 1995.

Charles Bronson, or Charlie as I called him, had been brought to Durham. He was kept in continual solitary, which meant he used the yard alone during his short time at Durham, and had to be kept inside a kind of lion's cage. He'd be in his cage doing press-ups for an hour, jogging on the spot, waving over to people looking at him from their cells. He had a bald head, a moustache and was very muscly. They couldn't keep Charlie anywhere long because he was such a dangerous man. A serial hostage-taker, we'd been writing to each other for a while.

He'd noticed me from the yard as I looked out of my window. He recognised me, and called out, "It's the Black Widow! I love you, Black Widow, and I'm going to call you the Black Rose! Black Rose! I love you!"

I had to laugh at that. Charlie proposed to me every three months, but this time, I told him I was marrying Danny.

He wrote back, saying, "You can have two husbands as long as you don't have sex with them."

He was truly, properly insane.

Mum visited me in Durham ahead of the wedding. She looked pale and older, probably from the stress of having me as a daughter, and she had grave concerns about my plans.

"Linda, darlin', please don't get married to him. It'll be bad for you. You don't know this man, and if you walk down the aisle with him they'll think you were in cahoots all along."

I saw my mum's logic instantly.

"Ok, Mum, I won't. You're right."

When I told the girls what Mum had said, they went bananas. I could see it was the most exciting thing that had happened to my unit for quite a long time, and so, against all the good advice, I decided to go along with it after all. I was wrapped up in that tiny world of prison, and I couldn't see past having a lovely wedding day, and the connection I thought I had with Ron's killer. Rashly, my thought process was, "They bloody found me guilty, so I might as well look it."

In the end, I wore my daughter Mel's dress, and both my bridesmaids, Bernie and Maria from the wing, wore black. They were both in for murder. It was a fitting gangster's wedding, my second in a prison, held in the small chapel at the centre of HMP Durham. Confetti was thrown. We ate cake, then the whole thing was over. Danny and I were allowed a visit, sitting across from each other at a table in Durham's visitor room, looking incongruous in our wedding garb.

Danny and I had made a huge mistake.

I'd mistaken our relationship for something more than it was, and so had Danny. More significantly, though, it made us look guilty. Our wedding made it seem like we'd planned to get rid of Ron and be together after all.

My mother had been right. I'd made the world believe I was guilty, just as the court said I was.

# CHAPTER 27
# DOING TIME
## 1995-99

I'm told the five stages of grief are denial, anger, bargaining, depression and, finally, acceptance. I'd been through two of those at the start of my sentence, and until my appeal, I had been trying to bargain my way out. When my hopes of early release were crushed by the Appeal Court judge, I could've sunk into deep depression, but something stopped me. Something made me dig in, put my head down and stay determined not to let the system break me. I don't know if it was the strength of character I inherited from my mother. I don't know if it was sheer bloody-mindedness, but I wouldn't let go of the fact that one day I would walk free.

So, what did I do to get through years of prison life? I adjusted my focus, got on with my cleaning jobs, my work serving breakfast or dinner, and was friendly and chatty to the girls I was banged up with. I listened to plays on Radio 4, I wrote to Danny, Reggie and Charlie, and I got on with it. I won't say there weren't days when I railed against my fate, but I was stubborn in my determination not to let that take over.

It takes strength to survive prison, especially high security jails where the rules are stricter, where inmates can be locked up for 22 of every 24 hours, where the size of our cells measured no more than 11ft by 5ft. Living alongside truly evil people such as Myra and Rose was the worst part of it. They had some indefinable darkness about them, which is why they were avoided by most of the girls. Neither Myra nor Rose showed any remorse or warmth in their personalities. Both were as cold-hearted as they were twisted, and neither ever spoke of their crimes – a fact that used to make me shudder. I witnessed so much that sickened me, and yet I got through it. I'm a survivor. I wouldn't just give up and go under, even when things took a very nasty turn.

"Bye Mum, bye Dad. I love you," I said, finishing my phone call.

I always felt a bit teary after speaking to them. I knew it can't have been easy for them, keeping an eye on Mel and Neil, keeping the family together while I was in prison. They had suffered as much as I had from the miscarriage of justice that saw their daughter incarcerated for a crime she didn't do. They must've battled feelings of unfairness, though they never said anything to me. That was their way of protecting me, carrying part of the burden themselves.

It was a Sunday morning in Durham and the wing was very short-staffed, but a screw was waiting to take me back, as we had to be locked in when there weren't enough guards to let us out.

Walking back, a buzzer sounded. It was loud and urgent.

"Keep walking, Linda, that's one of the self-harmers. I'll have to go and see her, but I can't get back up to put you back in your cell."

"It's ok, you go and help her," I said, "I'll pace up and down for a bit. Go."

"Ok, let me see what she wants." The screw grimaced, though in a friendly way.

None of the guards bothered me much. They knew I wasn't a trouble-maker, and so they didn't worry about me causing havoc at a time like this. I was enjoying being able to stretch my legs. Some of the girls would go crazy when they were allowed out to use the phone – they'd refuse to go back in their cells, kick up a stink of screaming and shouting. I couldn't blame them. It was hard being locked in a tiny space with little to occupy yourself, and many of the younger girls got very angry, even violent, as a result. I was never like that. I didn't see the point. Besides, it always annoyed everyone else on the wing because it ruined their peace, so kicking up a fuss wouldn't have made me very popular.

I watched the screw leg it up to the cells that lined the overhanging balcony area.

"Oh my God, Linda, LINDA!" the screw shouted.

"What is it?" I followed her up those steps as fast as I could in my pink fluffy slippers, which looked out of place against the polished floor and metal steps.

The screw turned to me and grabbed my shoulders. She was shaking.

My stomach flipped. If a guard was upset, then there was something nasty afoot.

"Linda, please go in there with her, while I call for an ambulance."

"Ok, of course I will," I said, and immediately regretted my decision.

Walking inside that girl's cell, I saw immediately that half her face was hanging off, revealing her cheek and jaw bones. There was blood pouring down her neck, spreading across her clothes and the floor.

"Oh darlin', what 'ave you done?" I said as calmly as I could.

My first impulse was to vomit, then run, but I couldn't leave that poor girl alone. My instincts were screaming at me to leave that cell, but I saw she needed help and so I stayed.

Sitting beside her as gently as I could, I said, "What's happened?"

"They told me to do it." The girl's voice was small. She didn't appear to feel any pain, but kept her eyes on the floor. She looked twitchy, unpredictable, and I realised that I was alone with her.

"Who told you, darlin'?"

"My voices."

"Which voices?"

"The ones in my head."

The girl, who had long lanky brown hair, started muttering to herself. She was young and tomboyish, and her grey jogging top and bottoms were soaked in her blood.

"You mustn't listen to them when they tell you to do terrible things like this," I said, looking around for something to quench the blood, and to hold the jagged flap of skin back onto her face. There was nothing suitable, no towels or clean sheets, just an old T-shirt on the floor.

"I'm goin' to have to hold your face back together with this, sorry, darlin'."

I reached for the T-shirt slowly, as I didn't want to frighten her. She was shaking now, and had started to stammer words I didn't understand.

I picked up the shirt and packed it against her face. She didn't wince, didn't respond at all when I pushed her flesh back against the bones it had been roughly separated from.

"What did you do it with?" I asked, wondering if she had smuggled in some kind of weapon. I was starting to feel nervous. The screw seemed to be taking forever to get help, and I'd been left with this highly volatile and extremely vulnerable prisoner.

"What did you do it with?" Was there a weapon to hand?

"This," the girl said simply.

She pulled her bedcover away to reveal a china dinner plate smashed in half. One part was covered in black blood.

That's when I realised how afraid I was. The broken plate was on the other side of the girl. I couldn't stop her if she grabbed it and used it on me. I had to think.

"Darlin', why don't we put the pieces of plate by the door." I smiled as soothingly as I could.

"It's alright, they like you," she replied, looking into my eyes for the first time. Her ripped face was grotesque, with severed skin and jutting bones, but I could see she must've been a nice-looking girl once. She was new to the wing and I hadn't had a chance to meet her, but it was obvious she had some kind of psychosis and should never have been put in a cell all alone.

"Who likes me?" I replied, momentarily puzzled. I could feel my arm starting to ache as I held the blood-soaked T-shirt up to her damaged face.

"The voices. They've told me not to hurt you."

"Ok darlin', tell them I don't want them to hurt you again, so I'm goin' to put the dinner plate by the door."

I put her hand where the soaked rag was, and told her to keep it there. She was muttering to herself again, and I knew she wasn't really here, with me, in this cell. She seemed to come and go out of her own troubled mind. It was very strange. I took the plate, easing it away from her side, and put it carefully by the door, pressing the red buzzer as I did so.

*Oh my God, they've left me here on my own. Where's that ambulance? Where's the screw?*

I looked round, half expecting the girl to have followed me. She was still sitting on the bed, staring at the ground.

"Is it hurtin' you?" I asked. I felt desperately sorry for her, and also very scared for myself. I wouldn't have left her, though, however frightened I was. She was clearly in need of care and help.

"No, no it doesn't, you're very kind." She had a northern accent, and I guessed she was from Newcastle way.

Then, just as I had given up on anyone coming to help, I heard the sound of footsteps on the stairs. They were slow, casual, and I felt anger flare up inside me. As the door was unlocked, a woman's voice said, "This is really inconvenient. I'm trying to do all the men's medication."

Thoughts were buzzing through my brain. *Why the delay? Why so slow? Did no-one realise how serious this was?* I moved away from the girl and as I did so, the top of her cheek flapped back down again. At that moment, the prison nurse walked in.

"Oh, for God's sake! This is an emergency! Why didn't you tell me? When you'd said she'd cut her face I had no idea..."

The nurse's voice was urgent now. I held the girl's face back up. The nurse left to call 999, and the screw stayed with the girl. Within minutes, an ambulance had arrived and the girl was taken away. It turned out she was only meant to be in Durham for a few days until they found her a bed in a psychiatric ward. A few days too many for her.

I spoke to Reggie soon afterwards, and I told him about the girl. In his usual kindly manner, he took pity on the girl and sent a pair of trainers to her in hospital.

When the governor called me to his office to thank me for helping her, I let rip. "I could've been attacked. I was left there alone with a very disturbed girl. I should never have been put in that situation." Mr Smith offered me a phone card as a reward.

"I don't want a phone card. I want to know that girls like her aren't put in here. She should've been in a hospital all along."

I was really angry. I felt that justice had let me down, but I was an unusual case, whereas girls like the self-harmer were everywhere in the broken prison system.

My time at Durham was coming to a close. I'd been there for four years, and was due to be moved to an institution in Wakefield – but before I went, an old friend of mine made a bizarre gesture of love.

One day I was told I had an incoming call. When I picked up, a voice said, "Hello, Black Rose."

"Hello Charlie. How are you?"

"I've come in to take a hostage for you."

I heard a door slam, then Charlie shouted, "You're all my hostages!"

"Charlie, what's goin' on? What are you doin'?" I couldn't work out if this was some kind of elaborate joke.

"I've took them hostage." Charlie sounded elated. He began to shout down the phone, high as a kite.

"What do you mean?" I said, puzzled, hoping he hadn't really done what he'd said he had.

"They let me in the guv'nor's office to call you, and now I've taken everyone in here hostage." He had done exactly what he'd said. "They've got to set you free, and I'm going to keep them until you are released."

"Oh my God, Charlie, you can't do that. I'm alright. I don't want to go home today," I flustered. "Please let them go, I really don't need it."

I was pleading with the man considered Britain's most dangerous criminal. There was a pause from his end.

"Ok, Black Rose doesn't want me to take hostages today. To say thank you to her, we're all going to sing." Charlie was obviously speaking to the people he had captured.

"We're going to sing 'He's Got the Whole World in His Hands', but we're going to change it to 'He's got the whole world in his sawn-off shotgun'. Ready?" He laughed. "When we get to the end of the song, you can take me back down and you won't be hostages any more."

I didn't know whether to laugh with him or to be scared for those poor people in the office.

He made them sing, then finished with, "Black Rose is so classy. She's got red varnish on her fingernails and gold varnish on her toenails."

I didn't want to contradict him. It was a truly bizarre way to end my time in that prison.

I was moved to Holloway, where the excitements included a visit from Elton John.

"Yeah, a couple of the girls on the wing have Aids," a screw explained to me, "and so he's comin' in to see them. Somethin' to do with a charity called Aids in Prison. Make sure you're about."

Well, I had nowhere else to go.

Elton did indeed come in. He was dressed in jeans and normal clothes and glasses, and I asked him why he wasn't dressed up as I'd always seen him.

"Do you think I walk around all day wearing a glittery shirt and glasses?" he replied. I giggled. He was a sweetie and we had a nice chat in the TV room. I wrote to him afterwards, and he generously sent a cheque for £5,000 to the person in charge of Aids in Prison.

Shortly afterwards, I was moved on to Newall, which was primarily a young offenders' institution in Wakefield. I was the only Cockney in there – the rest of the girls were from that area and spoke in northern accents. The screws paid them in Crunchie bars for blow jobs.

I couldn't believe some of the things I heard in Newall. One girl I knew had been done for prostitution. I was chatting to her one day when a male prison guard we hadn't seen before walked past.

She looked mildly surprised. "Hello again."

The guard ignored her as he went past. She raised her eyebrows and turned to me.

"He used to be one of my clients. Seems he's not so interested any more."

The double standards in our world never ceased to amaze me.

The young offenders in Newall called me "Ma", and came to me with their problems. One young woman had been sold by her father to a much older man for sex, just to pay off a gambling debt. She'd been 14 at the time. It was horrendous. Every girl seemed to have a tragic story to tell: mothers who were junkies, being pushed into prostitution to earn money, neglect and violence leading to drugs, abusive relationships and, finally, prison. In those days, I saw how lucky I'd been to have a lovely family, to have known the love I have.

Acceptance came easily to me then, and I felt something else: gratitude. Yes, I'd been imprisoned unfairly, but I also knew that I was one of the lucky ones. I had never experienced the degradation suffered by those poor girls, and I never would.

# CHAPTER 28

# FREEDOM

## 1999-2008

Myra let out a loud scream.

"Aaarghhhhh, a spider!"

The vilified murderess was sitting on a chair as I was dying her hair the dark shade of red she liked, when she suddenly jumped up and started shouting.

"Aaarghhhhh it's huge!" I shrieked, catching sight of the spider as it went hell for leather across the cell floor.

It wasn't like me to lose my head, but this one was as big as it gets. It had long thick legs and had scuttled out from under Myra's bed.

We both legged it to the corner of her cell, which was situated in a kind of no-man's land between the punishment block and the main wing of HMP Highpoint in Suffolk.

Myra had arrived a year after I had, and while I was kept in the regular cells, she had to be kept away from the other inmates, as she was still the most hated woman in Britain – or so the papers said. I don't think anyone could've disputed it. She had two rooms to herself, one for sleeping in and one for repairing library books. By contrast, my wing was only locked at the end of the corridor. The individual cells were open.

Highpoint was a Category C prison, meaning it was closed, but with fewer security measures. Myra would've been in danger from the other inmates if they had access to her. She lived right in the bowels of the building, which seemed fitting. I'd been told about Myra's arrival a few weeks ago by a gleeful screw who seemed to think she and I were pals.

"Did ya hear, Linda, Myra Hindley's comin' here. What d'you think of that?"

I looked over at the screw. She was leaning against the kitchen doorway as I helped prepare breakfast for the girls. It was hot and steamy in that room of stainless steel cupboards and surfaces. I was ladling out porridge.

"I don't mind where she goes. It's nothin' to do with me," I shrugged. "Who'd like some porridge? Don't touch the stuff myself." That made a girl in the queue for food laugh.

"You and Myra, eh," the girl joked. She can't have been more than 25 years old. She was doing time for arson and theft.

"But you know her from Durham, don't ya?" the screw went on. "That's what the guv'nor told us. Anyway, it'll have to be you who keeps her company."

"Oh, why's that then?" I asked. "There you go, darlin', there's sugar and milk over there." I winked at the young woman as she carried away her plastic bowl of porridge on a plastic tray and went to find somewhere to sit.

This wasn't really the time to be trying to engage me in conversation. Was the screw trying to make trouble?

"The guv'nor says you and Myra were friendly, like, so when she comes, you'll have to look after her."

I snorted at that. Putting down my ladle, I turned to the prison guard. She was tall and stockily built, with short brown hair. "I can tell you now that Myra and I were never friends. I worked in the library and she spent a lot of time there. That was that. Didn't you know I slapped her in the face once?"

"Good for you, Linda," hollered one of the girls who was still waiting to be served.

"You could always tell the guv'nor you won't do it," said the guard slyly, knowing full well I wouldn't dare. It didn't go well for you if you refused to do what you were asked, and I wanted to leave this place eventually and go home. I didn't want any black marks on my prison records.

So, here I was, coming to see the woman I loathed, whose crimes were so abhorrent to me that I found it difficult to be in her company, and having to wash her hair twice a week. Once a month I'd have to go back to dye her roots and give her a trim, though I was no hairdresser. She'd smoke constantly while I was there, one cigarette after another in a constant chain, which I hated, as I always left her reeking of tobacco.

"You kill it! You're the Black Widow!" Myra shouted, hiding behind me.

"I can't kill it, I'm frightened as well."

I was amazed that this woman who had killed children could be scared about ending a spider's life.

At that point, the spider ran back into the darkness under her bed.

"Check it's gone, Linda, go on." Myra drew heavily on her ciggie as she spoke.

I sighed. Crouching on the grey linoleum floor, peering under her single bed, I couldn't see anything, except for a battered-looking briefcase. That immediately struck me as odd, as we weren't usually allowed anything we could hide things in.

"What's that case?" I said, feeling emboldened by tackling the wayward spider.

"Oh that, that's mine." Myra seemed to hesitate. "That's got my papers in."

"Your papers?"

As far as I knew, we weren't allowed to keep private documents on the wing.

Myra pursed her lips and it was obvious she wouldn't say any more. I have often wondered what was inside that forbidden briefcase.

By then, Myra looked like any other middle-aged woman. She had brown hair, which was short on top and long at the back, pink nail varnish, and at the age of 57, apart from her flowing kaftan, she could've been mistaken for a suburban housewife anywhere in the land.

"My mum wants to speak to you," she said, sitting back down on the chair.

I picked up the bowl of dye and the small brush I'd been applying it with and got back to work.

"Your mum? Nellie?" I said. "Why does she want to speak with me?"

"Because you're my only friend."

I almost dropped the bowl. I think I even choked. I really didn't know whether to feel chilled by that, or pity for her. She was no friend of mine. I was there under duress, chatting, doing her hair, wafting away her endless cigarette smoke. She obviously thought I was there by choice, but how could she? Didn't she know how hated, how despised she was by everyone, including me?

"Oh, alright then," was all I could say, weakly. "I'll chat to your mum. How is she?"

Myra coughed, her lungs sounded terrible. "She thinks I'll get out soon. It was Brady. I was forced, you know."

Suddenly the air seemed cold. Her voice sounded like ice.

I didn't know what to say. Her words were so unexpected. It was the first time she'd ever alluded to the horrors she and Brady had inflicted on little Lesley Ann Downey and four other youngsters. I hadn't a clue what to say. My mouth felt dry and I stood, waiting to see what would come next. Her words hung in the air. Myra obviously realised what she'd said.

"You wouldn't understand."

She stopped abruptly, then continued as if nothing had happened. "I want to go home, Linda, that's all I want now."

When I'd finished her hair, she fished about in her cupboard and handed me a heart-shaped box of chocolates. "It's for you," she said, lighting another cigarette.

"Thank you, Myra," I said, opening the lid to find nothing inside. "Oh, well it's a pretty box."

Did Myra think she was buying my friendship with odd presents? Was she trying to appease me in some way for her awkward confession? She had always talked a lot about going home. She had a small band of supporters who were lobbying the Home Office to release her. Perhaps she counted me as one of her admirers? I don't think she had any idea that many of those closest to her would gladly have left her to die, rotting in prison until the end of her days for the heinous crimes she'd committed.

That evening, when Myra's mum Nellie Moulton rang, I was there to answer.

"Hello, dear." Nellie was an old lady, living in a care home near Manchester, but she sounded compos mentis.

"Hello, this is Linda Calvey. How are you?" I said, at a loss to know what to say to this woman. I felt instantly sorry for her. How agonising to have given birth to a monster, to know that your child killed all those children, and possibly more. I had no idea how that would feel.

"I'm so pleased Myra has a nice friend," she said, though in my mind I couldn't shut out the voice shouting *I'm not her friend, I never will be.* "Myra says you colour her hair, that's nice."

And so the conversation went on. I started speaking to that woman every Sunday, because I felt so sorry for her. She must've gone through hell, and the least I could do was play along with this bizarre friendship.

Another odd friendship that I struck during the next few years in prison was with a charismatic lawyer called Giovanni Di Stefano. His nickname was the Devil's Advocate, and he claimed he specialised in "defending the indefensible". It was rumoured he'd acted for serial killer Harold Shipman, Saddam Hussein and, later, Osama Bin Laden. One of the girls was seeing him in her bid for freedom, and she asked if I'd be interested in meeting him too. I'd heard he had managed to overturn Hoogstraten's manslaughter conviction, so I admitted I was intrigued.

"Hello Linda, it's a pleasure meeting you." Giovanni kissed my hand. He was charm personified, wearing an expensive suit, a colourful tie and wearing designer glasses. His hair was receding, but he was an attractive man.

"Can you help us?" I said, simply, referring to both Danny and me.

"Linda, I have looked at your case and you should not be in jail. I will fight for your freedom, I promise you." He was suave and sophisticated, clearly an influential man. In 2003, he managed to get my case put before the High Court to challenge Home Secretary David Blunkett's failure to pass my case to the parole board. We were arguing they were in breach of the European Convention on Human Rights.

I went to court to hear my case reviewed. My daughter Melanie and other members of the family attended. Mel was heavily pregnant with her third child – yet another grandchild I wasn't able to care for.

I was 53 years old, and I'd spent 12 years in prison by this point. I heard how my minimum tariff – set at just seven years by the trial judge – had been increased to 15 by the Secretary of State. Since then, the House of Lords had ruled on another case that minimum terms for mandatory lifers was "incompatible with human rights".

As I listened to my QC, a Mr Alan Newman, I gazed at my daughter, smiling at her, tears forming in my eyes. This time, *this time*, it would end well for me.

But I didn't walk out of that court room a free woman.

Afterwards, I asked to see Giovanni. My request was denied. Giovanni was under scrutiny. It turned out he was a fraudster, not a real lawyer at all, and unable to meet me any further. Sometimes, I look at my life and think that I couldn't have made it up. Fake lawyers, proposals from mobsters, hairdresser to Myra Hindley.

I asked Danny for a divorce. We'd both realised in time that the only bond between us was Ron's murder, and it wasn't common interests or real love for each other that had bound us together. Being married – though it was never consummated – had changed our friendship, and so I asked him if he didn't mind if we officially ended it, so we could get back to being pals.

Danny agreed, and we divorced amicably.

I spent years more inside, until one morning the same mousey-haired screw approached me.

"You're going to an open prison, Linda."

I looked at her like she'd told me I was meeting Mickey Mouse that day.

"Open prison? That means it won't be long before I go home…"

The screw nodded.

I felt a rush of joy. *Oh My God, I'm goin' home soon.* It could only mean things were changing for me. I rang Mel and Neil straight away.

"You won't believe it, they're sendin' me to East Sutton Park in Kent."

"That's amazin', Mum, I'm so proud of you!" Mel squealed. I knew a lot of the struggles both my children had been through: drugs, homelessness, chaotic lives. My family had tried to keep it from me over the years so that I wouldn't get upset. I wanted so much to return home to my kids, to show them I could go straight and be in their lives at last. I wanted to be a proper grandmother to their children.

"I'm proud of you too, darlin'. Give my love to those babies, won't you," I said, hanging up. I felt like my life was about to start again.

I was moved to East Sutton Park as I awaited the response to my parole application. I knew I was nearly there. Getting home was all I could think about, every hour of every day.

One day shortly after I arrived, another inmate in the open prison told me one of the screws was looking for me.

*Oh my God, is this it? Is it finally time?*

I hurried in to see her.

"You wanted me?" I asked.

"Yes, oh, Linda, I've been looking for you all over!"

"What's it about?" I asked, curious and impatient. Had they moved my release date forward?

But the guard shifted uncomfortably in her chair, and my heart sank. Her eyes were flitting about nervously.

"What is it?" I asked her urgently. "Is something wrong?"

"Ah, now that you're here, Linda, I don't know how to say this."

I frowned. *What was wrong? What have I done?*

"I find it helps to start from the beginning," I said. My nerves were beginning to get the better of me, and I was getting fed up with her evasiveness.

"Well," she said, "thing is, I was actually wondering…"

"Yes?"

She leant forward conspiratorially. "I was wondering, could you do a murder for me?"

I was dumbstruck. I stared at her in horror, searching her expression, trying to find out what on earth she was getting at.

"Stand up," I said slowly.

She looked at me quizzically. "What? Why?"

"Stand up, now," I snapped. Uncertainly, she obeyed.

"Where's your wire?" I demanded.

"What?"

"Your wire. Are you recording me?"

"No, Linda! I'm serious."

I approached her in a business-like fashion and patted her down. All of a sudden, it was like she was the prisoner and I was the officer.

"You're trying to set me up," I said, incredulously. "You're trying to get me to incriminate myself so you can put me away for longer."

"No, really Linda, I'm not trying to do anything. I'm asking you a serious question."

I narrowed my eyes. I searched her again, then checked under the table. There was nothing.

I stared at her.

"Linda," she began again, "I'm in trouble and I need your help. My boyfriend hits me, he does terrible things to me and I'm scared of going home. I need to get rid of him, but I don't know how. Can you do it?"

I was utterly shocked.

"There's no way I'd ever, ever consider doing such a thing. I'm no killer. I'm this close to release, and you're asking me to murder someone? How dare you."

I stormed out of the office and went straight to the governor, insisting on seeing him immediately.

"Sir, it's urgent. Someone's asked me to do a murder for them."

The governor's jaw dropped. "That's appalling. Tell me who it is and I'll get them shipped out immediately."

I hesitated. "Actually, sir, it's not one of your prisoners. It's one of your staff."

The governor stared at me blankly. Then his expression changed entirely. Suddenly, he looked relaxed and confident.

"That's not possible."

"Sir, this is serious." I told him the full story. "You've got to investigate. One of your own staff asked me to commit a serious crime on their behalf."

"Linda, I don't believe this and I will not investigate my own guards. My staff are honest, and I won't have them being accused by the very people they're looking after."

"In that case, sir, I'm going straight to my solicitor," I said. "Unless you call the police right now."

Reluctantly, he agreed. The police were called, I told them every detail of what had happened, and they questioned the officer responsible.

"It's true," they told the governor. "All the details the prisoner gave us about this guard's domestic situation are completely accurate. There's no other way the prisoner could have known all that." But, in another travesty of prison justice, they couldn't charge the officer. It was her word against mine, and as an inmate, a convicted murderer, I wouldn't be treated as a reliable witnesses in court.

"Sorry, madam, there's nothing we can do."

Once again, I was left speechless by the double standards in the system.

Every day, I was more and more convinced that justice was skewed against us prisoners. It wasn't long afterwards that a teacher was found murdered in the car park in the prison grounds – and it was automatically assumed that one of us inmates had killed her. The investigation was thorough and painful, and the authorities did their best to pin it on one of us, but the explanation turned out to be as simple as it should have been predictable. The teacher's jealous ex-boyfriend had murdered her, and he'd done it on prison grounds with the deliberate intention of framing an inmate.

"Move over and let Linda sit with you." A Chinese man at a nearby table gestured to a white-haired fella sitting nearby.

I'd been at East Sutton Park for a few months now, and they'd allowed me out on day release. My friend Kate Kray ran a restaurant not far away, and had invited me and a couple of friends over for Sunday lunch.

"Of course," the man replied. "It would be my pleasure if you ladies joined me."

"What a charmin' bloke he is," I whispered to my friend as we sat down.

"I'm George. And you're a friend of Kate's?" He smiled. He was rather a portly gentleman, but he had a kind face.

"I am," I replied. "My name's Linda."

"Are you married?" he asked.

"No, I'm widowed once and divorced once," I said. "Are you?"

"I'm divorced," said this lovely man, and a shadow passed over his features. I took it that he'd been through a difficult time, and didn't question him further.

We chatted all afternoon, and when it was time to go, George said, "Can I take you out for a meal?"

"You certainly can, but I'm only allowed out once a week."

George looked puzzled. "Why?"

"Because I'm in prison," I said, without an ounce of self-pity. I wasn't ashamed, and so I didn't see why I should hide it.

George burst out laughing. "Oh, you're *that* Linda! Linda Calvey," he snorted.

"Yes, I am," I said, and we both started to giggle. It all seemed utterly ridiculous all of a sudden.

We arranged for him to pick me up the following Sunday.

That day, I waited for him. All the other visitors came and went.

"He ain't comin', Linda," one of my friends on the wing said, giving me a pitying look.

We were sitting in the rather grand lobby of the prison, a former manor house which had 99 deer on the lands (only the Queen can have 100). I'd made myself up nicely, and had waited for almost an hour, but George was nowhere to be seen.

"If he takes any longer, it won't be worth our while goin' out at all," I said. "I'm not standin' here like a lemon. Give me a shout if somebody pulls up." I wandered off, leaving my friend in the lobby, convinced I'd been stood up.

Five minutes later, there was an excited shout.

"Linda, LINDA! There's a red Roller turned up, it must be for you!"

I couldn't believe my ears. A red Roller? I ran back and looked out of the entrance hall.

George was standing with his back to the shiniest red Rolls Royce I'd ever seen in my life. For a moment, I was 12 years old again, sitting in my dad's van, craning out the window to catch a glimpse of that remarkable sight, that red Roller, wishing I could have the kind of life that had such wonderful things in it.

I was spellbound, choked up by the memory, and, above all, delighted that he'd shown up. That young girl inside me was dancing for sheer delight. The red Roller had finally shown up. All that yearning had found its natural conclusion. I could only laugh at the irony of it all.

"A red Rolls Royce! I made it in the end," I laughed to myself. I'd endured 18 years in prison, and here I was about to be whisked away, like the ending of a Disney film.

"I hope he's not a crook," said a screw, whistling at the sight of the car. "I'll get someone to check his number plate."

That brought me down to earth with a bump.

Later, I told him that I was the Black Widow, but that nowadays I planned on being straight as a die. If he was a criminal, I said, it was best to leave things there.

George laughed merrily at that. He'd made his fortune selling bleach, of all things, proudly declaring that he was the first to put it in plastic bottles.

We shared stories about our lives, and I told him about that time I'd seen a red Roller and fallen in love with the high life.

He smiled kindly and looked into my eyes. "Well, now you've got one."

After that, we saw each other every weekend. He was so smitten with me, he turned up at my workplace in a local charity shop – a move strictly forbidden – and so I was moved back to a closed prison for two months as punishment.

"I'm so sorry, Linda! I wanted to see you. I hope this will make up for it."

George and I were sitting together like young love birds in the Cookham Prison visitors' room. He drew a small velvet box from his pocket.

"Go on, open it," he said, beaming.

I gasped. Inside was a large teardrop diamond solitaire ring. My sister Maxine had helped George pick out a ring for me.

"It's beautiful, George, oh thank you."

"Will you marry me, Linda Calvey?"

I couldn't speak. I thought I'd never find love with a kind, steady man, but I had.

I nodded, and he placed it on my finger. The wheel of fate had swung all the way back up again. There was only one last thing that would finish its full circle – and that came sooner than I thought.

"Linda, you got parole."

I was working in the kitchen back in East Sutton Park. I thought I'd misheard.

"Say that again," I said slowly, holding a large ladle in one hand. The prison governor was standing in the dining hall, smiling broadly.

"You got parole. Your release date is here. Linda Calvey, you're going home."

On 1 August 2008, my daughter Melanie's birthday, I walked out of prison. I was on probation, though, and wasn't allowed home yet. Instead, I was sent to a hostel for six months in

Maidstone. That was standard procedure for released prisoners while officials found them work, but I was already past retirement age. There was no purpose in my being there. I was meant to be a free woman, and I couldn't understand why I couldn't just go home with George. He accompanied me to the hostel the day I was released, and as we got out of the car, a man walked out of the door with a blow-up doll under his arm.

George was horrified. "Linda can't live in a place like this! She deserves somewhere far more respectable."

He lived in a lovely house just 45 minutes away in Canterbury, and my family were only 45 minutes in the other direction in Essex. I couldn't believe that I'd have to sit out six months in such a dingy place. I was only allowed out to see George for Christmas.

But those six months in the halfway house passed quickly enough, and I walked free. My prison life was over, and I was about to step into a bright new future with a lovely man at my side, my family intact and with a whole lot of grandchildren to love.

The sun shone as George drove me away, his red Rolls Royce winking in the sunshine.

# EPILOGUE

George and I married in a small village church in Kent, a fairy tale ending to a life lived mostly outside of society norms. Billy Blundell's youngest daughter was a bridesmaid.

You could say George and I were like chalk and cheese. He was placid, calm and steady, whereas I always had a rebellious streak: a woman prepared to risk everything, a woman burnt in the fire, but who rose like a phoenix from the flames of a badly-lived life.

When George passed away four years ago, the papers called it the curse of the Black Widow. My third husband and I knew the tragic truth. He died of cancer, a happy man, loved by me and my family, and his many friends.

The day we sprinkled his ashes, an old friend of my husband, a man called Simon, toasted us both. "Here's to George – and to you, Linda. A chapter of your life has ended – and a new one starts now. I hope it is happier for you, though I know it'll be just as exciting."

My new chapter starts now that I am finally able to lay to rest the many bizarre twists and turns my life has taken. I have been a bad woman, a sad widow and a mad gangster. I have lived on the edge of normality, always looking for the way to move forwards, the new path to take, never looking back – until now.

In telling my story, I have told the truth about Ron's murder – the blame lay squarely on Danny Reece's shoulders. He did not like the idea he was standing behind my skirt tails, and is happy for me to tell the world at last that it was him who wielded the weapon, him who killed Ronnie Cook. Danny has been taunted inside prison for what the prosecution said – that he lost his bottle and couldn't do the deed himself. He is happy for me to put the record straight. After all, he has done the time.

I served eighteen and a half years, and yet I made it out. I still have so much to live for, so many good things in my life. My grandchildren know me as their nanny, my daughter and son have me back as their mother, and it is my mission in life to return them the love I have been given tenfold, because I can, because I'm a free woman with her life, and who knows? Maybe I could even love again.

It's still a journey for all of us, though our family is strong. We still live with the impact of my imprisonment, my life choices and the death of my Mickey. I never gave up hope that I would one day walk free, put everything behind me, and make a fresh start.

Over the years, those notorious figures from the East End have died out. Brian Thorogood passed away three years ago, but he remained close to us all until his death. Ronnie and Reggie Kray died, Ronnie at the age of 61 in 1995, Reggie at the age of 67 in 2000. In 2002, Myra died as a result of a heart attack at the age of 60, while at the time of writing Rose West is still alive, housed in an all-female maximum security prison in Durham. Charlie Bronson is still campaigning for his release.

I have now been home 10 years. My children have been asking me for years to tell my side of the story, as so many tales have been told about me in books, magazines, newspapers and TV documentaries. After all this time, I felt it was time to put the record straight.

I have not received any money for writing my story.

I now live a very quiet life in a little chocolate-box 400-year-old cottage, bought for me by George. The only time I see any of the old villains – Freddie Foreman, Billy Blundell and the rest – is when we are asked to attend charity functions. Our criminal paths are behind us, and now we are wheeled out for these events, as people are curious to see the famous East End faces they have read about. Our notoriety is now put to worthy causes, raising money for various charities. Sometimes I feel like the bearded lady from Victorian times, being publicly exhibited as a curiosity from a bygone era.

Every year, there are fewer and fewer of us left. Once, we struck fear into people with our gun-wielding raids. Now, we are the dinosaurs of our time, fossils from an era that will never come again. The blaggers, the hard men and the protection rackets are things of the past now.

Sometimes I cannot believe my path has crossed those lives I've listed. Me, a girl born in Ilford and brought up in Stepney, daughter of an ironworker and a market trader. I must've had strange stars orbiting my heavens the day I was born. I hope I will live a quiet life now, spending time with my grandchildren and good friends.

My last words go to my first and only true love, Mickey Calvey. Never a day goes by that I don't think of him. He was a convicted armed robber, a blagger, a thief, and the man of my heart. It was his death that made me who I am today: the notorious Black Widow. A woman who was intent on fulfilling the destiny that was ripped from her more than 40 years ago. A woman with a burning hatred for authority, and love for the finer things in life. A bad combination, my mother might've said, but since when did I ever listen?

I was mad for Mickey. Handsome, charming, always impeccably dressed, and a crook, I was smitten. It was love at first sight for him too. I still can't believe he's dead, that all the vitality, the humour, wit and charm disappeared the day he was killed in broad daylight – a failed robbery leading to an ended life. The officer who fired that fatal shot left me a widow with two young children and a molten rage that burned deep within me, driving me to carry on Mickey's work, to provide for our kids the only way I knew how: by picking up a sawn-off shotgun and going on the pavement to do the robberies myself.

Mickey was a good teacher. I listened and learnt as he plotted around my kitchen table with hardened crooks, violent and dangerous men for who I poured tea and cut ham sandwiches, all the time taking in what they were saying, the tricks they used, the targets they went for, never knowing if one day I'd need to use that information. That day came. When he left us, dying on a cold hard street, the seed was planted within me. The die was cast in the moment he took his last breath.

# EPILOGUE

I am the Black Widow still. Mickey will always be in my heart. What happens next is down to me, though, and me alone. This time, God willing, I will walk an honourable path into my future.

# ACKNOWLEDGEMENTS

Thank you to Ajda Vucicevic at Mirror Books, without whom this book would never have happened, and to George Robarts, for his tireless work in bringing my story to life.

Thank you to Cathryn Kemp for her patience and hard work in helping me tell my story.

Thank you to Andy Jones for your friendship and support over the years.

Thank you to Julian Hardy, my solicitor, who promised he would get me free. I promised I would get him into the Masons. We both kept our promises.

This book is dedicated to my children, and to the memory of my wonderful parents, Charlie and Eileen Welford, my beautiful sister Maxine and, last but not least, my husband George. They were always there for me.